LOOKING BACK FROM THE CENTRE

LOOKING BACK FROM THE CENTRE

A Snapshot of Contemporary New Zealand Education

Edited by Joanna Kidman & Ken Stevens

VICTORIA UNIVERSITY PRESS

TE WHARE WĀNANGA O TE ŪPOKO O TE IKA A MĀUI

VICTORIA
UNIVERSITY OF WELLINGTON

VICTORIA UNIVERSITY PRESS
Victoria University of Wellington
PO Box 600 Wellington
victoria.ac.nz/vup/

National Library of New Zealand Cataloguing-in-Publication Data

Looking back from the centre : a snapshot of contemporary New
Zealand education / edited by Joanna Kidman & Ken Stevens.
Includes bibliographical references and index.
ISBN 978-0-86473-633-8
1. Education—New Zealand. I. Kidman, Joanna, 1963- II. Stevens, Ken J.
379.93—dc 22

Printed by Astra

We dedicate this book
to our colleague and friend,
Dr Jim Neyland
1953–2010

CONTENTS

Preface   9
Dugald Scott

Introduction   11
Joanna Kidman & Ken Stevens

Sociology of Education

Are We There Yet? Sixty Years of Educational Sociology and   19
Equality in Aotearoa/New Zealand
Jane Gilbert

Parking in the Margins: The Sociology of Education   41
Joanna Kidman

He Pārekereke: Māori Education and Pacific Education   52
Te Whānau o He Pārekereke

Education Policy

Educational Research and Democratic Debate: A Reflection   63
on the Centre
Hugh Lauder

Education: Commodity or Public Good? Twenty Years On   73
Gerald Grace & Martin Thrupp

New Zealand's Role in Education in the Pacific   85
James Irving

Understanding Why Radical Policy Reform Takes Time to   103
Embed: Illustrations from Policy on Assessment
Cedric Hall & James Irving

Early Childhood Education

Teaching Early Childhood Education at Victoria: Policy,   121
Discipline and Profession
Carmen Dalli & Anne Meade

Reframing Some Windows on Early Childhood Education: 139
An Unlikely Career
Helen May

Rural Education

An Open Learning Matrix to Sustain Education in Rural 161
New Zealand
Ken Stevens

The Introduction of a Collaborative New Zealand Model 173
to Sustain Rural Schools in Atlantic Canada
Ken Stevens

Human Development, Psychology, and Education

Diversity, Development and Educational Psychology: Keeping 189
Social Justice on the Agenda
Lise Bird Claiborne

Adolescent Identity Development: Implications for Teaching 202
and Counselling
Jane Kroger

A Capital Contribution: People, Proclivities and Programmes 213
Lex McDonald

Education Matters: Teaching and Philosophies

Reminiscences on Peace Education 227
Jim Collinge

Learning to Read and a Half-Century of Research 238
G. Brian Thompson

Mathematics After Efficiency: An Agenda for Action 252
Jim Neyland

Afterword: Contributions to Scholarship in Education from 263
the School of Education
Joanna Kidman & Ken Stevens

Contributors 267

Index 275

PREFACE

This book celebrates the work of the excitingly diverse group of scholars who have been part of Victoria University of Wellington's Department and later School of Education.

Dr Joanna Kidman and Dr Ken Stevens, themselves part of the tradition, have assembled a collection of works that are individually interesting, but, as a collection, are very effective in helping us understand some of the highlights and major shifts in the intellectual domain of education over the last few decades.

These are wise and passionate voices about educational issues and events, educational strengths and weaknesses, and personal challenges and triumphs in the study of education. The authors demonstrate strong allegiance to their discipline and to the issues that swirl around it, and, in doing so, help describe and record the ethos and purpose of the university Department and School to which they belonged.

Educational structures, plans, and policies can seem to be in constant flux. Other ideas, like the merger between the then training college and the university proposed by the University Council in 1925, can take decades. The contributors to this book provide a valuable commentary on a range of educational events and ideas, but also demonstrate the essential purpose of educational studies as a reflective and critical activity.

This is a welcome addition to our knowledge about the study of education.

Professor Dugald Scott
Pro Vice-Chancellor and Dean (Education)
Victoria University of Wellington

INTRODUCTION

Reflections on the Study of Education in New Zealand

Joanna Kidman and Ken Stevens

This book is about the study of education in Wellington, the capital city and geographic, political and cultural centre of New Zealand. We decided that this book needed to be written in 2008, when the School of Education Studies at Victoria University of Wellington was disestablished following a merger between the University and the Wellington College of Education and a subsequent restructuring of the new Faculty. The school was an integral part of the educational domain in Wellington for eighty-one years and during that time, many staff and students made significant contributions to the field. *Looking Back from the Centre* is our way of honouring the work of those colleagues who came before us and those who shall come after. As tertiary institutions grow and change it is important to look towards the future but we also need to remember and understand what happened in the past – this book then is both a way of remembering and a way of looking forward.

The following chapters have been written by past and present members of the Department of Education (later Educational Studies) of Victoria University of Wellington. Each chapter is a reflection on the intellectual pursuits that were followed by a few of the many faculty members who have worked in the department, many of whom are now at other universities in this country and overseas.

A feature of academic life in a university education department in the capital and geographic centre of New Zealand is, appropriately, educational policy studies. Gerald Grace, a former professor and chairperson of the department, now at the University of London Institute of Education, and Martin Thrupp, now a professor at the University of Waikato, reflect on some of the educational policy debates they were involved in from the late 1980s. Educational policy debates preoccupied many members of the department in its later years and from them a substantial number of academic policy publications were generated. Professor Hugh Lauder was appointed to the department following the departure of Gerald Grace and during his tenure he was deeply involved in public debate about educational policy. His chapter in this volume is a reflection on the neo-liberal policy agenda and his often very public debates with officers of the New Zealand Treasury and members of government during the 1990s. Professor Lauder has maintained his interest in New Zealand education policy from his current position at the University of Bath in the UK. Professors Grace and Lauder were educational sociologists and each contributed to this field during their time in the department. Cedric Hall and James Irving have worked together on educational assessment policy matters for many years. In their chapter they look at the reasons why educational policy takes time to embed, and explore strategies for developing policy that move beyond an implementation focus and incorporate professional development models. Drawing on their decades of experience in the field, Cedric and James provide unique insights into the way policy works.

Dr Jane Gilbert, now with the New Zealand Council for Educational Research, joined the department for a few years where she engaged in research and teaching in the sociology of education. Her chapter reviews the theoretical frameworks that have shaped this field in New Zealand and takes us through a number of perspectives from functionalism to more contemporary ways of considering society and its organisations and structures. Her chapter is a tour de force of the highest developments in the sociology of education in this country and beyond.

While policy debates were a prominent feature of the department, other areas of educational studies also flourished. Helen May, now Dean of Education at the University of Otago, writes about her involvement in the development of early childhood education at Victoria University of Wellington. Her chapter is accompanied by one written by her former colleague Carmen Dalli, now an associate professor in the newly formed Victoria University of Wellington College of Education, and Dr Anne Meade. They trace the development of early childhood education as a field of study as far back as 1947. Both chapters chronicle the background and growth of this now well-recognised area of educational research and teaching and remind readers of the many people who played a part in its development.

The study of educational psychology and human development in the Department of Education was an area of considerable scholarly activity over many years. Dr Lex McDonald sets out his reflections in one of the following chapters titled 'A Capital Contribution' reflecting his view of educational psychology at the University. Dr McDonald is currently the head of the School of Educational Psychology and Pedagogy in the new Faculty of Education at Victoria University. In his chapter he draws attention to the work of former faculty member Professor Deborah Willis, now Dean of Humanities and Social Sciences at Victoria University, Dr Don Brown, Associate Professor Carmen Dalli and Professors Cedric Hall and Wally Penetito. All contributed to the development of educational psychology at Victoria University of Wellington and beyond. There have also been many other contributors to the field at Victoria University in the past three decades, such as Professor Reg Marsh, Dr Bruce Ryan and John Panckhurst, who left his lectureship in educational psychology in the late 1970s to take up an appointment as the Principal of the former Wellington College of Education.

Over many years Dr Brian Thompson taught courses in educational psychology and attracted international attention for his work on reading. Numerous academic visitors spent time in the former department to work with Brian and his chapter outlines his many scholarly publications on reading, some co-authored with scholars in other parts of the world. Brian's work continues in his retirement and he continues to undertake research in the new Faculty of Education that has resulted in a continuing flow of publications.

Associate Professor Lise Claiborne, now at the University of Waikato, spent many years as a member of the Victoria University of Wellington Department of Education where she pioneered new ways of looking at developmental and educational psychology. Lise has had a long-standing interest in social justice issues and attracted many graduate students to her courses. She supervised a large number of doctoral theses during her time in Wellington and her published work has established her as an authority in this field. During the 1980s Lise taught a popular first year course in psychology and development with Professor Jane Kroger, now at the University of Tromsø in Norway. Jane's work on identity formation is internationally recognised.

The history, sociology and philosophy of education have a long history at Victoria University's former Department of Education. Jane Gilbert,

Hugh Lauder, John Barrington, Joanna Kidman and Ken Stevens all contributed to the development of the sociology of education in different ways and some of these are reflected in their chapters in this volume. Professors Colin Bailey and Rollo Arnold together with Dr Neil Daglish and Dr John Barrington undertook research in aspects of the history of education in this country. Jim Collinge and Jack Shallcrass taught courses in educational theory and philosophy and Jim later pioneered peace studies with popular courses he taught over many years. His chapter is a timely reminder that peace, and teaching the philosophies of peace education, is a radical act and one that challenges and disrupts the status quo in unexpected ways. As tertiary institutions move towards an uncertain future, Jim Collinge's reflections on peace and social justice need to be kept in mind. As educators, we need to ask ourselves *what* are we teaching and why?

Ken Stevens' background in the sociology of education led him to the study of both rural and distance education and eventually to a professorial position in Canada, where he was able to integrate his three research interests. One of his former students, Joanna Kidman, later took over his courses and developed a focus on scholarship in Māori education. Joanna writes about changes that have taken place within the department in which she was first a student and later a member of the academic staff. Her recollections provide readers with a view of academia based on her contributions to her discipline.

Māori education and Pacific education are two domains that have developed in a unique manner at Victoria University. Over the past seventeen years Māori and Pacific staff have worked closely together at He Pārekereke: Institute for Research and Development in Māori and Pacific Education and during this time they have formulated new ideas about education and indigeneity in New Zealand and the Pacific region. Their co-authored chapter explores some of the debates that have taken place as they built a working relationship.

Other scholars in the former department brought unique perspectives to the study of education in New Zealand. Jim Neyland's chapter about mathematics education was written shortly before his death in 2010. He proposes a radical agenda for action in an area of the curriculum that is central to the professional education of primary and many secondary teachers. Jim Irving, who taught comparative education and policy courses, provides a detailed examination of New Zealand's long involvement in the education of Pacific nations. His chapter is a comprehensive summary of Pacific Island education and the many difficulties that face educators and policy makers in providing opportunities for students in this large and diverse part of the world. The nature and extent of New Zealand's involvement in the provision of education in the Pacific may surprise readers.

Looking Back from the Centre is a look back on a university department that specialised in the academic study of education from the perspectives of multiple social science disciplines. There are many New Zealanders as well as people from other countries who were introduced to the study of education at Victoria University of Wellington. A considerable number of faculty members of the former Department of Education later had careers in other New Zealand universities and in universities overseas, some of which are outlined in the conclusion of this volume. In the meantime, the department has been physically moved from its home on the Kelburn campus to become part of a new faculty housed in Karori, through a merger with the former Wellington College of Education. We are grateful to our colleagues who have contributed to this book. In looking back over the landscapes of New Zealand education they have mapped an important part of the intellectual terrain.

THE SOCIOLOGY OF EDUCATION

Are We There Yet? Sixty Years of Educational Sociology and Equality in Aotearoa/New Zealand

Jane Gilbert

This chapter reviews the theoretical frameworks that have informed educational sociology as it has developed in Aotearoa/New Zealand, looks at the effect of these frameworks on equality of educational opportunity, and suggests that it could be time for a new approach.

In the modern welfare state, access to education is a basic 'social right'.[1] Universal, publicly funded education is critical to democratic, egalitarian societies because it provides the infrastructure for realising these ideals. Education's availability to all is supposed to remedy social disadvantage by providing everyone with a roughly equal starting point in life. In addition, providing everyone with certain kinds of knowledge, skills, and dispositions helps them to fit in with wider social norms, while having individual needs and aptitudes catered for allows people to find their particular niche in society. This, in theory, builds social cohesion, while at the same time also providing for the human resource needs of the economy.

These two rather different aims – providing a social right, and meeting the economy's human resource needs – are how state-funded education systems are justified and legitimated. They were the two main arguments used in the Parliamentary Debates preceding the passing of the 1877 Education Act that set up a national system of compulsory (primary) education in New Zealand.[2] Sixty or so years later, in 1939, these two goals were repackaged as part of an influential speech, written by Dr C.E.

---

1 This term is usually attributed to T.H. Marshall's (1977) distinction between the 'social' rights that developed as part of the 20th-century welfare state, and the individual rights of earlier political theory (such as the right to life, the right to liberty, and the right to own private property).

2 As outlined in Harker (1990).

Beeby (Director of Education at the time), but given by the Minister of Education, Peter Fraser, at the beginning of the term of New Zealand's first Labour government.[3] This speech, which emphasised the first goal over the second while retaining the second, was later known as the 'Beeby vision' because the values and aspirations it expressed were, at least in theory, the basis of New Zealand's public education system for most of the 20th century. Many years later (in 1986), Beeby argued for the need for such 'myths' (his term) in education: ideas that are 'big' enough to draw people together, to give a sense of unity, direction and purpose, while at the same time offering guidance to planners, administrators and teachers. However, his vision for education, as expressed in the 1939 speech, while it may have drawn people together and provided a rhetorical basis for policy building, has not been realised.

Why is this? Seventy or more years later, do we know any more about why this idea – and, therefore, the legitimacy of the system – have failed? Answering this sort of question is the territory of educational sociology. For a large part of the 20th century, sociologists of education have described and mapped the unequal distribution of educational opportunities and, later, attempted to explain these patterns. Decades of work have produced a large empirical and theoretical literature in this area, and some of this has influenced the direction of educational reform. However, 'the problem' still exists. The education system continues to make very little difference to the life chances of a great many people, and, in many cases, it actively reproduces social inequities. Why is this? Have policy-makers not listened properly to sociologists of education? Or does sociology of education continue to be an 'emerging' discipline, characterised by a lack of consensus on what its object of enquiry or theoretical frameworks actually are? In this chapter I review some different sociological approaches to the problem of educational inequality, and look at the solutions that arise from each approach. My purpose is to explore some of the strengths and weaknesses of contemporary

---

3   The part of the speech that is usually quoted is as follows: "The Government's objective, broadly expressed, is that every person, whatever his level of academic ability, whether he be rich or poor, whether he live in town or country, has a right, as a citizen, to a free education of the kind for which he is best fitted, and to the fullest extent of his powers. So far is this from being a mere pious platitude that the full acceptance of the principle will involve the reorientation of the education system." (Fraser, P., Appendices to the Journal of the House of Representatives 1939, pp. 2–3, quoted in Beeby 1986).

educational sociology, and to suggest some possibilities for rejuvenating it as the important field of enquiry it should be in 21st century Aotearoa/ New Zealand.

From learning the 'dignity of labour'[4] to 'diversity' and 'inclusiveness'

Two of the phrases used in the 1939 Beeby statement – "of the kind to which he is best fitted" and "to the fullest extent of his powers" – epitomise the functionalism that underpinned most educational sociology until the 1970s.[5] Functionalist sociologists see society as being like a biological organism, a collection of systems that work independently, but depend on each other. There is a 'natural' order of things, in which everything – and everybody – has a role. People have differing characteristics and aptitudes which fit them best for certain roles, to which they 'naturally' gravitate. Society is a steady-state system, which is disrupted if something (or someone) moves out of their natural place. Like other natural systems, because it has evolved into its present form over time, it is the most efficient way of doing things. Children learn the rules, norms and aspirations of their social group in families, and schools prepare them for their likely role in society. Schools decide who is best fitted for what, and channel students into activities that prepare them for that role, and, through this sorting process, reflect – and reproduce – existing social structures and roles.

In 1930s New Zealand, this meant, as T.B. Strong (Director of Education in 1929) put it, that Māori education should "lead the Māori lad to be a good farmer and the Māori girl to be a good farmer's wife" (cited in Barrington 1988, p. 55), a view that maintained the largely separate 'native schools' system for Māori until the 1960s. The mainstream curriculum was gender-differentiated (Tennant 1977, Fry 1985, Matthews 1988), and when secondary education became common,

---

4 The phrase 'the dignity of manual labour' was used in 1906 by George Hogben, who was Inspector-General of Schools in New Zealand, to advocate 'more practical' (i.e. less academic) forms of education for Māori (cited in Barrington 1988, p. 47).

5 The 'sociology of education' community in New Zealand in the late 1970s was very small. According to the author of a paper presented at the inaugural New Zealand Association for Research in Education conference in 1979, it consisted of "some two dozen people, roughly half of whom claimed to be engaged in actual research" (Bates 1980).

there were various – not entirely successful – attempts to differentiate it on class lines as well (McKenzie 1992). By the 1960s, equal educational opportunity for all was the official goal: however, the link between social origins and educational achievement remained. This was explained by functionalist educational sociologists as a consequence of 'cultural disadvantage', 'cultural deprivation', or 'sex role stereotyping', and various compensatory – or re-education – programmes, designed to help disadvantaged groups 'measure up' to white, male, middle-class norms, were recommended.[6] For these theorists, the problem lay, not with schools, but with 'deficiencies' in disadvantaged groups/individuals. As they saw it, the system has a responsibility to help people fit it: however, a spread in aptitudes is normal, and necessary for social equilibrium.

In 1980s New Zealand a sociological critique of this view of achievement began to emerge. Researchers influenced by the theories of what was then referred to as the 'new' sociology of education questioned this understanding of 'success' and 'failure', and the normal/deficient model it depends on (e.g. Ramsay 1985, Codd et al. 1990). In a body of work influenced by the phenomenological view of knowledge as socially constructed, researchers investigated how school curricula construct some students as normal, and others as deficient. Some researchers, using ideas explored in Michael Young's (1971) collection *Knowledge and Control*, and Basil Bernstein's (1971) work on the classification and framing of knowledge in education, focused on how 'school knowledge' is selected and organised to reflect and maintain the interests of particular social groups. From this, some argued that it is through institutional racism and sexism, not cultural – or linguistic – 'deprivation', that some students succeed, while others fail, and that this should be the focus of educational research and change. The idea that Māori knowledge and Māori pedagogies should be included in an explicitly bicultural or multicultural school curriculum was officially sanctioned and many schools developed taha Māori[7] programmes for all students. There were

---

6 For example, in the US, the Operation Headstart initiative, and the associated television programme Sesame Street. In New Zealand, official publications, like the Department of Education's 1971 handbook *Māori children and the teacher*, advised teachers how to compensate for their Māori children's cultural and linguistic deprivation, and there were a number of initiatives designed to address sex role stereotyping – the Girls Can Do Anything programme, for example.

7 Taha Māori is translated as 'the Māori dimension' or, literally, 'the Māori side'. See Smith (1990) for an explanation and critique of these policies.

also calls for the inclusion of the perspectives and/or preferred 'ways of knowing' of other groups, in particular women (e.g. Bell 1988)[8] and working-class people: however, they had less impact on the official school curriculum. Other researchers focused on what came to be known as the 'hidden' curriculum – the other, less overt interactions in classrooms (and outside them) that provide the background for students' construction of their identity in relation to school knowledge. One body of work, influenced by the phenomenological/interpretivist paradigm, investigated young people's everyday experiences in classrooms, looking in particular at their creative responses – and resistances – to events in the classroom, and analysing these experiences using the Marxist view of social class relations (e.g. Jones 1986).[9] Other work, also within this paradigm but using 'life history' approaches, studied how educational ideas are experienced and 'lived' by teachers and students over time (Middleton 1987a, 1987b, 1990), while yet another body of work focused directly on how classroom interactions construct students who are not male, middle-class, and white as 'other', or deficient (Alton-Lee et al. 1987, Jones 1988).

Marxist-influenced work looked for structural 'correspondences' between school culture and the division of labour in workplaces, arguing that these are key to the reproduction of existing inequalities (Bowles and Gintis 1976, Anyon 1980, 1981). Bourdieu's concept of 'cultural capital'[10] was widely used to account for the role of education and/or the family in reproducing inequalities (Nash 1981, 1983, 1993, Harker 1990, Middleton 1990), and researchers continued to collect and analyse quantitative data demonstrating the link between social class, school performance and further education and/or employment destination

---

8   This kind of work followed Belenky et al. (1986).

9   This ethnographic study, influenced by earlier British ethnographies of working-class young people's experiences of – and resistances to – school culture (e.g. Willis 1977, McRobbie 1978), looked at the secondary school experiences of two groups of girls, one a low-stream group of mainly Pacific Islanders, and the other a high-stream group of mainly middle-class Pākehā.

10 Bourdieu (1971, 1973, 1974) argued that, within the family, children pick up the language, competencies, habits of mind and tastes, or 'habitus', of their parents' class/ cultural group. Schools assume, but do not explicitly teach, the habitus or 'cultural capital' of professional, middle-class families, thus disadvantaging children from other social groups. Middle-class cultural capital is converted to financial capital via the school credentials that allow access to professional occupations.

(Lauder and Hughes 1990, Nash, Harker and Charters 1990, Waslander et al. 1994, Strathdee and Hughes 2006). Following on from this work, Roy Nash argued that family resources – that is, income, social connections and literacy practices – are the main determinant of educational success or failure (Nash 1993), and researchers from the Smithfield project[11] went on to collect data on the effect of 'school mix' – the social class composition of school intakes – on the academic achievement of individual students (Thrupp 1995, 1997). Later, as the 1990s progressed, these researchers and others focused on developing a critique of the New Right policies that produced the major reforms of New Zealand's education system in the late 1980s and early 1990s. There was a particular focus on the likely effect of 'school choice' and 'self-managing schools' policies in exacerbating existing inequalities (e.g. Lauder 1990, Grace 1990, Lauder et al. 1995, Waslander and Thrupp 1995, Gordon 1997, Wylie 1997).

Most of the post-1980s work focuses on structures and systems, and how these function in replicating the status quo. The functionalist account of cultural 'disadvantage' as the main cause of educational inequality is replaced by cultural 'relativism', the idea that society is made up of many cultural groups with world-views which are different from, but neither superior nor inferior to those of the others, and that each of these groups is entitled to schooling that acknowledges, and supports their particular 'way of knowing'.[12]

Mainly as a result of the work outlined above, cultural relativism is currently the official approach. Twenty-first century schools are required to be 'inclusive' and to address 'cultural diversity'.[13] The Ministry of Education's current mission is "to raise achievement and reduce disparity", and much of the research and teacher professional development it funds is designed to raise student achievement in poor areas and areas with high numbers of Māori and Pasifika students, and

---

11 The Smithfield project was a major Ministry of Education-funded research project which looked at changes in New Zealand school composition after school zoning was removed in the early 1990s.

12 Barrington (2008) describes the appearance of this idea in educational debate in New Zealand in the early 1930s.

13 'Inclusion' and 'cultural diversity' are two of the eight principles underpinning the most recent national curriculum document (see Ministry of Education 2007, p. 9), and a recent Ministry of Education's 'best evidence synthesis' outlines ten characteristics of "quality teaching to meet the needs of diverse learners" (Alton-Lee 2003).

to improve teacher practice in relation to these students.[14] However, these goals are unlikely to be achieved, for a number of reasons. One reason has to do with the way we think about 'achievement' in general, and about what it means to be 'poor'. Student achievement at primary school level is usually measured using nationally standardised tests, the results of which give a picture of how a student is doing *relative to* all other students at that particular age/stage. Because student ability – and therefore achievement – is assumed to be normally distributed, the results are adjusted to fit this distribution (that is, to produce a normal curve with a 'tail' of high achievers, a 'tail' of low achievers, and a 'bulge' of average achievers). This system thus *requires* that there be low achievers. The effect of one school raising the performance of its students (as measured on one of these tests – that is, relative to other students of the same age) would be to *lower* the performance of other students somewhere else. When we add to this the fact that our measure of 'poorness', the decile ranking system, was developed using factors chosen because they correlate with student achievement,[15] it is not surprising that students from poor areas turn out to perform less well. Nor is it surprising that the wider public see the decile ranking system as a proxy for quality. Because we expect students from poor areas to perform less well, we design the system so that this is what happens. At the end of the first decade of the 21st century we have a system which, while it officially emphasises diversity, inclusiveness and raising everyone's achievement, is structured in ways that make this impossible. Educational sociologists continue to collect data on the inequalities produced by this system to support their strong critique of neo-liberal policies and their material effects – the 'marketisation' of education, for example, or the 'disembedding' of individuals from social structures and systems to the extent that they are now 'responsibilised' 'entrepreneurs of the self' (Giddens 1991, 1998, Beck 1992, Du Gay 1996, Lash 1994, Rose 1999, Beck and Beck-Gernsheim 2002, Bauman 2005, Giroux and Searls Giroux 2009).

14 See for example the Picking up the Pace and Shifting Focus work, both of which are part of the larger Strengthening Education in Mangere and Otara (SEMO) project (Phillips, McNaughton and MacDonald 2002, Timperley, Phillips and Wiseman 2003); the Pasifika Languages Research and Guidelines Project (Franken, May and McComish 2005), and the Kōtahitanga research (Bishop et al. 2003). The Kōtahitanga work in particular aims to address what it refers to as teachers' 'deficit theorising'.

15 Ministry of Education spokesman David Lambie, quoted recently in Hunt (2009).

So what does this mean for the future of educational sociology? The functionalist focus on fixing deficiencies in individuals or groups has been replaced by structuralist interventions designed to fix deficiencies in the system. They have not had the desired effect, and while it is fair to say that many of these interventions were imperfectly implemented, that is not the reason for their failure. There are still major differences in the educational achievement of different social groups, and middle income groups are still the main beneficiaries of educational services. This, I think, tells us that a new angle is needed. If educational inequality is *not* caused by deficiencies in some social groups, and if it hasn't been solved by recognising and 'including' diversity, then what *is* the source of the problem? In the second half of this chapter I want to argue that there are a set of very deep, almost unconscious, assumptions underlying educational thinking and the systems it produces, and that it is these assumptions that make equality of opportunity impossible. My aim is not to present this argument in detail, as space does not permit this here: rather it is to contribute to a debate about the future of educational sociology in Aotearoa/New Zealand. I think it is important to have this discussion because, for a number of reasons, after strong activity in the 1980s and 90s, the field is no longer growing and is, I think, not especially well-equipped to contribute to the challenges being faced by mass education systems in the 21st century.

Towards a 21st century version of the 'Beeby vision'

Just as Marxist thought emphasises the importance of structures over agency, and environment over mind, contemporary social psychology views mind(s) as socially produced: that is, we are socialised to organise our thinking in particular ways through our immersion in complex social structures. Because of this, Marxist social theorists would argue, we cannot change people's thinking without first changing the social structures that produce it. For these theorists, social structures are the product of economic organisation, and so economic change must precede social change. However, there are other possible sources for the social structures that organise our thinking. Psychoanalytically oriented social theorists, for example, argue that social structures (and language systems) are the surface-level expressions of the much deeper symbolic systems that give us certain sets of categories to think with (and exclude others). This 'collective unconscious' is a self-replicating system, in that it produces the social structures that organise individual thinking in ways that reproduce those structures, and make it impossible to think outside them. These theorists argue, however, that in the context of specific processes and spaces, it is possible to begin to think outside these categories (e.g. Irigaray 1985, Piussi 1990, Whitford 1991, Sartori 1994, Schwartz 1999). In this section I want to draw on some of this thinking to look, *not* at how educational failure is produced by students (and/or their families), schools, or society, but at how it is produced by – and necessary to – our *ways of thinking* about education. To do this, I explore three of the 'big ideas' underpinning educational thinking to show how it is impossible for them to produce an equitable system, because they are premised at the very deepest level on excluding certain categories of person. These three 'big ideas' are individuality, equality, and knowledge. In the final section of the chapter I explore how we might begin to set up processes and spaces which would allow the deconstruction of these ideas and the emergence of alternatives.

We are all individuals, but some are more individual than others . . .[16]

Modern Western social, political, and economic thought is premised on the idea that all people are autonomous individuals, and that they have certain basic human and social rights, including the ability and freedom to participate in public life. A second key idea is the view of knowledge as a set of universal truths that are available to all. For this system to be legitimate, we must all be able to enter it as equals, as equally free and able to be the 'subjects' of political/social/economic life, and of knowledge. In modern Western democracies, education, health, and other social services are supposed to provide the platform on which this ideal can be achieved. However, as we have seen, these services do not always work as intended, and much of the work of modern social and political theorists involves analysing how and why this is the case. In the later 20th century, the focus of some theorists shifted to look, not at how these services might be improved, but at what allows them to *appear* to work, most of the time, for most people. In what follows, I review some of this work, focusing on the critiques of the 'standard' view of individuality, equality and knowledge it develops.

---

16 This phrase comes from Yeatman (1994a), p. 78.

Thirty or more years' work by feminist political theorists shows that, in Western European thought, while all individuals are people, not all people are individuals. In early modern political thought, the household was the main political unit, and the head of household was the main political actor, or 'individual'. The head of household 'stood for' all the other people in the household, and, because these people came under his protection and jurisdiction, they were thought of as if they were part of him.[17] Thus the 'individual' of early modern politics was a white, male, property-owning person. Women, children and servants were *not* individuals, in a political sense. These people, if they were considered at all in early liberal political theory, were seen as being part of the domestic (that is, non-public) sphere. They did not participate in the political, economic, and intellectual activities that are the basis of public life, and, importantly for later developments, they were not *conceptually* part of it (Gutmann 1980, Eisenstein 1981, Elshtain 1981, Pateman 1988, 1989, Yeatman 1994a). Women, children and servants were *not* thought of as autonomous rational thinkers, they did not have equal access to knowledge, and they could not be the 'subjects' – or creators – of knowledge. They were not equal, they did not vote, and they did not have the same human rights as those who were individuals. Thus the modern conception of individuality did not, when it was first developed, include women and other non-property-owning people (the 'working classes' for example). Nor did it include the indigenous peoples of the countries that were later colonised by Western European powers.

This way of thinking is of course no longer legitimate. It has been destabilised by several generations of activism on behalf of women, working-class people, indigenous people and disabled people. These people are now formally included in this model of individuality. In theory, they have equal rights. They can vote, own property and demand redress if treated unjustly. However, because of the way it originated, this model of individuality is inherently problematic. One problem, which has implications for our model of public education, has to do with the logic of equality. Social justice, in the modern political system, depends on the concept of equality. When it can be shown that a person or group has not had an equal opportunity to succeed in society, this is an injustice and, for the system to be legitimate, it must be rectified. However – and this is important – because equality is taken to mean *sameness*, this means

---

17 Within this system, known as patrimonial democracy, it was quite legitimate for adults who could not establish their own households to depend on those who could.

that if the person or group is to prove that they have been treated unjustly, logically, they must first show that they are *the same as* all the other people or groups in the society (Rancière 1992).

This requirement produces some difficulties. For example, in order to argue that women should have the same rights as men, the early feminists had to claim that women are the same as men. While this claim eventually achieved formal equal rights for women, it didn't work very well in practice, as women and men are *not* actually the same. However, we don't have the conceptual tools for thinking outside the one-size-fits-all, male-as-norm model of individuality, with the result that women's differences from men can *only* be seen as lacks or defects. In the modern political framework, equality *with difference* is not possible. The experiences of other previously excluded groups have been similar. They too are not, at a deep level, *recognised* as being 'fully' equal. However, political activism in the late 20th century emphasised difference, which produced a proliferation of many new and different 'identity categories' – women, black, indigenous, gay, disabled and so on – each arguing for recognition and inclusion in competition with the others. There were fractures between these groups, and separatism became the main strategy. The critics of this approach called it 'identity politics' or 'essentialism' (Riley 1988, Fuss 1989). While these developments were important for pointing out how the standard, one-size-fits-all model of individuality does not include everyone, they did not solve the problem of how to argue against injustice from a position of difference. Post-modern political thought has developed out of this difficulty.

Post-modern political theorists are interested in the concept of *difference*, not as the antithesis of equality, but as an interdependent term. This has, I think, some interesting implications for educational sociology, some of which are explored in the final section of this chapter. First, however, I review the (related) post-modern critiques of the 'standard' view of knowledge.

Knowledge, subjectivity and equality/difference

Post-modern theorists argue that, just as women, working-class and indigenous peoples were excluded from the conceptual categories that underpin individuality, so are they excluded from the 'standard' view of knowledge, and from 'subjectivity' of that knowledge. For example, feminist theorists influenced by psychoanalytic theory have argued that Western thought is organised so that meaning is produced in a binary, A/not-A system in which one term of a pair of terms achieves its meaning through being whatever the more highly valued term is not (Jay 1981). 'Woman', for example, is whatever is 'left over from' or not wanted by the category 'man' and, following from this, 'the feminine' is whatever is *not* included in categories such as rationality, objectivity, knowledge, and so on traditionally associated with 'the masculine' (Irigaray 1985, 1987, Walkerdine 1989, 1990, Lloyd 1993). Thus, they argue, despite all the years of feminist struggle, and notwithstanding that many women do occupy positions of power, it is difficult, if not impossible, for a woman to position herself *both* as a woman *and*, simultaneously, as the authoritative 'speaking subject' of some branch of knowledge. In the unconscious symbolic realm, women have no 'authority' of their own, so that the only role available to them is in support of and 'next to the man' (Sartori 1994). This pattern, feminist scholars of science argue, is especially obvious in science, which, at least traditionally, has been seen as exemplifying objectivity, rationality, and so on. Science, they say, only becomes possible through its exclusion of everything seen as being part of the feminine (Keller 1985, Irigaray 1987, Lloyd 1993). Similarly, post-colonial theorists have shown how indigenous peoples are also unable to participate both as themselves *and* as the speaking subjects of Western knowledge (Spivak 1987, Bhabha 1994, Willinsky 1998, Ziarek 2001).

There is plenty of evidence that these ideas are replicated in our education system. For example, high-achieving girls (and Asian students) are pathologised as not really 'having what it takes' (masculinity), as getting the results they do through hard work and/or excessive conformism (Walkerdine 1989, 1990). Similarly, Māori, when they are successful in the education system, are constructed as not 'really' Māori (McKinley 2002). More recently, the emergence of the 'under-achieving boys' problem tells us, not that girls have taken over, but that the areas in which middle-class girls now predominate are no longer the areas that matter. For example, medicine and law are not the high-status professions they once were: their practitioners are now 'service providers'. The 'real game in town' is in the IT and financial sectors, and it is here that the new locus of reason and masculinity is located. The traditional role of women, as stagehands and service providers, and/or a reserve army of labour, has not actually been disrupted.

Just as it is impossible to argue against injustice from a position of difference, within the standard view of knowledge it is difficult to make a case for different 'ways of knowing'. As outlined earlier, the 'new' sociology of education in the 1970s produced calls for the 'voices' and knowledge systems of other groups to be recognised and included in the school curriculum. More recently, arguments are being made for curriculum development based on epistemological pluralism and/or the recognition of mātauranga Māori (Cooper 2008, Andreotti 2009). However, just as difference is reconstructed as deficit in the standard view of individuality, in the 'standard' view of knowledge, epistemological pluralism can only be seen as relativist (e.g. Moore and Muller 1999, Moore and Young 2001, Young 1998, 2008). If these questions are considered within the existing conceptual categories, there is no easy way around this, and, because our thinking is, at a very deep level, organised by these categories, we can't just get rid of them. Thinking outside the 'old' categories involves working with them differently, foregrounding different things, and working in the spaces between them. The final section of this chapter reviews work that could help us do this.

Spaces and processes for thinking differently

Post-modern political theorists argue that we need ways of thinking about personhood that allow difference to be expressed *as* difference, not as deficiency, lack or exclusion (Yeatman 1994a, Young 1990). For example, many Māori educators have been resisting the 'closing the gaps' policies of recent years, arguing that Māori don't want to be measured by Pākehā standards. They want an education system that can build, not damage, the capacity of Māori to *be* Māori, and to live *as* Māori (Durie 2003, Penetito 2002, Jenkins and Jones 2000). This approach, known as the 'politics of difference' to distinguish it from the 'identity politics' it rejects, does *not* involve abandoning egalitarianism and individualism. Rather, these ideas are seen as the starting point for debate and deconstruction. Some scholars maintain that simply doing this is enough to produce change. They say that simply bringing the assumptions that underlie an idea out into the open changes the way the idea 'works' (Fuss 1989). Political activism then no longer involves trying to achieve equal rights and/ or access to existing structures and systems. Rather, the focus is on developing contexts and processes that allow previously excluded groups to have a voice, but, more than this, to just *be*. Difference is the focus, it is central to the debate, and the goal is to allow it to be expressed on its own terms, not in relation to existing norms. This, it is argued, will allow previously excluded groups to work out their own *different* conception of individuality.[18] Separatism does not necessarily follow from this, and, in the longer term, this would not be a helpful strategy. Rather, the aim is to 'work difference together', to think in the spaces *between* existing categories, and to build relationships that allow the partners to acknowledge and genuinely recognise each other's differences – *as* differences, not deficiencies (Young 1990, Yeatman 1994a, Yeatman and Wilson 1995). Thus in this work there is an emphasis on plurality, difference, process and relationships, and on 'deliberative' forms of democratic participation.[19] For the psychoanalytically oriented feminist theorists, this involves finding ways to build the kinds of relationships that could allow the development of a genuinely female symbolic realm (Cicioni 1989, Piussi 1990, Whitford 1991, Sartori 1994). Alongside this, post-modern theorists of knowledge argue that we are seeing a shift in knowledge's core meaning. The standard view of it as an ideal to be aimed for, a 'thing', developed and stored in experts, and able to be organised into disciplines, is being replaced by a view of it as a process, a form of energy, or a system of networks and flows, defined not through what it *is*, but through what it can *do* (Lyotard 1984, Castells 2000, Gilbert 2005).

This shift away from universal ideals and concrete 'objects' to a focus on processes, relationship-building, negotiation and 'third spaces' provides an opportunity to look at the 'inequality' question through a new and more productive lens. To take one recent example, the 'new' or 'post-bureaucratic' model of public management emphasises difference, ongoing change, and negotiation in the spaces between traditional government departments and between government services and their clients. Government services are now in theory 'joined up', project-based, and client-focused. There is a focus on 'mutual adjustment', on listening to, and assuming a capacity for judgment and trust in the client, and an

---

18 See the collection of articles in Yeatman and Wilson (1995) for some examples of how people have thought about these ideas in the New Zealand-Australian context.

19 Deliberative democracy is government via discussion/dialogue/debate between citizens, in 'little polities' and thus involves an emphasis on 'voice', dialogue and process, in structured and informed contexts. See, for example, Gutmann and Thompson (2004) or Hajer and Wagenaar (2003).

expectation that services will be 'co-produced' in ways that genuinely meet client needs (Yeatman 1994b, Parker and O'Leary 2006). Working in this way requires a focus, not on shiny new structures, but on the messier work of relationship-building, context-setting and space negotiation, work that would be difficult to do in the existing outcome- and accountability-oriented agenda. This 'personalised' services model has been taken up by some educationists interested in transforming schools for the 21st century (e.g. Miller and Bentley 2003, Bentley and Miller 2006, Leadbeater 2004, 2006). Leadbeater, for example, advocates a model involving the development of 'prosumers', in which students, with scaffolding from older, more knowledgeable others, carry out their own needs analysis and conceive and design their own programme of learning. Personalising learning was a major feature of the British government's education policy in 2003–04, and the same occurred in New Zealand in 2006–07 (Ministry of Education 2006, Maharey 2007). However, in these contexts it meant flexible, multilevel study that allowed students a certain amount of choice in assembling customised programmes of study. For Leadbeater, this is a very limited form of 'mass customisation' of the traditional curriculum which is unlikely to allow co-produced learning, and, because it is an 'add-on' to existing structures, is likely to exacerbate rather than reduce inequalities.

Personalising learning of the kind advocated by Leadbeater *could* be the basis of a schooling system which allowed and encouraged difference to flourish. However, it would call into question most of what we do now. For example, in a process-oriented, locally negotiated curriculum what would happen to the traditional canon of universal knowledge? How would we assess achievement and progress without reference to some sort of norm? If schools no longer see sorting people for their future employment destination as a key function, who or what will replace them? How will the tendency for new approaches to be mobilised to serve old interests be resisted? How these questions are answered is critical to whether personalising learning (or some other idea) can transform the education system or whether it follows 'diversity' and 'inclusiveness' in becoming a 'politically correct' but empty slogan, an add-on to the existing system that doesn't change anything.

The issue of *who* should answer these questions is also important. The personalised learning idea arises in the new public management model, which is in turn linked with the move towards 'deliberative' democracy:

that is, organising decision-making about the delivery of public services so that it happens, not in centralised bureaucracies, but in community-based 'little polities'. These ideas go together. Because reorganising our schools to deliver personalised learning programmes would require major changes to current practices, there would first need to be a new 'policy settlement' (Openshaw 1995), a new public consensus on what we think our education system is, and what it is for. We collectively would need to develop a 21st century version of the 'Beeby vision', one that aims to improve people's chances of living a good life by developing and extending their ability to be – and live as – who they want to be.

Educational sociologists can, I think, make a contribution to this process. Firstly, as outlined in the first half of this chapter, past work has accumulated a large body of data showing that the current system does not produce equal opportunity. This work must inform the new policy settlement. Secondly, the traditional role of independent critic will obviously be important as the debates progress. Thirdly, there is also, I think, an important place in these debates for 'prospective' thinking: that is, thinking which aims to creatively shape the world as we *want* it to be, as opposed to thinking that simply reacts to developments as they occur (Homer-Dixon 2006).

This chapter has reviewed educational sociology in Aotearoa/New Zealand over the last half century or so in terms of how it has contributed to reducing disparity, and made a case for a new focus. It has suggested that this new focus could emerge from a synthesis of recent developments in political theory and epistemology, and that putting these ideas together will allow us to see beyond the 21st century goal of liberation through universal knowledge and equality/sameness, to new spaces that, by encouraging differences to assert and develop themselves, allow people to realise their full potential. However, 'operationalising' this shift away from absolute ideals to processes and intermediate spaces requires a new intellectual infrastructure. The 'old' theories of knowledge, current theories of social change, and our ways of thinking about cognitive capacities won't serve us well in this new environment (Kegan 1982, 1994, 2000, Garvey Berger 2004). The work of developing 21st century versions of these theories is, I think, educational sociology's future challenge.

References

Alton-Lee, A. (2003). *Quality teaching for diverse students: best evidence synthesis.* Wellington: Ministry of Education.

Alton-Lee, A., Nuthall, G. & Patrick, J. (1987). Take your brown hand off my book: racism in the classroom. *SET: research information for teachers*, 1, 8.

Andreotti, V. (2009). The knowledge society debate: cognitive adaptation versus epistemological pluralism. TLRI position paper in progress: available at wiki. canterbury.ac.nz/download/attachments/5801107/TLRI+position+paper+VA. pdf?version+3

Anyon, J. (1980). Social class and the hidden curriculum of work. *Journal of Education.* 162, 1.

Anyon, J. (1981). Social class and school knowledge. *Curriculum Inquiry.* 11, 1.

Barrington, J. (1988). Learning the 'dignity of labour': secondary education policy for Māoris. *New Zealand Journal of Educational Studies*, 23, 1. pp. 45-58.

Barrington, J. (2008). *Separate but equal? Māori schools and the Crown 1867–1969.* Wellington: Victoria University Press.

Bates, R. (1980). Sociology of education. In New Zealand Association for Research in Education (Ed.). *Research in education in New Zealand: the state of the art.* Palmerston North: New Zealand Association for Research in Education .

Bauman, Z. (2005). *Work, consumerism and the new poor.* Buckingham UK: Open University Press.

Beck, U. (1992). *Risk society.* London: Sage.

Beck, U. & Beck-Gernsheim, E. (2002). *Individualisation.* London: Sage.

Beeby, C. E. (1986). Introduction. In W. Renwick, *Moving targets: six essays on educational policy.* Wellington: New Zealand Council for Educational Research. pp. xi-xiv.

Belenky, M., Clinchy, B., Goldberger, N. & Tarule, J. (1986). *Women's ways of knowing: the development of self, voice and mind.* New York: Basic Books.

Bell, B. (1988). Girls and science. In S. Middleton (Ed.). *Women and education in Aotearoa.* Wellington: Allen and Unwin. pp. 153-160.

Bentley, T. & Miller, R. (2006). Personalisation: getting the questions right. In *Schooling for tomorrow: personalising education.* Paris: OECD. pp. 115-126.

Bernstein, B. (1971). On the classification and framing of educational knowledge. In B. Bernstein (Ed.). *Class, codes and control: volume 3 – towards a theory of educational transmission.* London: Routledge and Kegan Paul.

Bhabha, H. (1994). *The location of culture.* London: Routledge.

Bishop, R., Berryman, M., Tiakiwai, S. & Richardson, C. (2003). *Te Kōtahitanga: The experiences of year 9 and 10 Māori students in mainstream classrooms.* Wellington: Ministry of Education.

Bourdieu, P. (1971). Systems of education and systems of thought. In M.F.D. Young (Ed.). *Knowledge and control: new directions for the sociology of education.* London: Collier-Macmillan. pp. 189-207.

Bourdieu, P. (1973). Cultural reproduction and social reproduction. In R. Brown (Ed.). *Knowledge, education and social change.* London: Tavistock. pp.71-112.

Bourdieu, P. (1974). The school as a conservative force: scholastic and cultural inequalities. In J. Eggleston (Ed.). *Contemporary research in the sociology of education*. London: Methuen. pp. 32-46.

Bowles, S. & Gintis, H. (1976). *Schooling in capitalist America*. London: Routledge and Kegan Paul.

Castells, M. (2000). *The rise of the network society*. (2nd Ed.). Oxford: Blackwell.

Cicioni, M. (1989). "Love and respect, together": the theory and practice of *affidamento* in Italian feminism. *Australian Feminist Studies*. 10. pp. 71-83.

Codd, J., Harker, R. & Nash, R. (Eds.). (1990). *Political issues in New Zealand education*. (2nd edition). Palmerston North: Dunmore Press.

Cooper, G. (2008). Māui, Tawhaki, kaupapa Māori and ... "progress"? In *Making progress – measuring progress*. NZCER Conference Proceedings. Wellington: NZCER Press.

Department of Education (1971). *Māori children and the teacher*. Wellington: Department of Education.

Du Gay, P. (1996). *Consumption and identity at work*. London: Sage.

Durie, M. (2003). *Māori educational advancement at the interface between Te Ao Māori and Te Ao Whanui*. Paper presented at the Hui Taumata Mātauranga Tuatoru, Turangi, March 2003.

Eisenstein, Z. (1981). *The radical future of liberal feminism*. New York: Longman.

Elshtain, J. B. (1981). *Public man, private woman: women in social and political thought*. Princeton NJ: Princeton University Press.

Franken, M., May, S. & McComish, J. (2005). *Pasifika languages research and guidelines project: literature review*. Hamilton: Wilf Malcolm Institute of Educational Research, University of Waikato.

Fry, R. (1985). *It's different for daughters*. Wellington: New Zealand Council for Educational Research.

Fuss, D. (1989). *Essentially speaking: feminism, nature and difference*. New York: Routledge.

Garvey Berger, J. (2004). Dancing on the threshold of meaning: recognising and understanding the growing edge. *Journal of Transformative Education*. 2, 4. pp. 336-351.

Giddens, A. (1991). *Modernity and self-identity*. Cambridge UK: Polity Press.

Giddens A. (1998). *The third way*. Cambridge UK: Polity Press.

Gilbert, J. (2005). *Catching the knowledge wave? The knowledge society and the future of education*. Wellington: NZCER Press.

Giroux, H. & Searls Giroux, S. (2009). Beyond bailouts: on the politics over education after neoliberalism. *Policy Futures in Education*, 7, 1. pp. 1-4. (Downloaded from www.wwwords.co.uk/PFIE March 2009).

Gordon, L. (1997). 'Tomorrow's Schools' today: school choice and the education quasi-market. In M. Olssen and K. Morris Matthews (Eds.). *New Zealand education policy in the 1990s*. Palmerston North: Dunmore Press.

Grace, G. (1990). The New Zealand treasury and the commodification of education. In: S. Middleton, J. Codd and A. Jones (Eds.). *New Zealand education policy today: critical perspectives*. Wellington: Allen and Unwin. pp. 27-39.

Gutmann, A. (1980). *Liberal equality*. Cambridge UK: Cambridge University Press.

Gutmann, A. & Thompson, D. (2004). *Why deliberative democracy?* Princeton NJ: Princeton University Press.

Hajer, M. & Wagenaar, H. (Eds.). (2003). *Deliberative policy analysis.* Cambridge UK: Cambridge University Press.

Harker, R. (1990). Schooling and cultural reproduction. In J. Codd, R. Harker, and R. Nash (Eds.). *Political issues in New Zealand education* (2nd edition). Palmerston North: Dunmore Press. pp. 25-42.

Homer-Dixon, T. (2006). *The upside of down: catastrophe, creativity and the renewal of civilisation.* Washington DC: Island Press.

Hunt, T. (2009). Apples with pears. *Education Review.* 3 April, 2009.

Irigaray, L. (1985). *This sex which is not one.* Ithaca NY: Cornell University Press.

Irigaray, L. (1987). Is the subject of science sexed? *Hypatia.* 2, 3. pp. 65-87.

Jay, N. (1981). Gender and dichotomy. *Feminist Studies.* 7, 1. pp. 38-56.

Jenkins, K. & Jones, A. (2000). Māori education policy: a state promise. In J. Marshall, E. Coxon, K. Jenkins and A. Jones (Eds.). *Politics, policy, pedagogy: Education in Aotearoa/New Zealand.* Palmerston North: Dunmore Press. pp. 139-156.

Jones, A. (1988). Which girls are 'learning to lose'? Gender, class, race and talking in the classroom. In S. Middleton (Ed.). *Women and education in Aotearoa.* Wellington: Allen and Unwin. pp. 143-152.

Jones, A. (1986). At school I've got a chance: social reproduction in a New Zealand secondary school. PhD Thesis. University of Auckland.

Kegan, R. (1982). *The evolving self: problem and process in human development.* Cambridge MA: Harvard University Press.

Kegan, R. (1994). *In over our heads: the mental demands of modern life.* Cambridge MA: Harvard University Press.

Kegan, R. (2000). What "form" transforms? A constructive-developmental approach to transformative learning. In J. Mezirow (Ed.). *Learning as transformation: critical perspectives on a theory in progress.* San Francisco: Jossey-Bass. pp. 35-70.

Keller. E.F. (1985). *Reflections on gender and science.* New Haven: Yale University Press.

Lash, S. (1994). Reflexivity and its doubles: structure, aesthetics, community. In U. Beck, A. Giddens and S. Lash (Eds.). *Reflexive modernization.* Cambridge UK: Polity Press. pp. 110-173.

Lauder, H. (1990). The New Right revolution and education in New Zealand. In S. Middleton, J. Codd and A. Jones (Eds.). *New Zealand education policy today: critical perspectives.* Wellington: Allen and Unwin. pp. 1-26.

Lauder, H. and Hughes, D. (1990). Social origins and differences in school outcomes. *New Zealand Journal of Educational Studies.* 25. pp. 37-60.

Lauder, H., Hughes, D., Watson, S., Simiyu, I., Strathdee, R. & Waslander, S. (1995). *Trading in futures: the nature of choice in educational markets in New Zealand.* Wellington: Victoria University.

Leadbeater, C. (2004). *Learning about personalization: how can we put the learner at the heart of the education system?* Nottingham UK: DfES/Demos. Retrieved September 2006 from http://www.demos.co.uk.

Leadbeater, C. (2006). The future of public services: personalised learning. *Schooling for tomorrow: Personalising education.* Paris: OECD. pp. 101-114.

Lloyd, G. (1993). *The man of reason: 'male' and 'female' in western philosophy*. London: Routledge.

Lyotard, J-F. (1984). *The post-modern condition: a report on knowledge*. Manchester: Manchester University Press.

McKenzie, D. (1992). The technical curriculum: second class knowledge? In G. McCulloch (Ed.). *The school curriculum in New Zealand: history, theory, policy, and practice*. Palmerston North: Dunmore Press. pp. 29-39.

McKinley, E. (2002). Brown bodies, white coats: post-colonialism, Māori women and science. PhD Thesis, University of Waikato.

McRobbie, A. (1978). Working class girls and the culture of femininity. In University of Birmingham Centre for Contemporary Cultural Studies: Women's Studies Group, *Women take issue: aspects of women's subordination*. London: Hutchinson.

Maharey, S. (2007). Organising secondary schools for personalising learning. Speech notes for an address to the Auckland Secondary Schools Principals' Association. Retrieved September 2007 from http://www.text.labour.org.nz/Our_mps_top/steve_maharey?speeches_and_releases/070314/i.

Matthews, K. (1988). White pinafores, slates, mud and manuka: Pākehā women's experiences of primary schooling in Hawke's Bay 1880-1918. In S. Middleton (Ed.). *Women and education in Aotearoa*. Wellington: Allen and Unwin. pp. 20-30.

Marshall, T. H. (1977). *Class, citizenship and social development*. Chicago: Chicago University Press.

Middleton, S. (1987a). Feminism and education in post-war New Zealand: An oral history perspective. In R. Openshaw and D. McKenzie (Eds.). *Re-interpreting the educational past*. Wellington: New Zealand Council for Educational Research.

Middleton, S. (1987b). Schooling and radicalisation: life-histories of New Zealand feminist teachers. *British Journal of Sociology of Education*. 8, 2. pp. 169-189.

Middleton, S. (1990). Family strategies of cultural reproduction: case studies in the schooling of girls. In J. Codd, R. Harker, and R. Nash (Eds.). *Political issues in New Zealand education* (2nd edition). Palmerston North: Dunmore Press. pp. 99-117.

Miller, R. & Bentley, T. (2003). *'Unique creation': possible futures – four scenarios for 21st century schooling*. Nottingham UK: National College for School Leadership/Demos.

Ministry of Education (2006). *Let's talk about personalising learning*. Wellington: Ministry of Education.

Ministry of Education (2007). *The New Zealand curriculum for English-medium teaching and learning in years 1-13*. Wellington: Ministry of Education, Learning Media.

Moore, R. & Muller, J. (1999). The discourse of "voice" and the problem of knowledge and identity in the sociology of education. *British Journal of Sociology of Education*. 20. pp. 189-206.

Moore, R. & Young, M.F.D. (2001). Knowledge and the curriculum in the sociology of education: towards a reconceptualisation. *British Journal of Sociology of Education*, 22, 4. pp. 445-461.

Nash, R. (1981). The New Zealand district high schools: a study in the selective function of rural education. *New Zealand Journal of Educational Studies*. 16, 2. pp. 150-160.

Nash, R. (1983). *Schools can't make jobs*. Palmerston North: Dunmore Press.

Nash, R. (1993). *Succeeding generations: family resources and access to education in New Zealand*. Auckland: Oxford University Press.

Nash, R., Harker, R. & Charters, H. (1990). Reproduction and renewal through education. In J. Codd, R. Harker, and R. Nash (Eds.). *Political issues in New Zealand education* (2nd edition). Palmerston North: Dunmore Press. pp. 61-73.

Openshaw, R. (1995). *Unresolved struggle: consensus and conflict in New Zealand state post-primary education*. Palmerston North: Dunmore Press.

Parker, S. & O'Leary, D. (2006). Re-imagining government: putting people at the heart of New Zealand's public sector. Available at http://www.demos.co.uk.

Pateman, C. (1988). *The sexual contract*. Cambridge UK: Cambridge University Press.

Pateman, C. (1989). *The disorder of women: democracy, feminism and political theory*. Cambridge UK: Polity Press.

Penetito, W. (2002). Research and context for a theory of Māori schooling. *McGill Journal of Education*. 37, 1. pp. 89-109.

Phillips, G., McNaughton, S. & MacDonald, S. (2002). *Picking up the pace: effective literacy interventions for accelerated progress over the transition into decile one schools*. Auckland: Child Literacy Foundation, Woolf Fisher Research Centre.

Piussi, A-M. (1990). Towards a pedagogy of sexual difference. *Gender and Education*. 2, 1. pp. 81-90.

Ramsay, P. (Ed.). (1985). *Family, school and community*. Sydney: Allen & Unwin.

Rancière, J. (1992). Politics, identification, subjectivization. *October*. 61. pp.58-65.

Riley, D. (1988). *"Am I that name?" feminism and the category of "women" in history*. London: Macmillan.

Rose, N. (1999). *Powers of freedom*. Cambridge UK: Cambridge University Press.

Sartori, D. (1994). Women's authority in science. In K. Lennon and M. Whitford (Eds.). *Knowing the difference: feminist perspectives in epistemology*. London: Routledge. pp. 110-121.

Schwartz, J. (1999). *Cassandra's daughter: a history of psychoanalysis in Europe and America*. London: Allen Lane/Penguin.

Smith, G.H. (1990).Taha Māori, Pākeha capture. In J. Codd, R. Harker, and R. Nash (Eds.). *Political issues in New Zealand education* (2nd edition). Palmerston North: Dunmore Press. pp. 183-197.

Spivak. G. (1987). *In other worlds: essays in cultural politics*. London: Routledge and Kegan Paul.

Strathdee, R. and Hughes, D. (2006). Socio-economic status and tertiary education attendance in New Zealand. *New Zealand Journal of Educational Studies*. 41, 2. pp. 45-89.

Tennant, M. (1977). Natural directions: the New Zealand movement for sexual differentiation in education in the early twentieth century. *New Zealand Journal of Educational Studies*. 12. pp. 142-153.

Thrupp, M. (1995).The school mix effect: the history of an enduring problem in educational research policy and practice. *British Journal of Sociology of Education*. 16. pp. 183-203.

Thrupp, M. (1997). How school mix shapes school processes: a comparative study of New Zealand schools. *New Zealand Journal of Educational Studies*. 32, 1. pp. 53-82.

Timperley, H., Phillips, G. & Wiseman, J. (2003). *The sustainability of professional development in literacy – parts one and two: a report to the Ministry of Education.* Wellington: Ministry of Education.

Walkerdine, V. (1989). *Counting girls out.* London: Virago.

Walkerdine, V. (1990). *The mastery of reason: cognitive development and the production of rationality.* London: Routledge.

Waslander, S., Hughes, D., Lauder, H., McGlinn, J., Newton, S., Thrupp, M. & Dupuis, A. (1994). *The Smithfield project phase one: an overview of activities.* Wellington: Ministry of Education.

Waslander, S. & Thrupp, M. (1995). Choice, competition and segregation: an empirical analysis of a New Zealand secondary school market 1990–1993. *Journal of Education Policy.* 10. pp. 1-26.

Whitford, M. (1991). *Luce Irigaray: philosophy in the feminine.* London: Routledge.

Willinsky, J. (1998). *Learning to divide the world: education at empire's end.* Minneapolis: University of Minnesota Press.

Willis, P. (1977). *Learning to labour: how working-class boys get working-class jobs.* Farnborough: Saxon House.

Wylie, C. (1997). *Self-managing schools seven years on: what have we learnt?* Wellington: New Zealand Council for Educational Research.

Yeatman, A. (1994a). *Postmodern revisionings of the political.* New York: Routledge.

Yeatman, A. (1994b). The reform of public management: an overview. *Australian Journal of Public Administration.* 53, 3. pp. 287-295.

Yeatman, A. & Wilson, M. (Eds.). (1995). *Justice and identity: antipodean practices.* Sydney NSW: Allen and Unwin.

Young, I.M. (1990). *Justice and the politics of difference.* Princeton NJ: Princeton University Press.

Young, M.F.D. (1971). (Ed.). *Knowledge and control: new directions for the sociology of education.* London: Collier-Macmillan.

Young, M.F.D. (1998). *The curriculum of the future: from the 'new sociology of education' to a critical theory of learning.* London: Routledge Falmer.

Young, M.F.D. (2008). *Bringing knowledge back in: from social constructivism to social realism in the sociology of education.* London: Routledge.

Ziarek, E. (2001). *An ethics of dissensus: postmodernity, feminism, and the politics of radical democracy.* Stanford CA: Stanford University Press.

Parking in the Margins: The Sociology of Education

Joanna Kidman

There is little that divides university staff more than the vexed question of campus car parking. In a fractured, market-driven tertiary environment it is one of those issues that generates a great deal of heat and occasionally a reasonable amount of newspaper copy – these days the geopolitics of the academic power structure are played out in the parking lots of universities. Debates over who shall have access to scarce resources (in this case named or reserved parking spaces), claims and counter-claims over contested territory (covered parks near the centre of campus) and complaints about the cost of occupation are all a reflection of a conflict that is being waged over the changing nature of university hierarchies. It is a kind of academic class war writ small across an expanse of asphalt.

For myself, there is a particular campus parking lot that evokes a certain sense of nostalgia. It is a pay-per-hour car park at the top of Kelburn Parade that marks the place where, until the bulldozers arrived in 2005, Victoria University's former Department of Education used to be. This paper is not a discussion about the institutional machinations of vehicle management, it is about the sociological study of education, but it does, tangentially, concern car parks.

The sociology of education has an interesting history in New Zealand. The Department of Education at Victoria University of Wellington was established as a separate entity from the teachers' training college under the leadership of the first professor of education, J.S. (John Smaillie) Tennant. Tennant had previously headed the teachers' training college in Wellington but in 1920, the same year as the first professor of education was appointed at the University of Canterbury, he was appointed to a part-time Chair in education at Victoria University College. He held positions at both institutions until 1927 when the fledgling Department of Education at the university required his full-time attention (Barrowman 1999, p. 43).

41

The early professors of education were instrumental in developing the study of education at Victoria University as a field of scholarship that was distinct from teacher training. They each shared a commitment to the sociology of education, and this was particularly true of the educational sociologist Professor Crawford Somerset. Later, educational historians, philosophers, anthropologists, psychologists and comparative education specialists joined the staff and the sociological study of education at Victoria University expanded in an increasingly vibrant and diverse intellectual environment.

When I joined the Department as a student in the early 1980s, the staff had long since moved from their offices in the Hunter Building to 'temporary accommodation' in a set of dilapidated prefabs that had been erected in a car park behind the Maclaurin Building. This 'temporary' state of affairs lasted from 1974 until 2005 when the buildings were demolished. In winter, cold southerlies blew through cracks in the un-insulated walls, and in summer the sun beat down on the corrugated iron roof. But the Department was a place where various Ministers of Education and former Directors-General of Education dropped by for meetings or a cup of tea; the staff were congenial and the courses were well taught; the study of education nudged me into thinking about the world in new ways; and every September, a magnificent wisteria bloomed outside my office covering the thin walls of the prefabs. I decided to stay.

At that time the Department of Education was a kind of one-stop shop for a variety of academic disciplines and one might reasonably assume that the presence of so many different specialists would foster the development of a range of interdisciplinary or multidisciplinary collaborations – but one would be quite wrong. The physical proximity of people from different subject areas bears little relation to the kind of research that is done– indeed, the boundaries between disciplinary territories are often strengthened rather than weakened when people with various disciplinary affiliations are clustered in a single organisational unit. In the Department of Education, psychologists and sociologists chatted over coffee in the staff room and attended the many of the same social functions; they supported their colleagues' course proposals through the Faculty Board vetting process and sometimes baby-sat each other's children on the weekends, but they didn't co-author books, share the supervision of postgraduate students, or in the main, read each other's work.

This is hardly surprising. Burton Clark reminds us that "academic territories are first of all subject territories" (Clark 1996, p. 19) and there are many subjects and territories in education. Indeed, the various disciplinary fields that make up the study of education remind me of Desmond Tutu's description of the fellowship of the Church of England – untidy but rather lovable. There is no single field of knowledge that properly belongs to education, rather there are many – this is one of its greatest strengths, but it is also perceived by some as a weakness. One may wonder what the central questions of education are or who the foundational theorists might be; or ask which fundamental principles students must learn – there is no single answer. This is true of most disciplines but it is particularly true of education, because academic staff as a whole do not share allegiances to a common discipline or body of knowledge, and consequently those outside the domain sometimes view educational studies as a series of disciplinary tics rather than a coherent field of inquiry.

Nevertheless disciplinary allegiances were fostered by educational studies staff at Victoria University in much the same way that subject loyalties are built in other academic domains. The processes involved with academic socialisation are important. If academic territories are indeed subject territories as Clark suggests, and if we see academic socialisation as a cultural act; a deep level of engagement with a particular branch of knowledge and the culture, disciplinary language, and intellectual structures that surround it (the *habitus* of the discipline), then the unique academic identities forged alongside those subjects will be central to the way that a department's research strengths are developed and maintained across time.

At Victoria University during the 1980s, undergraduate students moved freely between the disciplinary fields that were on offer in the Department of Education. Jack Shallcrass and Jim Collinge taught courses in educational philosophy, Ken Stevens taught educational sociology, Rollo Arnold and Neil Daglish taught the history of education, John Barrington taught comparative education and New Zealand educational history, and there were several others teaching in the field of educational psychology. Professors Gerald Grace and later, Hugh Lauder, were sociologists who encouraged sociological readings of education, albeit from different theoretical perspectives. Students were quickly made aware that in the broad domain of education they needed to be familiar with a range of disciplinary approaches if they wished to enter postgraduate study in the field. However by the time students enrolled in master's degrees they had usually begun to develop distinct intellectual and disciplinary loyalties. In this respect education can be seen as an aggregating device (for different kinds of academic identities and intellectual biographies) rather than an integrating one. For example, as an undergraduate I moved between the fields of educational sociology and philosophy guided by my supervisor Jim Collinge, but on the completion of my Masters degree, Jim encouraged me to expand my horizons beyond the department and conduct my doctoral studies in a fresh academic environment. Today I have a PhD in Sociology from the Australian National University and whenever people ask what it is that I do, I say that I am a sociologist, because that *is* what I am. Working in a faculty of education I am probably more insistent about this iteration of my professional identity than I would be if I was based in a sociology department, but in the crowded, noisy, and multiple fields of education, this is what we do.

There are ebbs and flows in academic disciplines that affect the development of research priorities and decisions about which courses are taught within a department. These decisions are often motivated as much by departmental budgets as they are by academic concerns. In times of relative financial stability within the tertiary sector, staff and students in education get on with their various disciplinary interests, with occasional squabbles over the big questions of educational policy or practice. And, in accordance with the adage that academic politics are so intense precisely because the stakes are so low, there is, as there is in university departments everywhere, a certain degree of feuding. But in times of economic uncertainty or restructuring when there are cutbacks to university funding, the circling of wagons around academic disciplines tends to be played out most fiercely amongst departments, like education, with diverse disciplinary affiliations and knowledge bases.

During the economic restructuring of the late 1980s and 1990s the provision of New Zealand tertiary education veered towards a new ideal, that of user-pays and Rogernomics – a particular blend of radical monetarism, privatisation and free-market ideologies. It was not simply a matter of breaking a few eggs to make an omelette – it was more as if the ownership of eggs had been auctioned to offshore investors and besides, in the pared down economic environment of benefit cuts, layoffs and plant closures, there was no one left to cook them anyway. The breadth of the reforms and the speed with which they were implemented took many academics by surprise. But once the smoke had cleared and the charred landscape of the welfare state came into view, the creep of managerialism into the universities had already begun and this ultimately affected not only the governance and management of universities but also, in subjects like education, the way that certain branches of disciplinary knowledge were perceived. Indeed, it was during this period that many academic and disciplinary hierarchies were substantially revised.

By the late 1980s it was evident that there was a new impatience on the part of many government officials towards social inquiry that deviated from the free-market policies that were driving health, education and social reform. It was not a simple matter of censorship; the 1989 Education Act embedded academic freedom, and the notion of the academic as a 'critic and conscience' of society, in legislation. It was more the case that the sources of funding for certain kinds of social research dried up, while in other instances, those academics who were openly critical of the reforms found that their membership of various government and Ministry advisory committees was not renewed or their advice was no longer sought. These changes had a profound impact on research in the sociology of education – a field in which awkward questions about the nature of power and ideology are frequently asked.

Part of the government agenda was to drive the economic reforms through at great speed, and indeed many New Zealanders who found themselves without jobs or financial security during that period experienced the restructuring as a series of radical shocks. Roger Douglas, the Minister of Finance responsible for implementing the programme, has said as much himself. In his book, *Unfinished Business*, he writes, "[d]efine your interests clearly, and move towards them in quantum leaps, otherwise interest groups will have time to mobilise and drag you down." (Douglas 1993). During this period there was a closing down of public spaces for dissenting voices, leaving many Wellington-based academics with research interests that did not mesh with those of the government in a difficult position.

The economic restructuring and the 1989 Education Act triggered changes in the way academic management and knowledge hierarchies were conceived but in the Department of Education at the University, other related influences were also at work. In the decade following the reforms several of the educational historians, sociologists, anthropologists, comparative education specialists and philosophers in the department either retired or took up positions elsewhere. University funding, always constrained, continued its downward spiral throughout the 1990s and early 2000s and consequently, staff who left the department were not generally replaced. This opened substantial gaps in the institutional memory as experienced academic 'politicians' within the department were no longer on hand to give advice. Moreover, prior to the progressive introduction of the new tertiary funding system between 2004 and 2007, student enrolments were a crucial part of a department's budget. Thus, the number of courses on the books was not greatly reduced but younger staff with less experience and disciplinary training in specific fields such as history and sociology were called upon to teach a wider range of subjects. This had a considerable influence on the way that knowledge in the various fields of education was organised and passed on to students by individual instructors within the school. Knowledge territories within the department were reorganised as education courses became increasingly pan-disciplinary, although not, it should be noted, more interdisciplinary.

At the same time, the public domain of education was undergoing its own sea change. Educational policy across all sectors was revised to embrace new ideas about globalisation, global economies and global citizenship (Duhn 2006, p. 193). Public education in New Zealand has always been hitched to government economic policies but this horse-and-carriage coupling entered a new phase throughout the 1990s and 2000s as the New Zealand government sought entry into new international markets. The discourses of curriculum policy began to incorporate a greater focus on the value of young people becoming 'entrepreneurial', 'international citizens' willing to enter into a global workforce with a marketable set of skills. These ideals were couched in the language of well-being, equity and equality, social justice, fairness, resilience, diversity and inclusivity and it seemed churlish to rail against this new-found optimism about the future. Didn't we (the nay-sayers sitting in our university offices), after all, value fairness and diversity? Well, yes, but our attention was fixed on those 'other' demographic groups – young people who had fallen through the cracks of the global marketplace and who kept on falling; students who would not ever dine at the free-market feast although they might get minimum-wage, casual employment without holiday pay in the kitchens. We were also watching those young people who, upon finding the entrance to the international market was blocked, adapted the lessons of the curriculum to establish those subversive economies at the edges of the global marketplace in everything from bartering and Marae-based economies to the drug trade. It seemed then, as it does now, as if there was some critical 'disconnect' between the rhetoric of educational equality and the practice. Meanwhile education, with its central role in the new economy, became increasingly fractured, dispersed, and prone to the vicissitudes of the international market.

In many ways the reforms were a successful experiment at least as far as the architects of the system might perceive it. Recent research shows that the generation of children educated in the years following the economic reforms frequently construct identities and make employment and educational choices in the context of the free-market discourses that surround them. Nairn and Higgins argue that young people have been "immersed in discourses of competition and enterprise throughout their schooling in education and other marketplaces." (Nairn and Higgins 2007, p. 266). They add,

> Repetition of these discourses over more than two decades in New Zealand constitutes such discourses as natural or normal and it is not therefore surprising that many (although not all) of our participants incorporated the norms of the entrepreneurial subject in their discussions of their imagined and actual lives. (ibid.)

Nairn and Higgins show that some young people have picked up on the opportunities on offer within this neo-liberal framework but I suspect there have also been certain costs, particularly in terms of a narrowing of the imagination that has tied them to a vision of the future that promises much but doesn't deliver equitably to all. In this respect there has been plenty of material for the sociology of education over the past two decades, particularly in that area of sociology that is so important to many of us – the relationship between structure and agency – and some important work has been done. However during the 1980s and 1990s another challenge emerged that, for a while at least, slowed the passage of debate.

The sociology of education as it was practised in New Zealand during the 1980s owed much to the work of British sociologists, particularly those who had developed social class analyses or analyses of power relations. Included in this canon were writers like Basil Bernstein, Anthony Giddens, Michael Young, A.H. Halsey, Paul Willis and others from the former Centre for Contemporary Cultural Studies at Birmingham University. Beyond the United Kingdom, New Zealand sociologists of education were familiar with the work of Paulo Freire, Pierre Bourdieu, Max Weber, Georg Lukacs, Louis Althusser, Antonio

Gramsci, Jurgen Habermas and the Frankfurt School, amongst many others. But in Britain, the power structures were changing, as they were in New Zealand and elsewhere. Social class didn't disappear and neither did capitalism but the modes of production, patterns of consumption, traditional occupational structures and organisation of labour diversified in new ways. These changes took place alongside the advancement of increasingly sophisticated technology, the growth of the media, and the mobilisation around the globe of different peoples, which led to new trends in immigration as well as the rise of new social movements. The 'New Sociology' of the 1970s and 1980s still had much to say that was relevant but was unable to account for some of the patterns that were emerging. Traditionally the sociology of education, at least as it was practiced in New Zealand, offered a bridge between governance and civil society, but by the 1990s the structures of power were multiplying rapidly, and so too were the forms of human agency and resistance. I have considerable sympathy here with the views of Jordanian-born sociologist, Mohammed Bamyeh, who has likened the modern institutionalisation of power in civil society to the spread of colonisation, insofar as the structures of governance are frequently set up without much consultation in the assumption that once the institutional shell is in place the people will arrive "merrily to live in it" (Bamyeh 1998). He adds that there is a widespread supposition in the West that society will eventually catch up with its systems of governance – a premise, he suggests, based on centuries of colonisation.

Mohammed Bamyeh has an interesting point and it has been made by others (e.g. Choudry 2007). The 1989 Education Act created several new institutional layers of educational governance and a number of organisations were created for the purpose of managing practically every aspect of the education system. The New Zealand Qualifications Authority was established along with the New Zealand Vice-Chancellors' Committee and the Tertiary Education Commission, and in the climate of decentralisation that accompanied *Tomorrow's Schools*, regional education boards were abolished and Boards of Trustees were given the power to govern their own affairs. Deregulation permeated the entire social and economic system although the changes to the education system as a whole were particularly acute. New Zealanders caught up with the systems of governance eventually but in many cases the costs to individuals and local communities were high (Dalziel 2002).

In universities, the role of the Vice-Chancellor was recreated as a Chief Executive Officer, and many academic staff saw this as a shift from the former relationship, where Vice-Chancellors had acted as scholarly leaders, to a more directorial role as employers and managers (Kidman 2001, pp. 207–211). The institutions of higher education grew new managerial shells around ideologies that promoted and rewarded competition and corporate enterprise – signs went up in university car parks reserving spaces for the directors and managers of this and that, and certain areas were cordoned off for vehicles owned by those who brought status and funding into the university coffers. If the shift in the discourses and geopolitics of higher education was not quite Orwellian in scope, at times it seemed to come very close.

Over the same period, teacher education was brought into closer alignment with competency-based paradigms and market-oriented philosophies. Basil Bernstein has argued that teacher training is increasingly focused on producing pedagogical identities with short-term priorities that can be adjusted to the shifting demands of the marketplace (Bernstein 2000). In New Zealand this kind of 'short-termism' can be seen in the construction of permeable teacher identities, with a primary emphasis on developing non-specialised technical practices that are flexible enough to adapt to fast-changing educational and curriculum settings. These identities seem to have few allegiances or ties to a particular body of knowledge or practice; rather, education workers are taught to enact what might be described as 'travelling' practice – the ability to parcel up a collection of generic 'best practice' skills that can be readily transported between various educational contexts. While this approach meets the need to establish a mobile educational workforce equipped to deal with unpredictable situations and changeable market demands, theorists such as John Beck contend that without a general theory connecting pedagogic discourse with key concepts of power and control to a comprehensive analysis of the State, these self-referential formulations of identity reveal a curious emptiness (Beck 2002, pp. 623–624).

This hollowness at the core can also be seen in the reconstruction of academic hierarchies and the corresponding move towards rewarding technical inquiry that incorporates a substantial performance component. In recent years a new cadre of university-based educational researchers, focused on providing generic solutions that can be applied in diverse contexts, has begun to emerge. At the same time there is a drive towards conducting micro-level investigations that offer technical responses to questions formulated in the absence of a theory of the economy, the State, agency, and the exercise of power. Moreover, in most New Zealand universities the number of education courses that emphasise technical, practice-based material has increased but there has been a corresponding reduction in courses that offer alternative discourses including critical theories of education and social control. In this respect, the philosophy and sociology of education have not fared well.

As a sociologist of education I often feel like a professional scold in the face of unrelenting optimism about globalisation and the economy – this savage, endless cycle that weds academic researchers, education workers and young people to the boom and bust of free-market enterprise. So what then can be retrieved? Here is an answer of sorts. More than twenty years ago I took my first undergraduate course in the sociology of education at the Department of Education at Victoria University. The classes were held in an old chemistry lab in the Easterfield building and it was there that I first encountered the ideas of Pierre Bourdieu, Basil Bernstein, Talcott Parsons, Emile Durkheim, Bowles and Gintis, and others. The course was run by Ken Stevens, an extraordinary teacher and the co-editor of this book.

Each week, Ken created for us a unique pedagogic persona, weaving stories about his upbringing on a King Country sheep station with tales about his life as a young teacher in the Waikato. As he worked through complex theoretical material, he recounted conversations he'd had with his wife or his daughters, or he recalled horseback riding with his father on the farm – big theories interspersed with small narratives of rural and village life in the farmlands of New Zealand. In this way, he incorporated his own intellectual biography with complicated and occasionally rather opaque theoretical narratives in ways that were always immediately accessible to students.

Nowadays I run that sociology of education course and it is held in the same old chemistry lab in the Easterfield building. At the moment the class is rather preoccupied with theories about continuity and change and last week, on one of his trips back to New Zealand, Ken came in to give a guest lecture. I sat with my class and a PhD student of mine who is tutoring on the course and found myself thinking back to the time when my lifelong fascination with the sociology of education began in that very same lecture theatre. Looking around the class I wondered which of my students might find themselves, twenty-two years hence, remembering their own intellectual awakening in this curious field.

We are no longer based on the Kelburn campus although we do our undergraduate teaching there. After Ken's lecture I had two slips of paper in my pocket – a note to return a call to Jim Collinge, my former thesis supervisor, and another reminding me to email the eminent educational sociologist and erstwhile member of the school of education, Jane Gilbert. As the taxi took us back past the parking lot where the school of education used to stand and into the leafy suburb of Karori where the Faculty of Education is located now, I saw Jack Shallcrass entering a café and Wally Penetito, my professor and colleague, packing books into the boot of his car and I thought, yes – this is what it's about. Those people who came before us and those who will follow behind. These are the stories we tell. This is what we do.

References

Bamyeh, Mohammad, A. (1998). Sociology, civil society, and the unbounded world. *Canadian Journal of Sociology*. 23. pp. 2-3.

Barrowman, R. (1999). *Victoria University of Wellington 1899–1999: a history*. Wellington: Victoria University Press.

Beck, J. (2002). The sacred and the profane in recent struggles to promote official pedagogic identities. *British Journal of Sociology of Education*. 23, 4.

Bernstein, B. (2000). *Pedagogy, symbolic control and identity: theory, research and critique*. Revised Edition. Lanham, Md.: Rowman & Littlefield.

Choudry, A. (2007). Transnational activist coalition politics and the decolonization of pedagogies of mobilization: learning from anti-neoliberal indigenous movement articulations. *International Education*. 37, 1.

Clark, B. (1996). Diversification of higher education: viability and change. In V.L. Meek, L. Goedegebuure, O. Kivinen and R. Rinne (Eds.). *The mockers and mocked: comparative perspectives on diversity, differentiation and convergence in higher education*. Oxford: Pergamon.

Dalziel, P. (2002). New Zealand's economic reforms: an assessment. *Review of Political Economy*. 14, 1.

Douglas, R. (1993). *Unfinished business*. Auckland: Random House New Zealand.

Duhn, I. (2006). The making of global citizens: traces of cosmopolitanism in the New Zealand early childhood curriculum, Te Whāriki. *Contemporary Issues in Early Childhood*. 7, 3.

Kidman, J. (2001). Travelling in the present historic: a case study of socialisation in an academic community in New Zealand. PhD Thesis. The Australian National University, Canberra, Australia.

Nairn, K. & Higgins, J. (2007). New Zealand's neoliberal generation: tracing discourses of economic (ir)rationality. *International Journal of Qualitative Studies*. 20, 3. pp. 261-281.

He Pārekereke: Māori Education and Pacific Education at Victoria University

Te whānau o He Pārekereke

There was a lot going on back in 1992. It was the year the Sealord deal was signed off and the year that Te Whare Wānanga o Awanuiārangi first opened its doors. It was a year in which nearly half of all Māori teenagers in the labour force were recorded as being unemployed[1] and the year that Paul Holmes and Hine Elder got married. There were big things happening in small places. Much like most years. It was also the year that the Victoria University of Wellington Council ratified a new research institute called He Pārekereke: Institute for Research and Development in Māori Education.[2]

A small group of Māori staff in the School of Education had argued successfully that Māori education was a viable avenue for academic and externally funded contract research for the University. This was no small feat. Prior to the appointment of Kathie Irwin in 1988, there were no Māori education courses that were taught from a Māori point of view and a critical mass of Māori researchers had not been developed. By 1992 several Māori education courses had been set in place and they were proving an attractive option for increasing numbers of Māori students. Many of these students enrolled in education courses at the University after they were personally shoulder-tapped by Kathie Irwin, who worked tirelessly over a period of several years to establish a Māori student body within the School of Education. Her personal approach worked well and as word spread amongst Māori working in the government ministries and schools around Wellington, a nucleus of Māori students began to form around the courses she taught in the BA and Master of Education programmes. By the early 1990s this group had grown large enough for Kathie to think seriously about training Māori graduates in educational leadership and He Pārekereke was subsequently established.

---

1   Cook (2000).

2   Irwin (2002).

The founding philosophy

The name He Pārekereke reflects the kaupapa of the staff and students; the pārekereke is a sheltered area where seedlings are nurtured before being planted out in the main garden. It was intended that Māori students and the growing number of junior Māori staff in the School of Education would find in He Pārekereke a safe place where they could begin their intellectual journeys through the academic world. Above all, it would be an environment where a commitment to Māori scholarship would be validated by Māori academics and students. The institutional context of the university at that time was a difficult one for many Māori, who fought to have their concerns taken seriously. Kaupapa Māori theories were only just beginning to make an impact in academic scholarship in New Zealand and Māori staff and students often found themselves in situations where they were defending practices and protocols that were taken for granted in Māori communities but which were viewed with distrust and, on occasion, overt hostility within the university walls.

The establishment of He Pārekereke was a response to these experiences – it was seen as a forum where new intellectual 'growth' would be nourished and encouraged within a Māori context – a place where, to borrow a phrase from Basil Bernstein, Māori could think the 'unthinkable'.[3] This kaupapa was set in place long before He Pārekereke was formally established, and its development was led by Kathie Irwin, who insisted that kaupapa Māori philosophies would drive the activities, protocols, decisions and practices of its members. She was right to take this approach. As the years passed, and changing government policies created a confusing and complex mix of institutional demands, He Pārekereke members have based their responses on the values drawn from Māori worldviews that were set in place at the outset.

Pacific Education

A growing interest in education in the Pacific region led to the appointment of a lecturer in Pacific education in the School of Education in the mid 1990s. The lecturer, 'Ana Koloto, a Tongan educator, joined the School on the understanding that the Pacific education component of the degree programme would grow over time and more Pacific staff would be

---

3   Bernstein (1996), p. 43.

appointed. However, there were substantial cuts to university funding during this period and each year, the goal of increasing the number of Pacific education staff in the school was put on the back burner.

In 1996, Kathie Irwin raised the possibility of inviting 'Ana to become a member of He Pārekereke. The rationale behind this suggestion was that the situation for Māori academics could be improved if we joined forces with other indigenous peoples in the academy. She argued that the priorities of Māori academics were frequently sidelined within the wider university, but the concerns of Pacific staff were often even less visible. She had also been placed in situations where Māori and Pacific academics were pitted against each other in competition for scarce university resources. Her response was that, as Māori staff, we should simply refuse to compete with Pacific colleagues over these institutional scraps. Moreover she argued that He Pārekereke should open its doors to Pacific staff and act jointly to secure resources and intellectual spaces. Turoa Royal had joined He Pārekereke by then and he strongly supported this idea.

The suggestion was made that Māori staff in the School of Education would host Pacific staff and students, sharing equally whatever resources were available, and commit to fully supporting each other's initiatives within the school and the wider university. Māori staff, it was argued, would make this commitment until the time came when Pacific staff and student numbers had grown to a point where they were ready to establish their own separate intellectual forums within the school. To that end, the idea was that Pacific staff would decide if, when, and how to make the move to establishing an independent research forum and they would never be asked by Māori colleagues to hurry the process. In effect, they would be members of He Pārekereke until they decided otherwise. In addition, He Pārekereke members would establish intellectual spaces within the institute that 'belonged' to Pacific staff. In other words, there would be Māori cultural 'spaces' and Pacific cultural 'spaces' within He Pārekereke that were managed separately.

The idea of joining forces with Pacific educators was one that the Māori staff accepted on an intellectual level, and strong friendships had already been established with the new Pacific education lecturer, so there was a great deal of good will. However, there was much debate within He Pārekereke about whether or not it could work in practice. At the time, Māori academics around the country were engaged in ongoing battles with their institutions for Māori concerns to be recognised and embedded in university policy. Every small victory seemed like a hard-won fight and it was exhausting. Some of the younger Māori staff at He Pārekereke had emerged from these skirmishes feeling bruised, and like many of their Māori students some had only just begun to reconnect with their own Māori identities. These reconnections were important – at that time, many Māori who had grown up at a distance from their papakainga were incorporating kaupapa Māori philosophies into their intellectual journeys and this had allowed them to construct new ways of being Māori and 'thinking' Māori. Not surprisingly, there was an enormous emotional investment in these newly formed intellectual territories and they were fiercely guarded.

The older members of He Pārekereke knew it would be difficult to set up a shared intellectual environment with Pacific staff at a time when Māori were fighting to establish their own spaces and identities within the university but they were equally determined to make it happen. They acknowledged that, while Māori concerns would always be paramount for Māori academics and students, there would also be times when as responsible hosts, Māori staff would make strategic decisions to place Pacific priorities at the top of He Pārekereke's agenda. It was possible, they argued, to share scarce resources *and* manaaki Pacific colleagues without losing ground as Māori. As it turned out, they were dead right. 'Ana Koloto joined He Pārekereke in 1996 and since that time, Māori and Pacific staff and students in education at Victoria University have worked together to build a shared vision of indigenous education in New Zealand and the Pacific that honours the diverse nature of our communities and celebrates our combined strengths. It has not been uniformly straightforward or easy – there were many more debates ahead and the nature of these collegial relationships have evolved over time – but once the decision was made, we were committed to making it work.

Shifting terrain

Marie McCarthy and Joanna Kidman became joint Directors of He Pārekereke in 1997 when Kathie Irwin went on research and study leave but the founding principles of He Pārekereke remained in place and they carried on the work she had begun. Building research capability and capacity continued to be a primary concern and the means by which we worked towards these goals were drawn from Māori and Pacific value systems. Wally Penetito joined the staff in 1998 as a full-time senior lecturer but at around that time, other colleagues were moving on. By 1999, the three founding members of He Pārekereke – Kathie Irwin, Dina Fuli and Marie McCarthy – had moved to new jobs outside Victoria University and 'Ana Koloto had also left. The staffing of He Pārekereke was suddenly much leaner and there were gaps in capacity that proved extremely difficult to fill. Government cuts to university funding also made it impossible to replace all of those who had left and there were times when the future of He Pārekereke looked very shaky indeed.

However, we weren't ready to give up and in 1999 Wally Penetito took over as Director of He Pārekereke when Joanna Kidman went on research and study leave. In the same year a new staff member, Kabini Sanga, joined He Pārekereke, bringing a renewed energy to the operations of the group. The name of the institute changed to reflect the Pacific membership, and was thereafter known as He Pārekereke: Institute for Research and Development in Māori and Pacific Education. Cherie Chu joined He Pārekereke in 2002 and taught alongside Kabini in the Pacific education courses. By this time, He Pārekereke had two directors – Wally Penetito had oversight of the Māori capability-building programmes while Kabini Sanga managed the Pacific programmes. Hazel Phillips joined He Pārekereke in 2005 and she immediately began to work on a range of externally funded Marsden, FRST[4] and HRC[5] projects that broadened the scope of our research activities. She has been involved with several studies relating to environmental health (including biotechnology), youth transitions, and kapo Māori. In addition she was heavily involved with creating mentoring programmes for Māori and indigenous PhD students in South Island universities and this was an important contribution to a range of new developments that were taking place at He Pārekereke.

Since its inception, staff at He Pārekereke were committed to increasing the numbers of Māori graduates, but progress was slow. That was to change in 2003 when He Pārekereke became a founding member entity of a new Māori Centre of Research Excellence hosted by the University of Auckland. This organisation, known as Ngā Pae o te Māramatanga, was led by joint Directors Linda Tuhiwai Smith and Michael Walker. Together they wove a national research body from the scattered groups of Māori academics around the country and they did so in a way that enacted the values of kaupapa Māori theory. This was heady stuff – for

4   Foundation for Research, Science and Technology
5   Health Research Council of New Zealand

the first time university-based Māori scholars had an opportunity to see the principles that had been talked about for years put into practice within a nationwide tertiary education context. More than that, for the first time, Māori academics and students had a formal mechanism for talking to each other across institutions and disciplines.

As members of He Pārekereke, we threw ourselves enthusiastically into the opportunities that this new organisation offered. We were particularly excited about a programme that was established by Ngā Pae o te Māramatanga to support Māori and other indigenous students through to the successful completion of their PhDs. The aim of the programme, known as Te Kupenga o MAI, was to establish a nationwide and international network of Māori and other indigenous scholars that would facilitate 500 Māori PhD completions within five years. It seemed an enormous and practically impossible task but it was one that we supported. The programme is managed by Professor Les Williams and under his guidance, a series of support mechanisms were set up that included regional mentoring programmes, doctoral writing retreats, doctoral conferences, a grants and fellowship programme and an online journal. In addition, specialist mentoring and support was established at Te Whare Wānanga o Aotearoa and Te Whare Wānanga o Awanuiārangi. Members of He Pārekereke set up a MAI group that served Māori and other indigenous doctoral candidates in the Wellington region and within a couple of years we began to see an impressive increase in the number of Māori doctoral completions. We have been assisted in the delivery of these programmes by PhD candidate Margaret Wilkie and our kaiwhakahaere, Pine Southon.

In many ways, our involvement with Ngā Pae o te Māramatanga was a turning point. Several He Pārekereke members were finding the demands of academic life difficult to reconcile with the concerns of the Māori communities to which we belonged and we were experiencing the high levels of isolation that came from having only a very small indigenous intellectual community to which we could turn. The advent of Ngā Pae o te Māramatanga changed that – suddenly we found ourselves in almost daily contact with Māori and other indigenous academics around the country. We were also impressed with the way that this organisation fostered active international connections with indigenous scholars. These kinds of international relationships were also embedded in the Māori-Pacific partnerships at He Pārekereke, and as a result the founding philosophy expanded in new ways.

An evolving philosophy

When Kabini Sanga joined the School of Education, our eyes were opened to new aspects of the Māori-Pacific relationships at He Pārekereke. Kabini had studied in Canada and the Pacific but he came to New Zealand via his homeland in the Solomon Islands. Previously we had framed Pacific education in terms of the priorities of Polynesian nations but we hadn't thought much about the role of Melanesian education. In addition, he was particularly committed to ideas about educational development in the Pacific that were drawn from local priorities and conceptual frameworks. Most of the other He Pārekereke members were trained in the sociology of education but in the early 2000s our understandings of educational aid and development were still based on outdated centre-periphery and dependency theories.

Kabini and Cherie Chu immediately began to develop an extensive programme of teaching and collaborative research in this domain and over time this led Māori staff to rethink the sorts of power relations we were reproducing in our own professional and academic contexts. Kabini and Cherie both provided opportunities for Māori colleagues at He Pārekereke to see their work in action. They regularly convened international educational leadership conferences in different Pacific nations, which were attended by large numbers of their graduate students. Between 2001 and 2006 they ran conferences in five nations including Fiji (2001, 2004), Vanuatu (2003), the Marshall Islands (2005), the Solomon Islands (2006) and New Zealand (2004). These conferences, and the extensive involvement of graduate students, brought Pacific concerns into focus in new and rather uncomfortable ways. Like many other New Zealanders, some of us saw the Pacific as a series of exotic destinations where people sang gloriously in church choirs and wore hibiscus flowers in their hair or swam in clear blue lagoons all day long. We had heard, but didn't fully acknowledge, that another Pacific lay behind the package holidays at leafy resorts where smiling locals in crisp white shirts served margaritas on the beach. We knew, but didn't quite appreciate, that another Pacific existed, with its histories of colonisation, conflict, resistance and endurance. We also hadn't really thought much about the role of the New Zealand government in the economic, political and social concerns that affect the contemporary Pacific. Kabini and Cherie never told us these things. They just pointed the way. We needed to discover those other Pacific places ourselves.

For the Māori staff, these realisations were more like a series of quiet shocks than a sudden, overwhelming realisation but our focus shifted from the way that Māori-Pākehā power relations worked (or didn't work) to looking for different ways of thinking about indigeneity as a constructive, positive force in our lives here in New Zealand. We also came to a fresh understanding that Māori struggles for self-determination can not be seen in isolation – they are part of a much wider, more nuanced picture. Thus, if we want to understand our own situation better, we need to look outside our immediate contexts and establish meaningful connections with indigenous peoples beyond our own shores. This is easy to say but more difficult to put into practice – nevertheless this is the foundation of a genuinely international indigenous scholarship.

Somewhere along the way, Māori staff ceased to act as hosts to Pacific colleagues. He Pārekereke is now focused on Māori education and Pacific education in equal measure. We are neither guests nor hosts, rather we are partners and colleagues in a joint venture and we draw meaning from each other's work, ideas and experiences as indigenous peoples. These relationships have become the basis of our professional identities – they make us who we are.

He Pārekereke today

Much has changed at He Pārekereke since its beginnings. Paul Holmes isn't married to Hine anymore, but the Sealord deal is still in place, and we watch with much pleasure the growth and expansion of wānanga programmes that have opened so many doors for so many Māori. We are still here and our original values are still in place. We have gained a new colleague since the College of Education merged with Victoria University. Fuapepe Rimoni is a teacher educator who provides much needed insight into the domain, and she is also guiding us through the newly merged institutional environment. There is a large group of Pacific graduate students who work with He Pārekereke staff and several have been engaged in collaborative writing projects which have led to publication. Our members regularly provide advice to the governments of the Solomon Islands and New Zealand, as well as to the administrators of other countries in the Pacific region. We have also had a writing fellow and two postdoctoral fellows under our supervision in recent times and a number of Fulbright scholars have also passed through our doors. In addition, we are all engaged on a variety of externally funded research projects, many of which have enabled us to extend our international indigenous networks. Our long-held dream that the University might one day appoint a professor of Māori education was realised in 2008 when Wally Penetito became our inaugural professor. This appointment was a significant move for the University but it is also perceived as a validation of Māori education in general.

We have worked hard over the past seventeen years to create a space where Māori and Pacific education can flourish. These are the things that matter most to us – the creation of Māori and Pacific intellectual spaces within the University and the professional relationships that draw us together at He Pārekereke. All of that, and the fact that we are still here.

References

Bernstein, B. (1996). *Pedagogy, symbolic control and identity*. London: Taylor and Francis.

Cook, L. (2000). *Looking past the 20th century: a selection of long-term statistical trends that influence and shape public policy in New Zealand*. Statistics New Zealand. http://www2.stats.govt.nz/domino/external/web/nzstories.nsf/0/a95f3e9878c148a7cc256b2500of548e?OpenDocument

Irwin, K. (2002). Māori education: from wretchedness to hope. PhD Thesis. Victoria University of Wellington.

EDUCATION POLICY

Educational Research and Democratic Debate: A Reflection on the Centre

Hugh Lauder

When I first arrived at Victoria in 1990 I was surprised at the intensity of debate over education in the capital city and in the Department of Education. It was one thing to pen a critique of New Right policies from the garden campus of Canterbury, another to face the full force of argument and counter argument over the New Right with colleagues, Treasury officials and Ministers.

From the centre there were complexities surrounding educational policy that vanished somewhere over Cook Strait. For a start, it was a Labour government that was embracing New Right or, as they are now more commonly called, neo-liberal policies, and for many there was a loyalty to the intentions behind the reforms if not the methods. Then there was the point made by one of my colleagues in the Department, John Barrington, that the Picot Report (1988) and the government's response to it, *Tomorrow's Schools* (Department of Education 1988) had elements within them embracing community oversight of school governance that any left-thinking academic initiated into politics through the student unrest of the 1970s would embrace.

Indeed, it was only when Labour lost the election in 1990 that it became clear how much its educational policies of the late 1980s were an attempt to reconcile different aspects of the traditions of the New Zealand Left with Chicago-style New Right emphases on 'efficiency'. The National government commissioned Stuart Sexton, a New Right 'identity' in Britain, to fly out to Aotearoa/New Zealand and deliver his blessing to a set of policies that any young Treasury official could have deduced from neo-liberal first principles in ten minutes on the back of an envelope. Out went the non-negotiable equity objectives in the school charter, schools were de-zoned in order to open up competition and the question of the devolved funding of teachers' salaries was reintroduced.

As we noted in *Trading in Futures* (Lauder et al. 1999) in describing this period of struggle over educational policy:

> The new system of schooling was imposed. It had little popular support but was driven by an ideological blueprint supported by rather scant evidence . . . However, true to the idea that New Zealand had become a social laboratory for the world, the fact that a relatively uniform market regime was established in education did allow for many of the claims made by market proponents to be tested. If you will, the New Zealand education system after 1991 constituted a natural experiment. (p. 41)

And, as we noted, it was our good fortune that we were able to undertake the testing. In fact, it was not a matter of good fortune but of the courage of Ministry of Education officials that enabled the research to be undertaken. What more stringent test of these reforms could there be than to ask a known critic of the ideology underpinning the reforms to conduct research on their outcomes?

The point of revisiting this period is to use the research (known as the Smithfield project) that led to *Trading in Futures* and its reception as something of a case study about the role of the researcher and research in democratic debate over policy.

Politics and the research process

One of the characteristics of the politics of the use of research, which vexed me then, and still does, is that educational research and indeed social science research is often seen as no more than a weapon to be used against perceived 'enemies'. In debates as sharp as those in the late 1980s and early 1990s in New Zealand, any scrap of evidence that could be legitimised as research could be hurled into public debate: it is as if all forms of research have methodological equivalence when it comes to knowledge claims. As such, the practice of the use of research in political debate embraces a form of relativism that may chime with elements of post-modernist thought but provides no sense of the quality and therefore the epistemic warrant that different kinds of research carry. A further difficulty is that when politics and research are brought into the same domain questions of warrant are lost. The problem here is that warrant and objectivity in research do not come from individual researchers but from the community of researchers: the critical mass of 'experts'. Yet in political debate the probity of research is often reduced to that of the individual researcher. Educational researchers are trained to adopt rules of evidence in relation to their theories and to be critically aware (reflexivity) of the limits and possibilities of the claims they are making. However, the warrant for research does not come from individual researchers but emerges over time through intellectual debate within the community of researchers. Here then is a further hiatus between research and the demands of policy makers. The latter often want answers to questions more or less on the instant, but given the time it takes for the warrant for research to be established there is a temporal problem in when research should be accepted as worthy of guiding policy.[1]

Underlying these issues is a fundamental problem that post-positivist epistemology has identified: that theories are always underdetermined by evidence and this leaves room for judgments that might favour the particular political or ideological orientation of researchers: indeed it is quite possible to make the claim that ethical values should be considered as a criterion in the appraisal of theories as one of my colleagues as argued (Balarin 2008). It is for this reason that the judgment of a critical community is so important. Yet when the research community gets caught up in political debate, as it inevitably does when it seeks to guide policy, that debate can be caught in claim and counter claim in which the personal, the academic and the political become mixed into a heady cocktail.

In a capital like Wellington, where politicians, civil servants and academics meet at a circuit of events that can range from the Beehive to the Cake Tin, there is both an intimacy and an intensity to debate. As a relatively young and certainly naïve researcher (in the social sciences academics are young until 50), I was shocked at the personal attacks by politicians and ideologues that came my way when we first started producing findings from the Smithfield project, a study aimed at finding out how parents choose schools for their children. Now and again there were moments of unexpected 'rescue'. On Morning Report, Roger Kerr from the Business Roundtable criticised a paper I had written for its sociological jargon that no one could understand. There was a break before I was on to respond and the presenter, Kim Hill, came out to the 'green' room to talk to me about the questions she would be asking. As we went back into the studio she told me that the paper was perfectly comprehensible, what were less so were the footnotes, but that was allowed! A point she then made on air.

---

1   See James Ladwig (1994) for a Bourdieuian view that the field of education research is different from that of policy.

Given the hiatus between academic research and policy there is one abiding question, for me, that has come out of this period: theories and the evidence used to test them are born, live and die. At what stage should the results of this process enter the public domain and inform policy? One way of examining this question is to look back at *Trading in Futures* and compare it to subsequent research on the question of markets in education in Aotearoa. I should hasten to add this is not an attempt to settle old scores; life is too short for that. Before doing so an account is needed as to why this question is so difficult.

Appraising theories

The fundamental task of social science researchers is to develop, 'test' and appraise theories, because as Brian Haig (1987) has noted the most significant insight of post-positivist epistemology is that it is through our best theories that we provisionally come to know the world. In terms of the question about when research should inform policy, the most important question is one of theory appraisal – how can we best judge between competing theories (and related evidence) that may inform a policy issue or problem? Here the question of how well developed a theory is and how good the warrant for it is crucial. These are difficult tasks and they are made more so because many studies in educational research are one-off, making questions of theory development and warrant difficult. When empiricism was the dominant epistemology these questions were much easier to address. For a start, the idea that evidence was in some ways theory impregnated could be ignored. That meant that researchers could engage in the classic 'literature review' in which a range of relevant studies were listed. Where there were conflicting findings, that gave a rationale for a further one-off study that could in principle adjudicate between the conflicting findings. However, once we understand the crucial role of theory in developing knowledge then such an uncomplicated view of educational research should be abandoned.

The problem is that one-off studies do not allow for theory development, in the way that longitudinal studies sometimes can (although one-off studies may point the way to further development). These studies may enter the life cycle of theory growth at a particular juncture, but it is not always clearly signposted: it often takes a rational reconstruction of the life of a theory or a theoretical tradition to see where a one-off study fits into to its development. Moreover, the range of possible criticisms that can be raised include fundamental or metaphysical assumptions about human nature and society, the substantive theory employed, the operationalisation of the theory and the interpretation of the data – and this is not an exhaustive list. Under these circumstances making judgments between theories is very hard indeed.

However, there are reasons as to why policy-makers are not keen to engage in debates about the relative virtues of theories even when they may be of direct relevance to their concerns. The first is that theories are explanatory; they not only provide evidence and insight into policy problems but they also offer an explanation for the phenomena under study. But policy-makers are not always keen on such explanations because they can challenge their political agendas. It is perhaps for this reason that policy-makers prefer research findings where they can 'fit' the evidence to their agendas. Arguably, it is for this reason that neo-classical economics, which has always eschewed sophisticated explanatory structures, is popular.

There is a further research strategy being employed by policy-makers that is problematic but should not be dismissed: meta studies, which seek to establish best evidence by reviewing the findings from a range of, typically, one-off studies. The latter case is somewhat different from the former; while it is true that theory and methodology, rather than method (e.g. tests of significance), have to be ignored in such meta reviews of the literature, it is always possible to generate theory for further testing and analysis to be developed from them. And in New Zealand, where funding for primary educational research is limited, such reviews clearly have a place, but they should always be treated with caution precisely because they can ignore theoretical and methodological differences between studies. When this strategy is supported by a systematic peer review, then it provides an important source of evidence as a substitute for national or regional longitudinal studies.

Three points emerge from this discussion. Theory appraisal is difficult at the best of times; this is especially so if one-off studies are being appraised, because they may be difficult to position within wider theoretical traditions; and finally, theoretically driven studies may not be welcomed by policy-makers since they will provide explanations that challenge policy-makers' agendas. With these points in mind, I shall turn to a retrospective consideration of the findings of the Smithfield project as presented in *Trading in Futures*.

Looking back to look forward

What we attempted to do with the Smithfield project was to conform to the tenets of what elsewhere I have outlined with Phil Brown and A.H. Halsey (2004) as post-empiricist policy science. The project attempted to judge between two competing theories: one from the pro-market advocates that took their theoretical assumptions from neo-classical economics and its offspring such as Public Choice Theory, and the other that of market critics who used the resources of sociological analyses of reproduction theories in education. A set of propositions were developed that could be 'tested' in such a way that they would enable judgments to be made about the merits of the respective theories. In this way the project was about theory appraisal that could inform policy.

In order to do so it had to link three distinct approaches to the question of markets in education. The first concerned the question of parental choice: in particular whether all parents had a degree of freedom of choice in where they would send their children to school, as neo-classical theory predicted, or whether such choices would be class based. Studies in the UK by Ball and Vincent (1998) had looked at this issue but could not provide a decisive judgment about the merits of markets. And here it should be noted that a one-off study will not necessarily provide strong evidence if, as Gorard, Fitz and Taylor (2001) have argued, working-class parents will have greater freedom of choice over time, once they understand the rules of the market game. In other words, this aspect of the study of markets requires longitudinal analysis before anything fairly certain can be claimed about their effects.

We therefore started by looking at the dynamics of parental choice over the year prior to when our sample of families were sending their children to secondary school. Our findings were salutary because, in contrast to the British studies, we found that at the start of the year there were no class differences in the type of school parents thought would be 'ideal' for their children: all thought that the more elite, often single-sex, schools were the ideal. But over the year this changed for the working class parents, who by the time their children entered the school gates were far more likely to choose a working class school. This element of the study was not explained as we simply did not have the resources. Yet providing plausible explanations for parents' decision-making is an important future task. However, the question of markets is no longer topical, in New Zealand because zones were reintroduced and in England because markets in education have become broadly accepted. What is important and what is topical can be different, and in terms of policy-makers it is the latter that wins.

The second phase of the study charted the flows of students between schools over time in relation to the kinds of decision-making that parents exercised and which we had documented. This phase of the research was labour intensive and we were criticised for having only a small subsample of schools where we could chart the changes wrought by the introduction of the market. However, there is one element to our findings that was subsequently followed up by Roy Nash and Dick Harker (2005) which is significant and that concerns the penalty imposed on schools that experience a spiral of decline due to falling rolls. School rolls can decline for a number of reasons that may include demographics as much as market mechanisms but the *prima facie* evidence as to the effects of the market on falling rolls is important.

Having followed children through the school gates the next question was: how did the distribution of children according to their social class affect school performance and pupil progress? Here we were testing another aspect of the conflicting claims of market proponents and their critics. The former see school management and teacher performance as crucial to pupil progress, while the latter have argued that composition of the student body can have an effect on individual pupil outcomes. Martin Thrupp (1999) crucially provided an explanation of how student composition could impact on schools using his study of a subsample of the Smithfield schools to develop the explanatory account.

We found that indeed there was a composition effect which we could trace back to the changes in the flows of students as a result of market policies. This finding was contested by Nash (2003), while a year later that Harker and Tymms (2004) were able to find a reasonable explanation for the differences in findings between their Progress At School study and those of the Smithfield project. This interrogation of conflicting findings has led to a better understanding of the specification of sampling techniques required to test the composition effects hypothesis.

There were many criticisms of our work, curiously enough mainly from Britain, and in particular by Gorard, Fitz and Taylor (2001), who failed to understand the New Zealand context and some of the data sets we used. Some of the criticisms were no doubt well founded but in itself this was an interesting phenomenon since the debate was being conducted across the globe when what we know of markets (and indeed the generation of data) is that they are context dependent. In the event, Gorard, Fitz and Taylor's (2001) apparent demonstration that working class parents could 'learn' the rules of the market game raises precisely the question of when research should enter the public domain. Instead of developing a specific data set for the research, they, along with many others in Britain, used the measure of free school meals as a proxy for those in poverty. But it is now clear that this is an unreliable measure, raising questions about the warrant of research that uses such a proxy measure (Kounali et al. 2008).

It is difficult to judge precisely from the Smithfield project as to when findings are sufficiently reliable to be a guide to policy. Such a judgment is made all the harder because many other policies were introduced at roughly the same time as the market reforms, so that disentangling the various effects would always be difficult. But we did identify some features that make research more reliable for guiding policy decisions. These are:

* the research should be longitudinal.
* it should involve theory development and appraisal.
* it should develop databases that directly address the questions being investigated; where proxies are used a very good case has to be made as to their reliability.

In the end though, and this is the key point, it is only with benefit of hindsight that both research and policies can be judged. In 2005 Roy Nash and Dick Harker published 'The Predictable Failure of School Marketisation: The Limitations of Policy Reform'. This provided an account, with the benefit of admittedly less-than-perfect official data, that there was no overall improvement in performance as a result of marketisation, despite the cost in resources and stress involved. The conclusion here is not of the 'I told you so' kind but something altogether different, and it goes back to something David Lange rather enigmatically said about the reform process he was introducing, to the effect that the reforms should stop at the classroom door. As Nash and Harker suggest there was a faulty link made between market success and pedagogical success. Whenever macro reforms are introduced the question of how they might affect the micro processes of the classroom is always a fundamental question. Pro market advocates had an answer: markets would spur teachers on through fear of losing their jobs if schools entered a spiral of decline and through the incentives of being part of a successful school. In the end this proved to be an impoverished account of teacher professionalism and its associated motivations.

Updating the story

In my current university I sit on a committee that awards a prize for the postgraduate student who is undertaking the most promising research from across all faculties. Invariably the prize is won by a student engaged in research in an area such as the biology of cancer. It has not been won by a social scientist. One reason is that research into the causes of cancer may produce tangible results that clearly improve human lives on a large scale; social science research rarely does that. It may provide guidance for policy-makers but that is a matter of chance. In fact it has a different role, especially if the explanations that it generates are at odds with the story policy-makers want to hear. In this case the research may have the effect of disrupting and challenging policy agendas. In other words, the merit of the research is that it may contribute to the tide of democratic policy debate, where outright victories are never gained but in which the taking part in the process is more important, if rather more humbling.

The Smithfield project and the lessons we might take from it about the research-policy relationship could not have been undertaken in any other place but in New Zealand at that time. The intense relationships between researchers and policy-makers inevitably throws up the kinds of issues raised in this paper. Personally, wrapped in the body armour of a conviction that research should be important to the policy process, I found the armour becoming increasingly thin as the debate over issues became a debate about individuals. But if I was beginning to develop a thinner skin, there were compensations. David Hughes and I managed to build a team of young researchers, many of whom are now 'stars' in the global educational research firmament and whose subsequent progress, for me, is the most important thing to have come out of the project. Martin Thrupp, after a distinguished academic OE in England, now has a Chair at Waikato; Sietske Waslander, a Chair at Tilburg. Sue Watson was offered a senior position as an education advisor in government before developing her own company. Rob Strathdee is Head of the School of Education Policy and Implementation at Victoria, Ann Dupuis is Associate Professor at Massey, and David Hughes probably did the sanest thing of all and left academia to build a rare breeds farm in Lyttelton. Given how sparky these young people were, the Smithfield project was not an easy ride, and in true Kiwi fashion the research was done on the smell of an oily rag when compared to the funding of research elsewhere. Whether it influenced the return to school zoning is hard to say. As social science researchers, we often do not know what impact we make, and when we do make an impact it is not always in the ways intended. Yet it would be absurd, despite all these personal and professional conundrums, to deny that systematic analysis of the key issues of the day is of paramount importance in the social sciences. And such issues are many.

References

Balarin, M. (2008). Post-structuralism, realism and the question of knowledge in educational sociology: a Derridian critique of social realism in education. *Policy Futures in Education.* 6, 4. pp. 507-527.

Ball, S. & Vincent, C. (1998). 'I heard it on the grapevine': 'hot' knowledge and school choice. *British Journal of Sociology of Education.* 19, 3. pp. 377-400.

Department of Education. (1988). *Tomorrow's schools.* Wellington: Government Printer.

Gorard, S., Fitz, J. & Taylor, C. (2001). School choice impacts: what do we know? *Educational Researcher.* 30, 7. pp. 18-23.

Haig, B. (1987). Scientific problems and the conduct of research. *Educational Philosophy and Theory.* 19, 2. pp. 22-32.

Harker, R. & Tymms, P. (2004). The effect of student composition on school outcomes. *School Effectiveness and Improvement.* 15, 2. pp. 177-199.

Kounali, D., Robinson, T., Goldstein, H. & Lauder, H. (2008). *The probity of free school meals as a proxy measure for disadvantage.* Education Department, University of Bath.

Ladwig, J. (1994). For whom this reform? Outlining educational policy as a social field. *British Journal of Sociology of Education.* 15. pp. 341-363.

Lauder, H., Brown, P. & Halsey, A.H. (2004). Sociology and political arithmetic: towards a new policy science. *British Journal of Sociology.* March, 55, 1. pp. 3-22.

Lauder, H., Hughes, D., Watson, S., Waslander, S., Thrupp, M., Strathdee, R., Simiyu, I., Dupusi, A., McGlinn, J. & Hamlin, J. (1999). *Trading in futures: why markets in education don't work.* Buckingham: Open University Press.

Nash, R. (2003). Is the school composition effect real? A discussion with evidence from the UK PISA data. *School Effectiveness and Improvement.* 14, 4. pp. 441-457.

Nash, R. & Harker, R. (2005). The predictable failure of school marketisation: the limitations of policy reform. In J. Codd and K. Sullivan (Eds.). *Education policy directions in Aotearoa New Zealand.* Southbank Victoria: The Dunmore Press.

Picot, B., Ramsay, P., Rosemergy, M., Wereta, W. & Wise, C. (1988). *Administering for excellence.* Wellington: Department of Education.

Thrupp, M. (1999). *Schools making a difference: let's be realistic.* Buckingham: Open University Press.

Education: Commodity or Public Good?
– Twenty Years On

Gerald Grace and Martin Thrupp

Introduction

In his 1988 inaugural lecture Gerald Grace refuted the claim that education should be seen as a commodity instead of a public good. He did this by rejecting the narrowly economistic conception of education used by Treasury under the fourth Labour government (1984–1990), arguing instead for alternative conceptions of education as a public good, centred on its role in developing and enhancing citizens and securing the foundations of democracy.

In the first section of this chapter we are concerned with the extent to which New Zealand education has become commodified over the subsequent two decades and what is known about the effects of this commodification. We take a broad view of what constitutes the commodification of education, including all developments that have reinforced a market or business orientation to education. We give a brief overview of these commodifying developments and their impact in the early childhood and compulsory schooling areas[1] and then provide some general observations about the patterns of commodification seen in New Zealand education. In the second section of the paper Gerald Grace urges the citizens of New Zealand/Aotearoa to resist the commodification and privatisation of their educational system, which was once a model for the world, designed on progressive and public good principles, and which could be so again.

---

1 The tertiary area has also had commodifying developments, most obviously 'user pays' for students and the system of EFTS (equivalent full time students) funding, however space constraints preclude discussion of tertiary education in this chapter.

An overview of commodification

Early childhood

Early childhood is the part of the New Zealand education system where commodification has been most obvious over the last two decades. Demand for early childhood education and care places has grown markedly, increasing from 110,000 to 185,000 between 1990 and 2007. Such growth is underpinned by increased birth rates, an increased number of women in the labour force and changing family structures with increasing numbers of single parents (Clough and de Raad 2005). Much of the increased provision to meet demand has been private. Thirty-four per cent of early childhood provision is now privately owned, including 62 per cent of home-based care networks and 58 per cent of education and care centres (Ministry of Education 2008) The heavily privatised nature of education and care centres is particularly noteworthy since they now represent 52 per cent of overall provision, have been growing by some 7 per cent per year since 1990 (whereas other kinds of provision are generally static or in decline) and often involve businesses setting up or taking over multiple early childhood centres. While some are small owner-operator businesses, others are large companies; for instance, New Zealand company Kidicorp owns and operates 115 centres, and international corporate ABC Learning also has over 100 New Zealand centres.

One reason the early childhood area has been so easily colonised by business is that early childhood centres have not been required to have Boards of Trustees in the same way that schools have. While these were recommended in the early childhood green paper *Education to be More* (Department of Education 1988a), they were dropped out of the subsequent white paper *Before Five* (Department of Education 1988b). After 1990, the National government further aided privatisation by both reducing regulation of the sector and increasing funding in a way that provided an increased profit motive. There were no restrictions on how government funding was spent, leaving business owners able to determine their own spending priorities (including any payments to themselves as managers and funding of capital works which could return a profit). After 1999 Labour substantively raised the teacher qualification requirements set in regulation, negotiated pay parity (with school teachers) for kindergarten teachers, and required employers to pay minimum rates for teacher salaries in education and care services. On the other hand, just before the 2005 general election

Labour extended its scheme to provide 20 free hours of childcare to for-profit centres. The recently elected National government has delayed implementing new regulations intended to raise minimum standards for facilities, services and safety. Lobbying by the Early Childhood Council, a body dominated by for-profit early childhood providers, appears to have been significant in influencing such policy shifts.

Along with the general impact of private sector lobbying on early childhood education policy, there is some evidence that in private centres the profit motive reduces investment in the quality of early childhood education, particularly in employment conditions, which represent a significant cost. Mitchell (2007) reports that, compared to their colleagues in community-based centres, teachers/educators in privately owned education and care centres are less likely to exceed the statutory minimum annual leave entitlement of four weeks, have less paid non-contact time and less involvement in decision-making. There is also a higher turnover rate for staff in private centres, which is likely to disadvantage the children that attend those centres.

Schools

Grace gave his inaugural lecture just before the Picot Taskforce announced its findings (Department of Education 1988c) followed by the *Tomorrow's Schools* reforms (Department of Education 1988d). While this set of reforms was by no means couched in the strongly neo-liberal Treasury discourse Grace was critiquing, they did have the effect of opening up schools to the market and business. The last two decades have involved some strengthening and some repudiation of the *Tomorrow's Schools* reforms but New Zealand schools remain individual business units, albeit with important constraints on their autonomy and now operating within a fairly regulated marketplace.

In relation to admissions and competition for students, the Education Act of 1989 started to encourage an education market by imposing maximum intakes on schools based on a very liberal interpretation of the capacity of their school buildings. Most schools then legally had to accept all enrolments and face market forces, although 31 secondary schools where there was a clear excess of demand over capacity were allowed to retain zones. At the same time the Act retained a measure of control on equity grounds. The right of students to attend their local school was protected and balloting was used to prevent discrimination by schools in pursuit of market advantage. There was also provision for schools to put a case to the Ministry to negotiate their maximum rolls downwards on educational or community grounds. National's 1991 Education Amendment Act brought a further shift towards a neo-liberal approach. Enrolment schemes could now only be put in place to avoid overcrowding – there were no other grounds on which to avoid unwanted enrolments. The Ministry no longer determined maximum rolls, schools had to apply to have overcrowding status approved. There was no longer a home zone specified by the government in the case of 'overcrowded' schools and the Act made no stipulations of the mechanisms of an enrolment scheme. This was now left up to the discretion of schools, although enrolment schemes could not breach the requirements of the Race Relations Act (1971), the Human Rights Commission Act (1977) and the Bill of Rights Act (1990). These changes signalled greater marketisation and the policies remained largely in place until 2000 when the incoming Labour government made some effort to pull back a market approach to school admission (discussed further below).

The impact of the admissions policies of the 1990s have been the subject of several analyses (e.g., Lauder et al. 1999, Fiske and Ladd 2000, Nash and Harker 2005). These have typically shown that there were marked flows away from the schools with the lowest socioeconomic intakes and those with the most Māori and Pasifika students, while movement of students to the highest socioeconomic schools was blocked by their overcrowding status. This led to greater segregation between schools, since those leaving the lowest decile schools tended to be their higher socioeconomic status students. Some studies have also provided insights into the responses of schools to their market position. Schools had a variety of responses including actively trying to respond to their market position by overt marketing, political responses which have sought to change the rules of the market or the terms on which school compete (such as lobbying government to get overcrowding status introduced) and networked responses which involved collusion or collaboration (Lauder et al. 1999). In some cases schools were also deliberately non-responding by avoiding actions that schools considered would be unacceptable, such as moving away from mixed-ability classes.

More recently, the Education Amendment Act (2000) brought in school admissions based on residential zoning, where all students living in-zone have the right to attend a school and there is balloting for out-of-zone places. With the outcomes of balloting never guaranteed, living in-zone is now the only sure way for children to be enrolled in a popular school. The post-2000 admissions policies have therefore shifted attention to the cost of housing in the zones of popular schools ('selection by mortgage'), and the rigour with which school zones are policed. The effects of the post-2000 policies on schools have been less researched but Pearce and Gordon argue that an absence of effective government control has allowed the zones of Christchurch primary schools to be drawn up in convoluted ways by schools to "bypass more deprived but closer areas in favour of further but wealthier suburbs" (2004, p. 7). Moreover they point out that school zones now often overlap, making them "less the tidy product of the old system of regional planning . . . [and] far more reminiscent of the free market where businesses compete for customers and little or no co-operation exists" (Pearce and Gordon 2004, p. 8). On the other hand, work on Auckland school zones by David O'Sullivan, Associate Professor of Geography at the University of Auckland, suggests most schools serve students who live locally and that both convoluted and overlapping zones are relatively uncommon. This in turn raises the question of how school-related decision-making is impacting on New Zealand housing choices (personal communication, 2008).

Making it necessary for schools to respond in some way to market competition for students is only one way that education policy has reinforced a market or business orientation to education over the last two decades. Other aspects of commodification have included new performance targets and financial and other accountabilities under the rubric of self-management, contestable rather than universal funding, increased incentive to build links to business in order to make up for shortfalls in government funding, and the required use of private sector management practices such as strategic plans, performance management processes and management information systems. All of these have fundamentally changed the role of principal to involve more business management. Particularly noteworthy were National's efforts over the 1990s to introduce the bulk-funding of teacher salaries. This was expected to lead to a breakdown of national awards, and allow for the implementation of performance pay on a school-by-school basis. However it was a policy strongly resisted by teacher unions and some schools. Salary bulk-funding was discontinued by Labour after it won the 1999 election. Labour also put a cap on government funding for private schools. This cap has been lifted by the recently elected National government.

The impact of all these managerial developments in schools has been complex (see, for instance, Wylie 1999). While many of the reforms have clearly often worked at the most obvious levels, there are two key concerns. One is that they have brought about a culture shift in schools to make them less authentically educational than in the past. For instance research in the 1990s showed that Education Review Office (ERO) reviews were leading teachers to begin to create artefacts and ritualistic displays of their work along with unreal assessment records and teaching performances (Robertson et al. 1997). ERO's assessment requirements meant teacher practices were becoming shaped by the touchstone 'This will be good for ERO!' even though teachers often did not believe these practices were in the best interests of students (Robertson et al. 1997). Indeed the recent emphasis of the Ministry on principals leading learning may be seen as tacit recognition that the self-management of schools got out of hand in the 1990s. A second concern is that the extent of success or otherwise of the shift towards business practices in schools has often been contingent on their contexts, especially the socioeconomic status of the communities they have served. For instance, the ERO found that low decile schools were more likely to lack financial and strategic expertise and therefore at greater risk of having financial problems and having only limited forms of evidence on which to prioritise and plan their spending on teaching and learning (Education Review Office 2006, p. 31).

The student experience of schooling has also become somewhat commodified over the last two decades. As well as the hidden curriculum of business practices and links into schools discussed above (sometimes with naming rights or product sponsorships and endorsements), there has been the growth of a formal enterprise curriculum in many schools. The way the senior secondary school curriculum is packaged into unit standards and achievement standards can also be seen to encourage a kind of consumerist approach to learning, where students choose particular fragments of curriculum rather than any necessarily coherent course of study.

Discussion

A number of general points can be made about the above. First, while Grace (1988) was particular concerned with critiquing Treasury's market discourses, many of the above developments reflect the managerial 'New Zealand model' of public management (Boston et al. 1998) promoted by the State Services Commission, which has also been an important commodifying influence by promoting a business culture within schools and other educational institutions. Second, there have been important differences across the sector, for instance, privatisation has advanced further in early childhood (and tertiary) education compared to schools. In this respect the non-compulsory parts of the education sector may act as testing grounds for compulsory schooling, which is politically higher-stakes and more unionised. Third, governments in power over the last two decades have differed in their enthusiasm for market and managerial solutions. Fourth, the stances of any specific governments have rarely been straightforward either. For instance, as noted above, the Labour government from 1999 to 2008 appeared to back away from commodification in the school sector by reintroducing school zoning, doing away with the bulk-funding of teacher salaries and capping subsidies to private schools. On the other hand it encouraged the growth of private providers in early childhood by allowing them to access government funding of twenty hours' free provision. It has also continued to favour consultancy and contracting out at times. Fifth, pragmatism clearly comes into the picture and helps create some of this complexity. For instance, the 1998 Education Amendment Act (no. 2 of that year) saw National make a step towards reregulating school admissions because its 'hands off' 1991 policies had proved unworkable. Sixth, the detail of policy is important. For instance, the bulk-funding of early childhood education seems problematic at first and yet the funding formula means that centres get funded more if they employ more experienced staff. Lastly, we would strongly reiterate a point already made, that the impact of reform has varied according to the social and historical contexts of schools.

What is clear from the experience of the last two decades is that, beyond any initial flush of enthusiasm (or indeed contestation), there has often been an ideological ratcheting up of commodification, where what once seemed unacceptable becomes unquestioned practice. A good example is the effort made to market schools, which once seemed over-the-top but is now just accepted as 'how it has to be'. The incoming National government has already signalled its enthusiasm for private sector involvement in education and we should not imagine that the threat to education as public good has disappeared. Business lobby groups such as the Education Forum, the Maxim Institute and the Early Childhood Council are involved in promoting commodification but don't always get their way. For instance, the Ministry of Education has not responded to business advocacy for an enterprise curriculum with any great enthusiasm. It has a place in the New Zealand Curriculum (Ministry of Education 2007) but it is still up to individual schools as to whether or not they wish to promote enterprise education and what form their enterprise curriculum will take. As well, the role of lobby groups for public education, such as the Quality Public Education Coalition, should not be overlooked. There are many groups and individuals in New Zealand who do not want to see education privatised and will resist commodifying steps towards that end.

A reflective postscript – twenty years on

I am grateful to Martin Thrupp for providing an up-to-date and scholarly survey of the research evidence in New Zealand relating to the commodification and marketisation of education and I also thank the editors of this volume for inviting me to reflect upon these developments.

When I arrived from the University of Cambridge in 1987 to take up the Chair of Education at Victoria University, I was immediately impressed by the principles upon which education in New Zealand/Aotearoa was based. Its founding charter was superior to anything that existed in the United Kingdom.

New Zealand's founding charter for education policy was that provided by Peter Fraser, Minister of Education in 1939, which said:

> the Government's objective, broadly expressed, is that every person whatever his level of academic ability, whether he be rich or poor, whether he lives in town or country, has a right, as a citizen, to a free education of the kind for which he is best fitted and to the fullest extent of his powers. So far is this from being a mere pious platitude that the full acceptance of the principle will involve the reorientation of the education system.

I remember thinking at the time, 'if only the UK had such a fine statement of citizen entitlement in education'! However, in that same year, 1987, the New Zealand Treasury issued a document entitled, *Government Management: Brief to the Incoming Government 1987: Volume II, Education Issues*. It was far from 'brief', being almost 300 pages long, and it was not, as would be expected from a public service agency, an objective and impartial analysis of education issues. It was quite clearly an ideological document designed to advance New Right ideas in New

Zealand, which suggested that education was not a public good service for citizens provided by the state but rather that it was a commodity that should be open to market forces and traded in the marketplace. This was stated explicitly:

> Education's investment benefits, which bring long-term benefits to society as well as the individual may lie behind the feeling that education does not belong in the marketplace. Education tends to be thought of as a natural sphere for government intervention because it is a social or public good . . .
>
> In the technical sense, used by economists, education is not in fact a 'public good' . . . education shares the main characteristics of other commodities traded in the marketplace. (Treasury 1987, p. 33)

This was, of course, nothing less than a brazen attempt by New Right economists in the Treasury to overturn the long-standing social and political concept of a public good in New Zealand, by a new 'technical' definition derived from what regarded itself as 'economic science'[2]. It was, in short, an attempted ideological revolution or coup d'état to take control of how education would be thought about and provided in the future in New Zealand.

I decided to devote my Inaugural Lecture at Victoria University in 1988 to a refutation of this ideological document and I subsequently developed my arguments in publications in 1990(a) and 1994. My position, in brief, was that New Zealand already had in place a democratic and progressive concept of education as a public good entitlement for all citizens, and that to replace this with 'a commodity in the marketplace' concept would be a backward step with deleterious consequences for equality of educational opportunity and for the overall quality of education in the country.

What does the subsequent review by Martin Thrupp show? On my reading of the first half of this chapter these things become clear:

Early childhood education

In Martin's review we read:

- 'After 1990, National further aided privatisation by reducing regulation of the sector . . .'
- 'the profit motive reduces investment in the quality of early childhood education, particularly in employment conditions . . .'

---

2 For a more developed analysis of the assumptions and presumptions of 'economic science' see Grace (1994).

• 'there is a higher turnover rate for staff in private centres which is likely to disadvantage the children . . .'

A central feature of New Right market ideology is to suggest that the 'regulation' of anything is counter-productive and merely an oppressive restriction of enterprise by 'state bureaucracy'.[3] In the field of early childhood education the existence of state regulation is not in fact counter-productive but is necessary to safeguard the interests of young children, the quality of their educational provision and the reasonable terms and conditions of their carers and teachers. What Martin Thrupp's evidence shows is that reducing 'regulation' while maximising the profit motive leads to a situation in early childhood education where economies are made in staff quality and costs to the detriment of the children's educational interests. The market, in short, puts profit before children.

Schools

Ranson (1993 p. 336), writing about the impact of market forces in education, gets to the heart of the matter when he observes:

> Action in the market is driven by a single common currency – the pursuit of material interests. The only effective means upon which to base action is the calculation of personal advantage: clout in the market derives from the power of superior resources to subordinate others in competitive exchange.

This is exactly what has happened in New Zealand's school system in the period 1988–2008. Thrupp reports the research of Lauder and colleagues (1999), Fiske and Ladd (2000), Pearce and Gordon (2004) and Nash and Harker (2005). These researchers show that when education is constructed as a commodity to be traded in competitive free market conditions, what results is a polarisation effect, a greater segregation whereby high decile schools grow even stronger and low decile schools become even weaker.

This, in effect, means that the principle of equality of educational opportunity has been weakened in New Zealand in favour of the visible (and much publicised) market success of culturally strong schools, while the fate of culturally disadvantaged and under-resourced schools has been conveniently ignored. The long-term social and economic effects upon

---

3   The present world financial crisis demonstrates the consequences of weakening regulation of the financial markets. The irony of this situation is that free marketers are now desperately requesting state intervention to rescue them from the resulting chaos and crisis.

the well-being of New Zealand society[4] have not been given sufficient attention in these developments. As Richard Pring, Professor of Education at Oxford University, observed:

> The market model of individuals all pursuing their own respective interests leads not to an improvement of the general good but only to an improvement of the positional good of some vis-à-vis other competitors and also to a deterioration of the overall situation. (Pring 1996, p. 65)

The formation of educational policy

In a progressive democracy such as New Zealand, the determination and making of educational policy should be in the hands of its informed citizens. It is the citizens and not the market ideologists or the academics who should make the final judgment between the contending principles contained in the Peter Fraser charter of 1939 and the New Zealand Treasury charter of 1987. Remembering, of course, that 'modern' or 'real world' ideas are not necessarily always superior to the wisdom of the past.

Acknowledgement

We are grateful to Linda Mitchell, University of Waikato, for advice on developments in the early childhood area.

References

Boston, J., Martin, J., Pallot, J. & Walsh, P. (1998). *Public management: the New Zealand model*. Auckland: Open University Press.

Clough, P. & de Raad, J. (2005). *Putting children first: early childhood education policies for a new tomorrow*. Wellington: New Zealand Institute of Economic Research & Early Childhood Council.

Department of Education (1988a). *Education to be more: report of the early childhood care and education working group*. Wellington: Government Printer.

Department of Education (1988b). *Before five: early childhood care and education in New Zealand*. Wellington: Government Printer.

Department of Education (1988c). *Administering for excellence*. Wellington: Government Printer.

Department of Education (1988d). *Tomorrow's schools*. Wellington: Government Printer.

Education Review Office (2006). *Schools' use of operational funding*. Wellington: Education Review Office.

---

4   As Roy Nash (2003, p. 74) so wisely remarked: 'The argument against market policies should be placed on a different level: it is the contribution they make to the erosion of communal wellbeing – of solidarity – that causes the real problem.'

Fiske, E.B. & Ladd, H.F. (2000). *When schools compete: a cautionary tale*. Washington, D.C.: Brookings Institute Press.

Grace, G. (1988). *Education: commodity or public good? Inaugural Lecture*. Wellington: Victoria University Press.

Grace, G. (1990a). The New Zealand treasury and the commodification of education. In S. Middleton, J. Codd and A. Jones (Eds.). *New Zealand education policy today: critical perspectives*. Wellington: Allen and Unwin. pp. 27-39.

Grace, G. (1990b). Labour and education: the crisis and settlements of education policy. In M. Holland & J. Boston (Eds.). *The fourth Labour government: politics and policy in New Zealand*. Auckland: Oxford University Press. pp. 165-191.

Grace, G. (1994). Education is a public good: on the need to resist the domination of economic science. In D. Bridges & T. McLaughlin (Eds.). *Education and the market place*. London, Falmer Press. pp. 126-137.

Lauder, H., Hughes, D., Watson, S., Waslander, S., Thrupp, M., Strathdee, R., Simiyu, I., Dupusi, A., McGlinn, J. & Hamlin, J. (1999). *Trading in futures: why markets in education don't work*. Buckingham: Open University Press.

Ministry of Education Website (as on 1st December 2008). *Education counts* http://www. educationcounts.govt.nz/statistics/ece/ece_staff_return//licensed_ ervices_and_ licence-exempt_groups/17812

Ministry of Education (2007). The New Zealand Curriculum. Wellington: Learning Media.

Mitchell, L. (2007). *Provision of ECE services and parental perceptions: results of the 2007 NZCER national survey of ECE services*. Wellington: New Zealand Council for Educational Research.

Nash, R. (2003). Dreaming in the real world: social class and education in New Zealand. In J. Freeman-Moir and A. Scott (Eds.). *Yesterday's dreams: international and critical perspectives on education and social class*. Christchurch: Canterbury University Press.

Nash, R. & Harker, R. (2005). The predictable failure of school marketisation: the limitations of policy reform. In J. Codd and K. Sullivan (Eds.). *Education policy directions in Aotearoa New Zealand*. Southbank, Victoria: Thomson Dunmore.

New Zealand Treasury (1987). *Government Management: Brief to the Incoming Government 1987: Volume II, Education Issues*. Wellington: New Zealand Treasury.

O'Sullivan, D. (2008). Personal communication, Auckland, 2 December.

Pearce, D. & Gordon, L. (2004). School zoning since 1990: a Christchurch study. Unpublished manuscript. University of Canterbury, Department of Education.

Pring, R. (1996). Markets, education and Catholic schools. In T. McLaughlin and B. O'Keeffe. (Eds.). *The contemporary Catholic school*. London, Falmer Press.

Ranson, S. (1993). Markets or democracy for education. *British Journal of Education Studies*. 1, 4. pp. 333-352.

Robertson, S., Dale, R., Thrupp, M., Vaughan, K. & Jacka. S. (1997). *A review of ERO*. (Final report to the Post Primary Teachers Association, Wellington). Auckland: School of Education, University of Auckland.

Wylie, C. (1999). *Ten years on: how schools view educational reform*. Wellington: New Zealand Council for Educational Research.

New Zealand's Role in Education in the Pacific

James Irving

Introduction

Any discussion on the Pacific must first take account of its complexity and diversity; there are many Pacifics. The countries which make up the Pacific vary greatly in geographic area, population, ethnic and linguistic diversity, and wealth. Countries range in size from continental Australia, to the large islands of New Zealand and Papua New Guinea, to medium-sized islands such as the Solomons and Fiji, to smaller islands such as the Cook Islands and Niue, and tiny atolls such as Kiribati and Tuvalu. Populations vary widely, from over 21 million in Australia, to over 4 million in New Zealand, over 900,000 in Fiji, nearly 600,000 in the Solomons, and 200,000 each in Vanuatu and Western Samoa. Tonga and Kiribati each have 100,000 inhabitants, the Cook Islands 20,000, Tuvalu 12,000, while Niue and Tokelau each have 1,500. At the extreme end is the tiny island colony of Pitcairn, with just over 50 people.

Six main ethnic groups are represented in the region. Melanesians occupy the west, including Fiji, Vanuatu, the Solomon Islands, New Caledonia and Papua New Guinea. Micronesians occupy the northern Pacific, including Kiribati, the Marshall and Caroline Islands, the Marianas and Nauru. Polynesians occupy the eastern and south Pacific, including Tuvalu, Tokelau, Samoa, Tonga, Niue, the Cook Islands, French Polynesia, Easter Island, and New Zealand. There also exist Polynesian outlier islands within Melanesia, including Rotuma within the Fiji island group and Tikopia within the Solomon Islands. In addition to the indigenous populations, nearly 40 per cent of the citizens of Fiji are of Indian descent and minorities of Chinese descent are also found throughout the region. While people of European descent make up the majority of the populations of Australia and New Zealand, European minorities are also found throughout the region. Finally, the Aborigines of Australia form a distinct ethnic group of their own.

Further complicating the ethnic map has been the growing migration of Pacific peoples to New Zealand since the 1960s, especially from Western Samoa, the Cook Islands, Niue, and Tokelau. New Zealand's Pacific population now stands at nearly 270,000, an increase of nearly 60 per cent since the 1991 census. The biggest groups are Samoan (50 per cent), Cook Island Maori (23 per cent), Tongan (19 percent), and Niuean (8 per cent). There are now far more people of Cook Island Maori, Niuean and Tokelauan descent living in New Zealand than in their home countries. Furthermore, the majority of New Zealanders of Pacific ethnicity have now been born in New Zealand, and it is a very young population, with around 50 per cent under 20 years of age. Two thirds of the New Zealand Pacific population live in the Auckland region, and the city of Auckland has the largest concentration of Polynesian people in the world.

The linguistic situation is also complex, particularly in Melanesia. Papua New Guinea has over 800 distinct languages, the Solomon Islands over 70, and Vanuatu over 100. Because of this complexity, Pidgin English has developed as an important lingua franca in these three countries. While the Fijian language is relatively uniform throughout that country, dialectic differences exist. Micronesia has a number of distinct Micronesian languages, I-Kiribati being the largest with nearly 100,000 speakers. In Polynesia each country has its own indigenous language such as Samoan, Tongan and Cook Island Maori, but a close linguistic family connection exists among all the Polynesian languages. Because of their colonial history, in addition to the indigenous languages, English is widely spoken throughout the region and is one of the official languages of many Pacific countries, and French is spoken throughout French Polynesia, New Caledonia and in parts of Vanuatu.

Wide disparities in wealth exist among Pacific countries. At one end are the wealthy developed countries of Australia and New Zealand. At the other extreme are some of the poorest countries in the world. On the United Nations list of the world's fifty least developed countries, five are in the Pacific. These are Kiribati, Samoa, the Solomon Islands, Tuvalu and Vanuatu. The UN classification 'least developed' is based on several criteria, including annual per capita GDP, life expectancy, per capita calorie intake, primary and secondary school enrolment rates, adult literacy, and economic vulnerability. The disparities in wealth mean that Australia and New Zealand exert a disproportionate economic influence in the region and the poorest countries remain dependent on external support and assistance.

Being a Pacific country has encouraged and enabled New Zealand to develop strong social, cultural, economic and political links with other Pacific countries. This has been particularly true for those countries for which New Zealand has had a colonial relationship. These links have facilitated an important two-way bridge for a traffic which enriches New Zealand society as a whole no less than that of its Pacific colleagues. As a result of this proximity and close relationship, New Zealand has established a long-standing involvement in the development and provision of education in the Pacific.

The colonial background

The Pacific represents a microcosm of colonial patterns and experiences. Over the years a number of countries have played their part or continue to be involved in the region. These include Britain, France, Germany, the United States, Japan, Chile, Australia and New Zealand. New Zealand's colonial experience began with the imperial and expansionist ambitions of Premier Richard Seddon in the late 19th and early 20th centuries, leading to the annexation in 1901 of the Cook Islands and Niue, which until then had been British protectorates. Further expansion occurred in 1920 after the defeat of Germany in World War I, when New Zealand was granted a League of Nations mandate over Western Samoa (a mandate which became a United Nations Trusteeship following the establishment of the United Nations in 1945). Finally, in 1925, Britain transferred the administration of Tokelau to New Zealand.

Western Samoa became independent in 1962, the Cook Islands in 1965, and Niue in 1974, while Tokelau remains a non-self-governing territory. Although independent, the Cook Islands and Niue have adopted constitutions for full self-government in free association with New Zealand, which allows their citizens to maintain New Zealand citizenship. Tokelau's status is reviewed regularly by the UN Special Committee on Decolonisation, but as recently as 2008 Tokelau voted to retain its existing association with New Zealand.

There have been three main stages of development in New Zealand's relationship with its colonies. The first can be described as a colonialist and expansionist phase from the period of Richard Seddon's premiership to the period immediately following the end of World War I; the second was a period of consolidation and paternalism lasting until the end of World War II; the third period saw a growing accommodation and partnership from post-World War II to the granting of independence for Western Samoa, the Cook Islands and Niue, and beyond to the present. The general trend has moved from being directive to being responsive. Initially, New Zealanders were somewhat uneasy colonialists, lacking the systematic thoroughness of the Germans in Western Samoa, or the broad and lengthy colonial experience of the British across the Empire. In Western Samoa this was evidenced by the mismanagement of the influenza epidemic which followed World War I, resulting in a large number of avoidable deaths. A second example was the inappropriate and heavy handed response to the Mau nationalist movement in Western Samoa, which resulted in unnecessary deaths in 1929. These unfortunate events scarred the relationship between New Zealand and Western Samoa for many years.

On the positive side, education and its provision came to play an increasingly important role in New Zealand's relationship with its Pacific territories, and also in Fiji and Tonga, where a close association developed. A significant outcome was that an increasing number of Pacific students came to be educated in New Zealand at the secondary school and tertiary levels. Many of these people subsequently became influential leaders in their own countries, such as long-serving prime ministers Ratu Sir Kamasese Mara in Fiji and Sir Tom Davis in the Cook Islands. The relatively large number of such individuals over the years, coupled with the growing number of New Zealand teachers, advisors and officials working in the region, facilitated a much better understanding of each other's needs. Both sides have benefited from this two-way educational exchange.

New Zealand's educational assistance

The major areas of New Zealand's assistance in education have included the provision of teachers under the Scheme of Cooperation; teacher training and development; the secondment of advisers and specialists;

the development of curricula; the provision of external examinations; advice and support for evaluation and assessment; the provision of school publications and resources; the provision of distance education; institutional development and support; and scholarships.

Teachers

The selection and provision of teachers under the Scheme of Cooperation became a significant area of educational assistance from 1925, when seventeen New Zealand teachers were appointed to serve in Fiji. Forty years later there were 191 teachers serving in eight South Pacific countries. The 1970s saw increasing localisation which steadily reduced this number down to 28 by 1988, the majority in the Cook Islands and Niue. This reduction, together with the changing composition of this teaching force, was a response to developing local needs and also to the improved quality of local teachers and teacher training. Initially, the majority of New Zealand teachers served in primary schools, but by the 1980s, with most primary schools staffed by trained local teachers, the majority of New Zealand teachers were employed at the secondary, tertiary and advisory levels. The trend has been away from the provision of personnel, towards supporting and improving the quality and training of local teachers.

The quality of an education system is only as good as the quality and training of the teachers available to it. Their prior educational level and entry qualifications, together with the length and nature of their training, largely determine their subsequent teaching competence and confidence, and their receptivity to innovation and change. In discussion of this issue it is instructive to consider C.E. Beeby's 'stages of educational development' thesis (1966). Beeby proposed that there are four stages in the qualitative improvement of a primary education system, with each stage more expensive than the one preceding it. He argued that improvement in quality depended on the prior level of general education of the teachers in the system and the amount and type of training they had received. The characteristics of the four stages are summarised as follows:

1. *The Dame School Stage* characterised by ill-trained or untrained teachers and an unorganised, narrow subject content based on the 3Rs, with low standards and rote memorisation.

2. *The Stage of Formalism* where the teachers are still ill-educated but have some training. The system is highly organised but teaching is

limited to 'one best way', one textbook, an emphasis on memorisation, and tight external discipline and examinations.

3. *The Stage of Transition* where the goals are similar to the Stage of Formalism but the teachers are better educated and trained. The goals are more efficiently achieved and there is a greater emphasis on meaning, but both are still rather formal and thin on content. While the curriculum and textbooks are less restrictive, teachers hesitate to use greater freedom because of restrictive leaving examinations.

4. *The Stage of Meaning* where the teachers are well-educated and well-trained. Meaning and understanding are stressed, the curriculum broadened, and there is variety in the content and methods. Individual differences are catered for with greater emphasis on activity methods, problem solving and creativity. Assessment is more internal and related to teaching and learning, discipline is more relaxed and positive, and emotional and aesthetic needs are catered for as well as intellectual. There are also better buildings, facilities and equipment, and closer relations with the community.

Beeby developed his thesis largely from his experiences in Western Samoa from 1945 during the period when he was Director of Education for New Zealand (1940–1960). Peter Fraser, the Minister of Education at the time (also Prime Minister) directed Beeby to undertake a review of education in New Zealand's Pacific territories with a view to raising and improving the low educational standards which existed. In Western Samoa Beeby found a New Zealand-appointed superintendent unsuccessfully attempting to introduce the innovative teaching methods that were proving so successful in New Zealand. What became clear was that such reforms were beyond the capabilities of the teachers who were trying to implement them, and Beeby found himself recommending procedures that he was actively trying to discourage in New Zealand. As a result, the unsuccessful implementation of new methods and ideas was replaced by a return to a tightly structured and organised system more akin to the Stage of Formalism and in line with the educational level and training of the existing teaching force.

In effect, what Beeby was emphasising was that the introduction of better, more innovative and effective teaching practices could only occur when the quality and training of the teachers had reached a sufficiently high level to enable them to meet the requirements for the Stage of Meaning.

New Zealand's move to increase support for and improve the quality and training of local teachers has therefore been of critical importance.

Some of the assistance in improving teacher education in the Pacific has been provided by New Zealand's Overseas Development Aid (ODA) programme, and the New Zealand Department of Education has assisted with a number of counterpart training programmes. It is also important to acknowledge the key role of New Zealand teachers colleges and some of the universities in working with local colleges on various projects over the years to improve the quality of teachers and their training. The programme to improve teacher training initiated by Dunedin Teachers College, working with the Solomon Islands Teachers College in the late 1990s, provides a good example of one such programme.

An example of an ODA programme aimed at enhancing the skills of Pacific teachers was the project in the late 1990s to provide opportunities for Pacific secondary school teachers to work with New Zealand counterparts in developing innovative but practical teaching and assessment techniques. This programme enabled Pacific teachers to tap into the knowledge and expertise of New Zealand teachers who had themselves experienced the development and introduction of new curriculum and assessment frameworks in the early 1990s. The project brought together the New Zealand teachers as resource people working with selected local teachers in workshops in several Pacific countries, in particular Samoa, Niue, the Cook Islands and Fiji.

More recent examples of New Zealand ODA assistance in facilitating teacher development are the Teacher Education Quality Improvement Project in Kiribati to strengthen the capacity of Kiribati Teachers College, and the Inclusive Education Programme in the Cook Islands to upgrade teachers' skills and qualifications in classroom teaching techniques. These programmes are similar to others that have over the years provided support to teachers and teachers' colleges throughout the region and are a cost effective form of overseas development aid to improve the quality and training of teachers in Pacific countries.

Examinations and curriculum

These two aspects of New Zealand's role in education in the Pacific are closely linked. Pacific countries adopting New Zealand external examinations necessarily committed themselves to following the requirements of the New Zealand curriculum. New Zealand's post-war development of School

Certificate (NZSC) at Form Five and University Entrance (UE) at Form Six saw these examinations and associated curricula being adopted by those countries for which New Zealand was responsible, and also in Tonga and Fiji. By the 1960s NZSC had largely replaced Overseas Cambridge as the secondary school leaving examination of choice in Fiji. Tuvalu and Kiribati were also later to adopt NZSC.

By 1986, 158 secondary schools in the Pacific were taking NZSC. This involved over 10,000 students, with two-thirds of the schools and four-fifths of the candidates coming from Fiji. In addition, about 100 schools from the region were taking UE, with about 6,000 students involved.

The adoption of the New Zealand examination system and curriculum was not without its problems, however, as some local observers saw the examinations as being imposed on the region by New Zealand and as being insufficiently responsive to the Pacific environment and its needs. To try and counter this perception, and as a result of the growing educational dialogue and partnership between New Zealand and the Pacific countries, from the late 1970s NZSC prescriptions were made more relevant to Pacific island candidates. This was achieved through the development and introduction of special South Pacific Option prescriptions and papers in English, mathematics, science, history and geography, and, for Fijian candidates, physical and biological sciences. A parallel development took place with UE English.

An unforeseen consequence of the adoption of New Zealand examinations was that it encouraged and reinforced an academic and elitist orientation to secondary education. This emphasis tended to be at the expense of recognising and rewarding the more practical education skills and learning required for such things as agriculture, fishing, basic engineering and building. As a result, it became difficult to persuade students and parents that practical education has the same value as that required for white collar occupations. No doubt this was an unintended outcome, and it would probably have occurred whatever overseas examination system had been adopted at that time. An illustration of this was seen in the late 1970s in Fiji when the decision was taken to provide rurally based non-academic Form 1–4 schools in remote rural areas. Initially these communities, which lacked secondary schools, welcomed the development, but were soon pressing for the schools to be extended to Form 5 and for NZSC to be available so that their children would have the same opportunities as their urban counterparts.

For many years Pacific schools preparing their students for New Zealand examinations received an annual oversight and advisory visit by education officers of the New Zealand Department of Education. These officers also consulted with and advised their local advisory counterparts, with the expectation that over time they would assume this responsibility. Other advisory visits in the 1970s and 80s included aid and advice on evaluation and assessment procedures and the development of educational standards testing programmes.

In addition to the provision of NZSC and UE, over the years New Zealand curriculum specialists were also working with Pacific Island departments of education, the South Pacific Commission and the University of the South Pacific (USP) to produce a wide range of books, and resource materials. These have included the Tate Oral English Scheme, readers in Cook Island Maori and Niuean, English language materials, the Shared Book and Book Flood programmes, mathematics textbooks and accompanying teachers' manuals, and social science and science units. New Zealand specialists have also been involved in working with local counterparts in reviewing curriculum needs.

One of the most encouraging developments in this area was the establishment in 1980 of the South Pacific Board for Educational Assessment (SPBEA) as an intergovernmental board to develop regional and/or national school leaving certificates. Initial operating costs were met by New Zealand, Australia and the United Kingdom, each providing 25 per cent, with the remaining 25 per cent coming from the Pacific member countries.

As the principal provider of external examinations at the time, New Zealand played a key role in helping to set up SPBEA. Prior to its establishment the New Zealand Department of Education, through the visiting education officers from its International Division, and also through staff from the Examinations Branch and the Curriculum Division, had been working with their Pacific counterparts in encouraging Pacific departments of education to think in terms of replacing the New Zealand qualifications with their own local or regional examinations. SPBEA was the successful outcome from this dialogue.

A further key player was the New Zealand Council for Educational Research (NZCER) in its work with local examinations staff. From the early 1970s, NZCER officers made regular visits to a number of Pacific countries to upgrade local staff skills in examinations and assessment techniques. That work continued until being taken over by SPBEA. NZCER's assistance with the development of examinations can be seen as part of a broader programme to aid the Pacific. This included studies of English language competence; research on reading and the preparation of reading materials; the development of performance tests; the provision of consultancy services; assistance with the establishment of a Psychological Assessment Unit at USP; and facilitating research by Pacific researchers and the publication of reports.

SPBEA offers two regional senior secondary school qualifications, the Pacific Senior Secondary Certificate and the South Pacific Form Seven Certificate, which began in 1989 and 2004 respectively. These qualifications have replaced the New Zealand qualifications except in the Cook Islands, Niue and Tokelau, which continue to use the New Zealand system through Levels 1, 2 and 3 of the National Certificate of Educational Achievement. SPBEA also assists member countries to improve assessment practices and procedures, to record and report results and to monitor standards in literacy and numeracy. The nine Pacific countries that form SPBEA are Fiji, Kiribati, Nauru, Tokelau, Tonga, Tuvalu, Samoa, the Solomon Islands and Vanuatu, plus New Zealand and Australia, who are the principal donors. SPBEA is a good example of a regional Pacific solution to the difficulties that face small countries in developing and operating viable examination systems which have international recognition.

Publications and libraries

For many years and on a regular basis, departments of education in the Pacific, and a number of schools, received publications from the School Publications branch of the New Zealand Department of Education. These included the School Journal, Bulletins and a range of curriculum resources. In addition, supplies of library books, advice on setting up libraries, and funds for the purchase of books were provided under aid programmes to schools throughout the region. With the disestablishment of the New Zealand Department of Education in 1989, and its replacement by a policy-focused Ministry of Education, School Publications became Learning Media, an independent publishing agency.

Learning Media produces material for the Ministry of Education which includes the Tupu series in Cook Island Maori, Niuean, Samoan, Tokelauan and Tongan. The series offers a range of genres at different curriculum levels and contains over 500 resources, with more added each year. The contents cover both Pacific Islands communities in New Zealand and the Pacific Islands themselves. The Ministry of Education sees the Tupu series as complementing other Pacific Islands language resources which it publishes for New Zealand early childhood centres and schools, and the programmes and guidelines for teaching Pacific languages. They also support the New Zealand Curriculum Statements for Pacific languages.

Learning Media resources are made available to Pacific school systems through Read Pacific Limited in Auckland, which for sixteen years has provided a range of books and school materials to most Pacific Island countries. Read Pacific has been involved in a number of Pacific aid projects and has developed an extensive knowledge of the region. Learning Media programmes promoted by Read Pacific include Pacific Literacy and Pacific Science booklets which have been developed specifically for Pacific primary schools. Pacific Literacy was developed by Learning Media in association with USP as a graded series of thirty books for Pacific children learning to read in English as a first or second language. The series can be used as a basis for bilingual reading programmes and is supported by a Teacher's Resource Book.

Distance education and communication

Not surprisingly, given the huge distances involved, this has been a significant feature of educational development in the Pacific. For many years and in certain circumstances, the New Zealand Correspondence School made courses available to students and teachers to supplement local teaching facilities. At the tertiary level, the Extramural Department of Massey University has played an important part, particularly in the field of teaching English as a second language, and the Open Polytechnic has provided a wide range of courses to Pacific students. New Zealand has also continued to support USP in strengthening its outreach capacity. Other New Zealand distance education providers have included a number of commercial colleges and religious education providers such as The South Pacific Bible College.

A significant example of regional cooperation in communication has been the development of the Pan Pacific Educational and Communication Experiment by Satellite (PEACESAT) set up in 1971 to meet the needs of sparsely populated, less developed areas in the Pacific. In 1972

PEACESAT became the first educational satellite network in the world, linking the University of Hawaii, Maui Community College, Wellington Polytechnic and USP in Suva, Fiji. PEACESAT has since expanded its network and has been operating successfully for 38 years. It is an important means of exchanging information on educational and technical subjects and provides education and training to help develop information and communication technology in Pacific countries.

Institutional support

Institutional support has been a significant feature of New Zealand's Pacific aid programme, ranging from early childhood to tertiary institutions throughout the region. Examples of this support include USP, which has been assisted by New Zealand since its founding in 1967. Initial assistance consisted of the buildings and site of the vacated Royal New Zealand Air Force base at Laucala Bay, Suva, which were donated by the New Zealand government. Subsequent aid has focused on further buildings and maintenance, books and resources at all levels, and secondment of personnel. The contribution of New Zealand staff to USP, both permanent appointments and shorter term secondments, has been very significant. Other institutional support has included the building of schools; the development of multicraft centres at the secondary level in Fiji and Tuvalu geared to meeting community needs; support for Alafua Agricultural College in Samoa; the development and ongoing support for the Fiji Technical Institute; assistance to teachers colleges in a number of Pacific countries; the provision of advisors and technical instructors throughout the region; and continuing support for the SPBEA.

Scholarships

For many years New Zealand aid has provided education and training at all levels for Pacific students to study in New Zealand. With the growth of Pacific institutions such as USP, scholarships have increasingly been made available for study in countries within the region, for example, New Zealand currently funds about 400 students from around the Pacific region to study at USP. This is likely to mean less cultural change and more environmental relevance for the students concerned.

Aid agencies and education

Some commentators such as Bauer and colleagues (1991) have questioned the long-term economic benefits from aid, saying that it encourages dependency and is more likely to benefit the donor than the recipient. It is my view, however, that educational aid has particularly beneficial outcomes through its role in developing human capital and widening opportunities for individuals to contribute to their societies. Successive New Zealand governments have recommitted to the United Nations goal of spending 0.7 per cent of gross national income on aid, but the current level of 0.23 per cent falls well short of that target. New Zealand's figure is similar to Australia's (0.25 per cent), but well below Norway's, which is the largest at 0.87 per cent. A number of New Zealand agencies have provided assistance to education in the Pacific over the years, but three stand out: the New Zealand government's Overseas Development Assistance programme (ODA), Volunteer Service Abroad (VSA), and the churches.

New Zealand government assistance

The principal provider of New Zealand's educational assistance to the Pacific has been the New Zealand government through ODA and the Pacific Division of the Ministry of Foreign Affairs, later to become the Ministry of Foreign Affairs and Trade (MFAT), but from 2002 a major review of the ODA resulted in the creation of the New Zealand Agency for International Development (NZAID) as a semi-autonomous body attached to MFAT. This has resulted in a reorientation of the education strategy for the Pacific improve quality and relevance of Pacific education by increasing support for basic education and strengthening leadership in education. These priorities align with the Pacific Forum Basic Education Plan (PFBEP) developed by Pacific Ministers of Education. The Pacific Regional Initiative for the Implementation and Delivery of Basic Education (PRIDE) has been developed as a mechanism for implementing PFBEP. Consistent with the Forum's priorities, NZAID supports initiatives aimed at strengthening educational planning and the delivery of basic education, raising education outcomes through student-centred learning, the rethinking of education by Pacific peoples, and ongoing research into the links between sustainable livelihoods and education.

On 1 May 2009, the new Minister of Foreign Affairs, Murray McCully, announced the reintegration of NZAID into MFAT. In doing so, the Minister indicated a revised aid mandate, focusing on economic development rather than poverty alleviation. However, these two goals should be seen as complementary and it remains to be seen what impact the revised emphasis will have on current educational programmes and the level and type of future New Zealand government assistance to education in the Pacific.

Volunteer Service Abroad

The main voluntary agency providing educational assistance to the Pacific has been VSA, founded in 1962. In 1964 a school-leavers programme began, which was to run for ten years. During that time 318 seventeen- and eighteen-year-olds served on one-year assignments, many of them in the Pacific. By 1974 VSA's objectives were expanded to emphasise a developmental role, an emphasis with considerable relevance for education. The understanding of what is meant by 'development' has evolved to place greater emphasis on the concept of 'we' in partnership, rather than 'us' and 'them'. Volunteers continue to work in Pacific schools, including two teachers in Tokelau, and there are recent vacancies for teacher-trainers in Papua New Guinea, Bougainville and Vanuatu.

The churches

It is not within the scope of this chapter to detail the role of the churches in assisting the development of education in the Pacific, but it is important to acknowledge the long history of that involvement. The first missionaries began working in the Pacific early in the 19th century and played a key role in transcribing oral vernacular languages into written forms. While the primary purpose was to enable Bible study and conversion to Christianity, it also enabled literacy in the vernacular to be established and the development of formal education to begin. The first secondary school in the Pacific Islands was established by the Methodist Mission at Tupou College in Tonga in 1866. The early part of the 20th century saw the churches still being the main provider of education, and even today secondary education, in particular, would be sorely pressed without the continuing contribution of the churches.

Some important issues

This chapter concludes with consideration of some important issues which are likely to have direct and indirect implications for education and its development in Pacific Island countries. These include problems of distance and isolation, demographic changes and migration, the health and physical well-being of the people, the maintenance of indigenous languages and literacy, the recruitment and status of teachers, economic growth, and political stability.

Distance and isolation pose ongoing problems for Pacific education, making contact and communication difficult to maintain, both internally and externally. These problems are probably more extreme in the Pacific than anywhere else in the world. Very small states have difficulty in providing a range of administrative and professional services for their education systems. For teacher improvement the role of advisory support is critical, but because of distance and isolation schools are visited infrequently, in-service courses are few and school servicing inadequate. Oversight and assistance are easier when only one island is involved, such as Niue or Nauru, but in countries with numerous scattered islands, such as Vanuatu or the Cook Islands, the problems are very difficult to overcome.

In the Pacific, demographic factors loom large for education and its provision. In most countries the proportion of the population that is of school age is very high, with between 35 and 40 per cent of the population under fifteen years of age. This places a considerable burden on already over-stretched education systems. Migration overseas has also had an important negative effect on the populations of many Pacific countries by removing well qualified people that these countries can ill afford to lose. There is also internal migration from the smaller, more isolated islands to the larger, more populated islands, which distorts the demographic profiles of already vulnerable communities.

The health and physical well-being of the people have significant implications for Pacific education. It is an unfortunate fact that the introduction of western foods, high in fat, sugar and carbohydrates, has had a detrimental effect on the health of Pacific Islanders. Changes in diet and lifestyle have resulted in high levels of childhood and adult obesity, and very high rates of diabetes, coronary heart disease, high blood pressure, and other associated ailments. Where more traditional lifestyles have been maintained the people are generally healthier. Education can play an important role in helping to counteract the lifestyle changes that have contributed to such negative health outcomes for Pacific peoples.

Language and literacy are key elements in any education policy aimed at improving the quality of education. Pacific Island countries face considerable difficulties in the area of language, as a facility in a major metropolitan language, such as English, is essential in order to participate in the modern world. It is necessary not only for trade, commerce and tourism, but also for the technology of development and for regional communication and cooperation. It carries with it, however, the very real risk that the indigenous languages will be eroded, and, as indicated by Benton (1981), is likely to result in some of the more vulnerable languages, with small numbers of speakers, dying out altogether. This is a critical problem as language is central to cultural identity. Thus, language policy for education and literacy needs to be based on the practical premise that the metropolitan language is a tool, a window to the wider world, but it should not be developed and taught at the expense of the indigenous languages and cultures. In practice this is difficult to achieve, but New Zealand can assist with, for example, the provision of reading materials in local languages such as the Tupu series. Assistance with language development and literacy can also be provided through the provision of effective, low-cost literacy programmes, such as the well documented Book Flood programme developed for the Pacific by Warwick Elley (2000).

As already indicated, the quality of teachers available to an education system is a major determinant of the quality of that system. In order to ensure the recruitment of suitable candidates it is essential that the status of teachers in the Pacific and their working conditions be improved. New Zealand is well placed to continue providing aid in support of teacher training and development, both pre- and in-service, and to help raise their status. One factor which works against teacher retention in Pacific countries is the general shortage of skilled and qualified people, which means that well trained teachers have marketable qualifications that enable them to move to other, often better paid, occupations. It is vital, therefore, that remuneration levels for well qualified teachers should be sufficient to retain them in teaching.

Economic imperatives are a significant factor in determining the resources available to education. Rapid population growth and the youth of populations place heavy burdens on overstretched systems, and Pacific countries vary widely in economic potential. The larger Melanesian islands have timber and minerals which can be exploited, but these are finite resources. Agriculture is well developed in a number of countries, such as Fiji, and tourism is a major source of income for many Pacific nations. However, for smaller atoll countries such as Tuvalu and Kiribati, fishing within their exclusive economic zones is the main revenue source, through licenses to countries such as China, Korea, Japan and Taiwan.

Political stability is essential to all aspects of life in the Pacific, including education. The ongoing instability in the Solomon Islands, for example, has for many years denied a proper education to a large number of children. Other examples of instability or potential instability include the secessionist movement in Bougainville, the campaigns for greater autonomy in the French territories, the repeated coups in Fiji, the 2006 riots in Tonga and campaigns for greater democracy in that country, and, throughout the region, problems of disaffected unemployed urban youth. Adding a further dimension over recent years has been the growing competition between China and Taiwan for influence in the Pacific.

Whatever the future holds for education in the Pacific, it is in New Zealand's interests to collaborate with and assist Pacific countries in attaining positive educational outcomes. No single solution or blueprint for success exists; what may work successfully in a relatively developed country such as Fiji will be less relevant for small atoll countries like Tuvalu. Rather than following the western model of individual competitiveness, appropriate solutions are more likely to be found within the Pacific way of community cooperation and partnership which recognises and acknowledges traditional values and culture.

Bibliography

Bauer, P., Siwatibau, S. & Kasper, W. (1991). *Aid and development in the South Pacific.* The Centre for Independent Studies, St Leonards, Australia and Auckland, New Zealand.

Beeby, C.E. (1966). *The quality of education in developing countries.* Cambridge, Massachusetts: Harvard University Press.

Beeby, C.E. (1992). *The biography of an idea: Beeby on education.* Wellington: New Zealand Council for Educational Research.

Benton, R. A. (1981). *The flight of the Amokura: oceanic languages and formal education in the South Pacific.* Wellington: New Zealand Council for Educational Research.

Campbell, I.C. (2003). *Worlds apart: a history of the Pacific islands*. Canterbury, New Zealand: Canterbury University Press.

Crocombe, R. (1992). New Zealand and the other Pacific islands: changing economic, social and political relations. In D.H. Rubinstein (Ed.). *Pacific history: papers from the 8th Pacific History Association Conference*. University of Guam Press and Micronesian Area Research Center. pp. 293-312.

Elley, W.B. (2000). The potential of book floods for raising literacy levels. *International Review of Education*. 46, 3-4. pp. 233-255.

Fischer, S.R. (2002). *A history of the Pacific islands*. New York: Palgrave.

Gadd, M. & Elley, W. (2003). Improving english literacy in Tonga's primary schools. In *Global/local intersections: researching the delivery of aid to Pacific education*. Research Unit of Pacific Education, University of Auckland.

Irving, J.C. (1980). New Zealand's role in the development of education in the South Pacific. In *Proceedings of the pre-congress conference, 4th world congress of comparative education societies, Seoul*.

Irving, J.C. (1984). Trends, options in islands education. *Development*. 7, 2. pp. 4-5.

Learning Media Te Pou Taki Korero (2007). *Passionate about learning – Learning Media*. Learning Media Te Pou Taki Korero. http://www.learningmedia.co.nz/ (accessed 5 December 2008).

Mangubhai, F. & Elley, W. (2008). *Literacy endeavours in Oceania: an historical overview*. Unpublished manuscript.

New Zealand's International Aid and Development Agency (2008). *Where do we work?* New Zealand's International Aid and Development Agency. August. http://www.nzaid.govt.nz/programmes (accessed 17 November 2008).

Read Pacific (2008). *Read Pacific: books and resources for education throughout the Pacific*. Read Pacific. January. http://www.readpacific.co.nz/ (accessed 5 December 2008).

South Pacific Board for Educational Assessment (2008). *About SPBEA*. http://www.stats. govt.nz/analytical-reports/pacific-profiles-2006/ (accessed 17 November 2008).

Volunteer Service Abroad (2008). http://www.vsa.org.nz/about/history/ (accessed 5 December 2008).

Understanding Why Radical Policy Reform Takes Time to Embed: Illustrations from Policy on Assessment

Cedric Hall and James Irving

Introduction

This chapter draws upon some of our reflections on three aspects of policy reform that are strongly associated with the timeframe needed to embed policy. The three aspects of interest are the role of *professional development* in spreading the change, the notion of *co-construction* in the design and particularly the implementation of reform, and the need for *specialist expertise* when the reform involves technical knowledge which the policy reformists (politicians and government officials) do not possess. We will illustrate our discussion with examples of policy change in educational assessment. Readers with an interest in other educational fields may find that some of the discussion resonates well within their own contexts.

It has long been recognised that educational change, from simple innovations to radical policy reform, appears to take an inordinate amount of time to bed down. The literature on change management identifies a number of factors that impede progress and the conditions that need to be in place to facilitate change. Various strategies have also been suggested to speed up change and enlist the acceptance/support of teachers and educational administrators. A glimpse into some of these strategies is provided by both Perris (1998) and Wood (1998) in their 'insider' reflections on the educational reform process of the 1980s and 1990s in New Zealand. These strategies are mentioned briefly in the following section.

This chapter is particularly concerned with policy reforms that run into problems despite being logical, valid, and/or based on sound research. The argument proposed is that while radical educational reform may be able to be driven through so that it is in place and operating, problems are likely to remain unless considerations relating to professional development and the co-construction of policy implementation with experts and practitioners are carefully addressed.

Problems in embedding change

There are clearly a wide range of factors that are linked to successful educational reform or change. Many of these are not new to the literature. For example, analyses of factors that impact on successful implementation have been provided by Miles (1964) and Morrish (1976). Morrish in particular addressed a large number of factors that either impede or facilitate the bedding down of change. Many of these resonate in the later debate that accompanied the educational reforms of the 1980s and 1990s in New Zealand. The following are examples of impediments to change which Morrish identified; brief commentaries are provided to give an illustration of the way the reform process considered each impediment.

Environmental resistance

The community at large does not usually encourage or expect major educational change unless a crisis in the system is detected.

Commentary: The educational reforms of the 1980s and 1990s were founded on at least two crises – the need for the education system to be far more responsive to the economic goals and directions of New Zealand within a global marketplace (Perris 1998, Wood 1998); and an apparent decline in the results of New Zealand students in comparative studies of achievement conducted by the International Association for the Evaluation of Educational Achievement.

Overcentralisation

The power in most systems is concentrated in the hands of a small group of senior officials; consequently innovations are filtered through bureaucratic processes that slow down change.

Commentary: The centrepiece of the New Zealand educational reforms, *Tomorrow's Schools* (Lange 1988), was designed with the main purpose of transferring power from the centre to parents and the community.

Teacher defensiveness

Resentment from teachers exists towards change in schooling that has not involved their participation; the situation is compounded when teachers are criticised for their existing practices.

Commentary: During the early stages of the reform process, schools and teachers were criticised on a number of grounds, such as ineffective reporting to parents, unwillingness to encourage competitiveness in their education, and inability to focus on the individual needs of all students. In addition, the secondary teacher union (The Post-Primary Teachers Association) was sidelined because of its opposition to the changes (Perris 1998).

Absence of change agent

An effective change agent is lacking, that is, someone in a major leadership role is needed who champions the change and acts as the mediator between the research that supports the innovation and the guidance provided to educational administrators and schools to help them through the change process.

Commentary: In relation to the structural changes in education that took place in New Zealand, Perris emphasised the major impact of particular people (e.g., Dr Russell Ballard, the last Director-General of Education) who held key change leadership roles during the reforms. In relation to assessment, the leadership provided by Lester Flockton and Dr Terry Crooks incorporated important aspects of educational change management under the umbrella of the National Education Monitoring Project (NEMP).

Underdeveloped scientific base

Whereas scientific inventions undergo rigorous testing, educational innovations are not usually as systematically investigated.

Commentary: The reforms were accompanied by various demands for accountability, such as schools being able to demonstrate, through reviews undertaken by the Education Review Office (ERO), that they had made a difference to students' learning. The current push for both national testing (again) and evidence-based teaching practice is also a reflection of the concern that teaching decisions and reporting should be guided by a more rigorous approach to evidence.

Confused goals

The aims and beliefs of teachers, administrators, school authorities and government officials are not in harmony, resulting in confused messages and competing directions. There is a need for all to sing the same tune.

Commentary: The emphasis given to 'seamlessness' during the reform process and the establishment of a single qualifications framework covering senior secondary school assessment, tertiary level education and industry training is an illustration of policy with a strong 'same tune' basis.

Uniformity of approach

Both students and teachers are diverse in their backgrounds, yet teaching methods focus on providing something that is applicable to the largest number of students rather than something appropriate for each child.

Commentary: The need for 'inclusiveness' is strongly evident in the rationale for the reforms in curriculum and assessment (Wood 1998). For example, the National Certificate of Educational Achievement (NCEA) was introduced in 2002 with a strong emphasis on social justice – that a system should be in place which supported the potential for all students, not just the elite going on to university, to succeed (Hall 2005).

It takes only a short reflection on most of these themes to recognise, as illustrated in the above commentaries, that the educational reforms of the 1980s and 1990s were consciously directed towards removing impediments to educational change.

Factors contributing to an improved timeframe

As noted earlier, Morrish looked at both the positives and negatives in relation to factors that impact on successful change. In looking at the conditions that are needed within a school to implement change, Morrish drew heavily on the analysis of creative teaching undertaken a year earlier by Nicholls and Nicholls (1975). In particular, Morrish noted the following points:

• Teachers should understand the change and be favourably disposed towards it.

• Teachers should have the knowledge, skills and confidence to implement the change.

- Essential resources should be provided.
- Administrative and organisational support should be available and appropriate.
- Effective channels of communication should exist for giving information, gaining cooperation, responding to concerns, and changing attitudes.
- In-service education (professional development) should be available to support teachers' understanding and implementation of the change.
- Adequate time should be allowed for the change to be communicated, understood, explored by teachers, supported, and embedded in practice.

The last of these has clearly been an issue. Exactly what constitutes 'adequate' time is contestable. For example, in reviewing the implementation of the education reforms in New Zealand over the period 1987–1997, Perris (1998) argued in support of the government's deliberate strategy that change should be introduced 'more quickly than is comfortable' (p. 25). The government's position was built on the rationale that change needed to be undertaken quickly in order to limit the ability of opposition forces to become organised. While Morrish would probably not have agreed with this position, he also expressed concern at the very slow rate of change associated with innovations and reform in education. He strongly supported the need for systematic attention to be paid to the change process so that innovations with obvious validity would be introduced more quickly.

Perris, who was Acting Secretary of Education for eighteen months over the period 1995–1996, identified fifteen factors which he thought were important for achieving successful educational change. These included:

- Change which taps into public support is likely to have a head-start.
- Any changes must be consistent with the supporting infrastructures.
- It is important to allow for mistakes and create incentives for transparency and learning. (Perris 1998, pp. 24–26)

Some of the other factors identified by Perris would appear to be less about *successful* change and more about making sure that strategies exist for driving the change through the education system. In the sense used here, *success* is indicated by a change that is embraced by all (or nearly all) participants in the process; success is also evidenced in the change becoming strongly embedded and positively valued within school practice.

Perhaps a distinction could be made at this point between policy that is 'operating' and policy that is 'working'. The former indicates that a policy is in place and running; the latter indicates something more: that the policy is widely supported and successfully embedded as an integral element of school practice. A policy that is driven through may well operate because it has been forcefully mandated, strategically managed, and associated with strong incentives and sanctions; determining whether or not it is successful requires detailed evidence about changes in school and system practices and achievement of policy goals (such as improved learning outcomes). On this point it needs to be acknowledged that Perris defined success in political terms; if a policy survives the transition associated with a change of government, then it has achieved a form of stability that is indicative of political success. However, Perris acknowledges that his review of the reforms focuses in particular on the processes related to their implementation, not on an analysis of the outcomes in terms of changed practices and student learning.

The 'driving through' strategies suggested by Perris include (comments are provided in parentheses):

• *Legislate the change.* (This shows that the government is serious.)

• *Find other opinion leaders who will help promote the change.* (This involves the use of credible leaders outside of the government who lend their support to the change.)

• *Use the communication media.* (This involves the use of media experts to help communicate the change positively to the profession, other stakeholders, and the public.)

• *Negotiate with and involve or isolate the pressure groups.* (This emphasises the need to engage with pressure groups, to attempt to get them onside, but to isolate them if they remain unsupportive.) (pp. 24-26)

It would be fair to suggest that the 'strategic' approach to change suggested by Perris differs somewhat in philosophy and practice from that recommended two decades earlier by Morrish. This is not intended to be a criticism of either position. What this chapter suggests is that stronger insights into the factors associated with successful policy implementation lie in looking at events through different lenses, and in recognising that different lenses may complement each other in providing an understanding of what is *working*, not just *operating*.

The role of professional development in implementing policy reform

A factor strongly emphasised by Morrish is the role of in-service education (professional development) in ensuring that educational change beds down successfully. A wide range of literature exists on what constitutes effective professional development in the educational context. For example, Mitchell and Cubey (2003) provided a synthesis of effective professional development in the early childhood sector within New Zealand. Significantly, most of the findings appear to generalise to other educational contexts and are consistent with the wider literature. They identified eight factors that were characteristic of effective professional development, including the following which have particular significance to this discussion:

- The professional development incorporates participants' own aspirations, skills, knowledge and understanding into the learning context.

- Participants analyse data from their own settings. Revelation of discrepant data is a mechanism to invoke revised understanding.

- Critical reflection enabling participants to investigate and challenge assumptions and extend their thinking is a core aspect.

- Professional development helps participants to change educational practice, beliefs, understandings and/or attitudes.

- Professional development helps participants to gain awareness of their own thinking, actions, and influence. (Mitchell and Cubey 2003, p. 81)

The remaining three factors focused on the need for inclusiveness, engagement with pedagogy, and engagement with theoretical knowledge and alternative practices. The significance of the factors quoted above is that they stress two important elements of relevance to the later discussion. Firstly, that participants need to see that the new development is not only relevant to them but is something that will positively change their own educational practice; a corollary of this is that the professional development should be structured such that participants engage in activities that are meaningful to their own practice and context. Secondly, that the professional development encourages participants to critically reflect on their own practices in a way that challenges their own assumptions, practices, beliefs and attitudes.

Similar conclusions were also reached from a major evaluation study of the 2005–2006 nationwide NCEA professional development initiative that was instigated by the Ministry of Education in New Zealand (Starkey et al. 2006). This evaluation not only looked at the professional development undertaken by teachers for NCEA, but also investigated the characteristics of professional development that teachers more generally value. One of the conclusions from this study was:

> Effective professional development was identified as including a strong focus on participants' subject needs, the understanding of such needs by the facilitator, and the engagement of teachers in examining good teaching in their own setting. (Starkey et al. 2006, pp. 3–4)

As mentioned, these ideas from the above New Zealand studies resonate with the wider international literature. For example, the model of professional development proposed by Guskey (2000) not only acknowledges the above points but also argues strongly that if professional development programmes are actually going to benefit students, harmonisation of a range of organisational provisions are needed to ensure that the outcomes of the programme become embedded in school practice. For example, changes to school policies and administrative procedures may be needed in relation to curriculum, assessment, resources, student guidance, parent education, and so on. This emphasis on underpinning change with structural support is consistent with the conclusions of Perris (1998), Morrish (1976) and Nicholls and Nicholls (1975).

Further reinforcement of the above ideas is evident from a recent major report on professional development published by the Ministry of Education (Timperley et al. 2007). This report reviewed New Zealand and international literature, focusing in particular on studies that indicated links with improved student learning. The findings are too many and complex to present in detail here, but again some of the key elements reinforce the points made above. The research recommends that prevailing discourses be challenged; that engagement in the new ideas and learning (the substance of professional development) is far more important than just being willing to participate; that the professional development should focus on matters that have consistency with wider trends in both research and policy; and that the professional development produces sustainable action by teachers and schools, that is, that the professional learning that takes place includes the knowledge, skills and reflective practices that further promote school and teacher investigation into existing and evolving practices.

Most of the research evidence shows that the requirements for both effective professional development and successful educational reform are very similar. The underlying ideas cannot be claimed to be entirely new but many are couched in ways or contexts that give them enhanced or new impetus.

We are reminded here of the literature relating to the notion of *experiential learning* that had considerable force during the 1980s and 1990s. Of particular interest, although far less in detail and more in general conception, is the *experiential taxonomy* developed by Steinaker and Bell (1979), which organises and sequences tertiary student learning through five levels of activities or experiences that progressively deepen the students' technical knowledge and skills. (Readers should transfer the descriptions below to their own experiences of in-service professional development.) The first level, 'exposure', requires that new ideas are communicated initially in a way that encourages a readiness in the learner to engage further. The second level, 'participation', provides activities that engage the learner in trying out the new ideas in ways or contexts that are meaningful to them. At the next level, the type of activities employed are designed to foster 'identification' of the learner with the ideas; the ideas become recognised as personally relevant and worthy of ownership. The fourth level, more than the preceding levels, takes the learning to a new plane. In formal educational contexts, instructional activities and experiences are designed so that the new knowledge and skills become 'internalised', that is, they become part of the learner's repertoire of skills, strategies and practices that are drawn upon, often tacitly, as a response to problems that are common in professional practice. However, there is a difficulty here that relates to the time needed to effectively internalise a major change; this is discussed shortly. The final level of the taxonomy, 'dissemination', provides activities or experiences that enable the learner to demonstrate their knowledge or expertise in drawing upon and applying the new ideas. In professional development contexts, someone at this level is in the position to lead others through the new ideas, to provide professional development opportunities for colleagues, and thus become an integral part of the change process that embeds the reform or innovation.

We do not want to make too much out of this sequence. However, the distinction between identification and internalisation is an important one because it offers at least a partial explanation as to why it takes time for a major educational innovation such as a radical policy change to become successfully embedded in everyday practice. The point is that genuine internalisation of significant ideas often requires a lengthy period of professional practice before the ideas become effectively integrated into professional behaviour. In reality, internalisation involves the learner not only understanding the new ideas, but knowing their limits or boundaries of application, recognising when to vary practice or explore further, and knowing how to critically examine their own competence in applying those ideas. In professional development contexts aimed at educational administrators and teachers, such as workshops or teacher-only days, internalisation can only take place following the initial engagement, through a lengthy period of everyday practice that is supported by school leadership and structural arrangements that are aligned to the changes. The complexities associated with internalisation are many. The next section highlights one complexity which has a professional development 'twist'.

The co-construction of policy with practitioners and experts

The preceding discussion identified some of the factors that are linked to successful professional development. Because professional development is usually a key element in ensuring that educational reforms bed down, there is a strong need to allow sufficient time for the majority of teachers and administrators to internalise the new learning. This raises a professional development issue of a different nature: If an innovation such as a radical reform in educational or school practices becomes policy, who will be the people to lead the change process out in the field? What is the prior experience of these people with the new ideas? Is this experience characteristic of internalised learning or more aligned with the earlier stage of identification?

As mentioned above, deep understanding of a reform or an innovation involves having the kinds of experiences that lead to recognising the practical strengths and limitations of the change, and knowing what the boundaries are, when to apply the ideas and when to leave them alone, and when to recognise that the policy requires adjustment if the implementation is to be successful. Arguably, the introduction of the National Qualifications Framework, the accountability reviews first undertaken in schools by ERO, and the implementation of NCEA, all involved 'agents' in the field who mostly did not have the kinds of prior learning and experiences that could be legitimately described as 'internalised'. For example, if the roles of school principals and ERO officers had been reversed, could the ERO officers have implemented school practices on assessment that would have dealt with the criticisms that were typically made in early ERO school reviews? It took some time before ERO itself recognised that there were too many achievement objectives in the curriculum to expect students to be systematically assessed against them all; it also took time for ERO to recognise that schools needed a range of assessment tools to assist them with their analyses of student learning and reporting progress to parents.

The point being made is that the very nature of a radical reform is such that widespread experience or expertise in understanding and applying the ideas is usually limited. Although many of the people appointed to the 'change agencies' during the early reform period (e.g., ERO and NZQA) were highly competent in their particular fields preceding their appointments, the work they were now asked to undertake lay outside their internalised experience and expertise. That these people identified with the reform is not questioned, but identification is not sufficient for recognising the kinds of practical problems that will arise from particular expectations, requirements or decisions that lie within the bounds of the policy.

There are therefore significant risks in introducing major policy changes. But the argument here is that radical reform should not be held back where the logic for its introduction is sound and/or the research evidence is very clear; what is needed is a process which involves 'co-construction' of the implementation between the reformers, the practitioners and, where technical knowledge is important for understanding the processes and consequences of particular aspects of the policy, experts in the field such as researchers in universities. What is being suggested here is a form of 'learning in tandem', a notion employed by Crowl and Hall (2005) to describe a process within educational aid programmes whereby the external expertise of consultants is blended with the local knowledge of the host community to bring about sustainable change; each learns from the other in the process.

It is very clear, in fact, that since the late 1990s (and in some cases before this time) the Ministry of Education's approach towards assessment reform has involved a significant element of co-construction. This is illustrated through developments in national monitoring (i.e., NEMP) and the provision of a range of assessment tools and strategies to help primary schools to inform their decision-making about student progress, and to report to the community and the government.

The NEMP project is a very good illustration of co-construction. National monitoring was a central recommendation of the Ministerial report on *Tomorrow's Standards* (Ministry of Education 1990); Otago University won the contract to undertake the monitoring. An important element in the acceptance of the Otago proposal was that its design dealt with a number of issues that were criticised in the UK system of 'key stage' testing against the national curriculum: that national testing narrowed the curriculum, was unmanageable and very expensive, and led to the creation of league tables that unfairly compared schools. Significantly, the leaders of the NEMP project were Lester Flockton and Terry Crooks, both with extensive experience in assessment within schools. Furthermore, the design was informed by a landmark international publication by Crooks (1988) that reviewed the literature on classroom assessment and evaluation practices.

A critical factor in the NEMP development was that throughout the policy development and implementation Ministry officials engaged meaningfully with both the teaching profession and assessment experts. An interesting contrast can be made with the design and implementation of NCEA, at least in regard to engagement with assessment experts.

As mentioned earlier, the NCEA policy was intended to provide the opportunity for all students to succeed, not just an elite that progressed to university or professional/technical programmes in polytechnics. The intent of this policy is not in any way challenged here; however, the design and implementation of the policy is. Key elements of the policy are described in Hall (2000, 2005); the essential ingredient is that the previously norm-referenced system of examination was replaced by a standards-based model which reported students' achievement in each subject against a number of separate standards (typically between three and eight per subject per year level), each having their own credit rating.

After the first year of implementation NZQA awarded itself a pass mark with headlines such as 'Hitch-free first year for NCEA examinations' (New Zealand Qualifications Authority 2003, p. 6). Two years later the storyline was vastly different. Media attacks on the failings of NCEA and Scholarship (the highest academic level of secondary school examinations) prompted the government to initiate two major reviews, one comprising a group of assessment experts and practitioners given the role of reshaping the 2005 Scholarship examinations, the other looking at the management and setting of Scholarship as well as the performance of the NZQA. The latter review was undertaken by a panel appointed by the State Services Commissioner.

Reports from the two reviews (Scholarship Reference Group 2005, State Services Commission 2005a, 2005b) resulted in major changes to Scholarship (Cabinet immediately accepted 25 out of 26 recommendations from the first of these reviews), and to the leadership and management of NZQA. For a detailed coverage of the pedagogical and technical problems relating to NCEA, readers are referred to analyses from Elley, Hall and Marsh (2005) and Locke (2004). It is sufficient to say here that over the first three years of these examinations, widely varying pass rates were obtained between standards across years that could not be accounted for by either cohort differences or changes in the level of student learning. Elley, Hall and Marsh found that the problems stemmed from the ideological approach to standards-based assessment that had been taken both in the design of NCEA (the responsibility of the Ministry) and in its operation over the first three years (the responsibility of NZQA). Throughout this time, the concerns of assessment experts were ignored; these concerns related to reliability, consequential validity (e.g., the impact on pedagogy) and manageability. All of these issues were specifically raised with the Ministry during the design of NCEA and in publications (e.g., Hall 2000, Locke 2001). In short, while some level of co-construction occurred in relation to NCEA through consultation with a forum of practitioners drawn mainly from the secondary school sector, this consultation did not include people with the technical expertise that was needed to deal with problems that were predicted, and subsequently arose, during the implementation of NCEA.

It is important to record that over the past two or three years NZQA has engaged closely with assessment experts in various developments related to NCEA and Scholarship. It is fair comment to suggest that

Scholarship is now *operating* and *working* effectively; however, NCEA is still struggling to overcome some of the design problems that were identified during its development.

Conclusion

As noted in the introduction to this chapter, educational reform is well recognised for the seemingly excessive time that the reform takes to bed down in practice. Factors that impede change centre on issues, at least in part, that limit acceptance of the change from schools and educational administrators. Although reform can be driven through using processes such as those identified by Perris (1998) – legislating the change, using the media effectively, and isolating pressure groups that remain in opposition – the bedding down of the change, so that it is widely and actively embraced by teachers and administrators, is still likely to take time.

Policy which is working, not just operating, requires something more than implementation strategies aimed at driving through the reform. Here we have focused on two provisions for successful reform: (1) that professional development relating to the reform is relevant to and accepted by the participants, challenges their existing practices and beliefs, and is followed up with a lengthy period of support to help them genuinely internalise the changes; and (2) that development and implementation of the reform involves the practitioners, and technical experts where required, to ensure that any potential problems with the reform are recognised and addressed.

A comparison of the reforms relating to national monitoring (NEMP) and secondary school assessment (NCEA) provides an interesting contrast. Although both engaged with practitioners, NEMP's design embraced the relevant educational research literature, the Ministry contracted people with curriculum and assessment expertise to develop and lead the project, and the project later drew upon international expertise to provide evaluations of the methodology and progress. In contrast, the development and implementation of NCEA by the Ministry and NZQA overlooked important literature, dismissed expert analysis of problems related to its design, and pushed forward ignoring what the assessment data were showing in relation to the validity and reliability of the grades obtained by students on a large number of achievement standards. NEMP has bedded down remarkably quickly; NCEA still has complex problems to resolve, which reflect difficulties that were exposed but ignored during its design. NEMP operates and works; NCEA operates but still has some way to go before it can be said to be working.

References

Crooks, T.J. (1988). The impact of classroom evaluation practices on students. *Review of Educational Research.* 58, 4. pp. 438-481.

Crowl, L. & Hall, C. (2005). Learning in tandem. In K. Sanga, C. Hall, C. Chu & L. Crowl (Eds.). *Re-Thinking aid relationships in Pacific education.* Wellington: He Parekereke, Victoria University of Wellington and Institute of Education, University of the South Pacific, pp. 420-433.

Elley, W., Hall, C. & Marsh, R. (2005). Rescuing NCEA: Some possible ways forward. *New Zealand Annual Review of Education.* 14. pp. 5-25.

Guskey, T.R. (2000). *Evaluating professional development.* Thousand Oaks, California: Corwin Press.

Hall, C. (2000). National Certificate of Educational Achievement: issues of reliability, validity and manageability. *New Zealand Annual Review of Education.* 9. pp. 173-196.

Hall, C. (2005). The National Certificate of Educational Achievement (NCEA): Is there a third way? In J. Codd & K. Sullivan. (2005). *Education policy directions in Aotearoa New Zealand.* Victoria Australia: Thomson/Dunmore Press. pp. 236-265.

Lange, D. (1988). *Tomorrow's schools: The reform of education administration in New Zealand.* Wellington: Government Printer.

Locke, T. (2001). English and the NCEA: The impact of an assessment regime on curriculum and practice. *Waikato Journal of Education.* 7. pp. 99-116.

Locke, T. (2004). The NCEA: 20 reasons for concern. *Education Review.* 8-9, 13–19 October.

Miles, M.B. (Ed.). (1964). *Innovation in education.* New York: Teachers College Press, Columbia University.

Ministry of Education (1990). *Tomorrow's standards: the report of the ministerial working party on assessment for better learning.* Wellington: Learning Media.

Mitchell, L. & Cubey, P. (2003). *Characteristics of effective professional development linked to enhanced pedagogy and children's learning in early childhood settings: best evidence synthesis.* Wellington: Ministry of Education.

Morrish, I. (1976). *Aspects of educational change.* London: George Allen & Unwin Ltd.

New Zealand Qualifications Authority. (2003). *QA news.* (Issue 44) February/March. Wellington: New Zealand Qualifications Authority.

Nicholls, A. & Nicholls, S.H. (1975). *Creative teaching.* London: George Allen & Unwin.

Perris, L. (1998). *Implementing education reforms in New Zealand: 1987-97. a case study.* Education, The World Bank.

Scholarship Reference Group. (2005). *A report prepared for the Associate Minister of Education.* Wellington: Ministry of Education.

State Services Commission. (2005a). *Report on the 2004 scholarship to the Deputy State Services Commissioner*. Wellington: State Services Commission.

State Services Commission. (2005b). *Report on the performance of the New Zealand Qualifications Authority in the delivery of secondary school qualifications*. Wellington: State Services Commission.

Starkey, L., Stevens, S., Taylor, M., Toia, R., Yates, A., Hall, C., McKenzie, L. & Meyer, L. (2006). *School/cluster based secondary qualifications professional development: Review of secondary schools' use of NCEA professional development resources, 2005–2006*. Wellington: Ministry of Education Research Division.

Steinaker, N.W., & Bell, M.R. (1979). *The experiential taxonomy*. New York: Academic Press.

Timperley, H., Wilson, A., Barrar, H. & Fung, I. (2007). *Teacher professional learning and development: best evidence synthesis iteration*. Wellington: Ministry of Education.

Wood, D.R. (1998). *The political origins of the New Zealand curriculum framework development*. Wellington: Unpublished paper.

EARLY CHILDHOOD EDUCATION

Teaching Early Childhood Education at Victoria: Policy, Discipline, and Profession

Carmen Dalli and Anne Meade

Setting the scene

Victoria University's contribution to New Zealand early childhood education policy stretches back many decades. In 1947 Professor Colin Bailey chaired the first government committee of inquiry on pre-school education, as it was then called. Forty-one years later, Dr Anne Meade, a graduate of Victoria and subsequent faculty member, chaired the third[1] government working group on early childhood education entitled *Education to be More*. Otherwise called the Meade Report (Department of Education 1988b), it was commissioned as part of the *Tomorrow's Schools* reforms. In 2001, between positions at Victoria,[2] Meade was invited to chair the fourth working group on early childhood education which resulted in the Labour-led government's ten-year strategic plan for early childhood education, *Pathways to the Future – Ngā Huarahi Arataki* (Ministry of Education 2002). These high-profile early childhood policy projects, led by Victoria University academics and involving the whole early education sector, helped put the Education Department at Victoria University on the world 'map' of early childhood policy. The involvement of the Education Department in starting the *Competent Children* longitudinal study in the early 1990s (Wylie and Hodgen 2001) added to Victoria's reputation in relation to early childhood education, this time putting it on the 'map' of early childhood education research. The appointment of the first professor

---

1 Clem Hill, a Professor of Education at Massey University, chaired the second committee of inquiry in 1971.

2 Meade was a member of faculty at Victoria on three occasions: in the 1970s while also a doctoral student; between 1989 and 1991 as a full-time senior lecturer; and again in 2004 and 2005 when she taught the masters education policy paper on a part-time basis.

of early childhood teacher education in the country, alongside the launch of the Institute for Early Childhood Studies as a joint venture with the then Wellington College of Education in the mid-1990s, further put the seal on Victoria's reputation as a leader in the field of early childhood studies, whilst also marking it out as the front runner in professionalising the early childhood teacher education sector.

In this chapter we tell stories about the introduction of early childhood education as an academic discipline at Victoria in the 1980s and 1990s and position this within the wider societal and educational policy context of New Zealand. Mirroring the fate of early childhood policy during those decades, the discipline of early childhood studies at Victoria underwent growth and development that saw it gain strength and visibility despite occasional setbacks. For three seminal years between 1989 and 1992, we (the authors) worked together to set up courses in early childhood studies within the BA and MEd programmes of the Faculty of Arts/Humanities and Social Sciences. Meade subsequently left to head up the New Zealand Council for Educational Research, leaving a senior staffing gap that remained, contentiously, unfilled till the arrival of the new professor of early childhood teacher education at the end of 1994. The story of that appointment is a story of collaboration and wise politics: we tell it here as a prelude to Helen May's story in another chapter in this volume of her 'unlikely career' to become that professor.

We conclude this chapter with some reflections on how the humble beginnings of the 80s and 90s have contributed to the development of early childhood studies as an academic discipline at Victoria, and to the development of early childhood teaching as a profession.

Early beginnings

In the late 1980s and early 1990s Helen May and Jill Mitchell – then at Hamilton Teachers College, which shortly thereafter became the University of Waikato – compiled two slim volumes celebrating New Zealand people who had made a contribution to early childhood education (May and Mitchell *n.d.* a and b). Among those profiled were two Victoria women: Geraldine McDonald and Anne Meade. A third Victoria woman, Marie Bell, was profiled separately by Helen May (1992) in *Te Timatanga*. A common theme in the stories of the three women is the struggle to get early childhood studies recognised as a valid scholarly area and, eventually, the importance of key people in opening the door for this to happen. All three have Victoria doctorates studying early childhood topics. McDonald and Meade were amongst the first five and graduated in the 1970s; Bell made history in a different way by graduating in 2004 aged 82 years.

In recounting her career in early childhood education Geraldine McDonald (May and Mitchell *n.d.* a) recalled the resistance she encountered at Victoria's Education Department while trying to conduct her masterate research on the relationship between playcentres and their local community. Refusing to be deflected onto the 'more worthy' topic of the study of reading, McDonald pursued her interest in early childhood education research and eventually took up a position at the New Zealand Council for Educational Research with a brief to establish a unit to carry out research into 'early childhood education'. Commenting on this aspect of her career, Geraldine McDonald noted that the name of the unit was not accidental but rather reflected a commitment to include a focus on childcare as much as on other 'preschool' services within the work of the unit 'right from the beginning' (p. 17). McDonald was later appointed to a number of governmental committees related to early childhood matters, including the Committee on Women in International Women's Year (1975) and the 1980 State Services Commission Working Group on Early Childhood Care and Education; the latter made the historic recommendation that government's administrative and policy responsibility for childcare services should be shifted from the Department of Social Welfare to the Department of Education. The recommendation was not acted upon till 1986. When implemented, it helped the growth of early childhood studies at Victoria. But even more directly, Geraldine McDonald has contributed to early childhood studies at Victoria through her guest lectures and research mentoring role. She has supervised or examined a number of early childhood doctorates within the School of Education and her research mentoring role – in early childhood issues and beyond – continues to this day.

Marie Bell's place in the history of New Zealand education will perhaps be most remembered for her pioneering role in setting up, and teaching at, the alternative school *Matauranga* in the 60s and 70s. She was also a pioneer of the Parents Centre movement, whose early history she documented through oral history interviews for her doctoral studies at the School of Education in the early 2000s, while in her eighties (Bell 2004). Bell can recall that as a young student in 1939 she attended classes taught by Professor Colin Bailey, who introduced child development as a legitimate component of Education 1 courses.[3] Bell also remembers Bailey as one of the first advocates for the early childhood years to be given their rightful importance in the study of education. For Marie Bell those lectures gave a glimpse into a world in which she later immersed herself as a young war widow studying in London under Dorothy Gardner, the protégé and successor of the influential psychologist and educational reformer Susan Isaacs (Gardner 1969).

Bell recalls that Crawford Somerset,[4] appointed as senior lecturer to the Department of Education in 1948 (Collinge 2000), also made strategic contributions to pre-school education, mainly through his great support for his wife Gwen's work within the Playcentre movement. Gwen Somerset taught for many years for Victoria's Extension Studies – a place where other early childhood people likewise made their contribution, notably Beverley Morris (e.g. 1967), a highly respected and internationally recognised advocate of children's play, and Val Burns, director of the early childhood division at the government Department of Education during the 1980s. Betty O'Dell, who became the Somersets' daughter-in-law about 1952, was already on the Victoria University Education Department's lecturing staff when Professor Somerset was appointed. She taught child development courses at Victoria until 1958, and also had some involvement in training kindergarten teachers and Playcentre supervisors. We believe she may have been the first woman lecturer in the Education Department at Victoria.[5]

After a long and distinguished career in education, Marie Bell became a ministerial appointee on Victoria University's Council and in the early 1990s continued her contribution to early childhood studies by her support for the case to appoint a professor of early childhood teacher education at Victoria University.

Meade was appointed to the Education Department for the first time as a part-time lecturer for one year in the 1970s, while she was completing her

---

3 Personal communication, March 2009.

4 The Somersets were to bequeath their house to Victoria University and for some years the School of Education was partly located in their refurbished house at the top of Kelburn Parade. Portraits of Gwen and Crawford Somerset hung for a number of years in this house and are currently located in the new premises of the Institute for Early Childhood Studies in the Gray Block of the Karori campus of the university.

5 The JC Beaglehole Room card index of Victoria University staff records lists Betty O'Dell as follows: 'Education: Jr lect, 1947-1954; Lecturer, 1955-1958'.

PhD under the supervision of Jim Robb from the Sociology Department and John Barrington from Education. Her thesis could be said to be the first early childhood education studies doctorate, as earlier doctoral theses had a child development or linguistics focus. She taught a course on the sociology of education.

The late 1980s – a period of convergence

The 1980s story of early childhood teaching at Victoria starts with the appointment of Carmen Dalli to a lectureship in Education in 1988. Dalli's appointment was to teach Human Development and Classroom Studies, areas she had studied as a Commonwealth scholar in the early 1980s at Bristol University while on study leave from her primary teaching position on the small island of Malta. Dalli had subsequently held a lecturing position at the University of Malta, where she had been employed to teach in the 'early and middle years' department of the Faculty of Education. One of her responsibilities within that department was to develop the new area of early childhood education as a scholarly field. On appointment to Victoria, Dalli was invited to a meeting with Professor Gerald Grace, who had not long arrived from England to take up the Chair of Education. It soon became clear that Grace was very interested in Dalli's short career teaching early childhood studies at the University of Malta, and in her time working in the early childhood division of the Head Office of the Department of Education in Wellington.

Dalli had arrived in New Zealand at the beginning of 1986, the year that New Zealand made international history (Moss 2007) through its shift of childcare policy and administration to the Department of Education. Working at the Department of Education at this crucial time, Dalli had been able to observe firsthand many of the sector's negotiations around this change. Through sitting in on consultation meetings, often as note-taker, Dalli acquired an extensive and detailed knowledge of the policy issues of the day; at the same time, her familiarity with the European educational context alerted her to the significance of the remarkable changes that were taking place in New Zealand's early childhood sector. Gerald Grace was keen to capitalise on Dalli's recent experience; he spoke about his plan to expand the course offerings of the department and to include in this a focus on early childhood education, which he rightly predicted would be an area of increasing policy and scholarly interest. Grace strongly supported Dalli's intention to focus on an early childhood topic for her doctoral research and urged her to start planning new courses in early childhood studies, with the aim of offering the first of these in 1990. As an initial step in this direction he asked Dalli to give a lecture on early childhood issues within one of the first year papers, Education and Society – the contemporary equivalent of Education 1 in the 1940s.[6]

Once her interest in early childhood education became more widely known, Dalli soon found herself involved in a range of early childhood forums. Almost immediately she was asked to convene the management committee of the university's staff early childhood education centre, just at the time that the *Before Five* policies – which emerged from the Meade Report (Department of Education 1988b) – started to take effect. This meant that she was involved at the practical level – developing a charter,[7] establishing new quality policies and ensuring that all staff were on the right training path – at the same time as she was considering the changes as policy matters to be taught in new education courses. Dalli also began to sit on the advisory committee of the university's student crèche and took over the role of university representative on the Wellington College of Education's early childhood advisory committee. This regular contact with early childhood staff at the College laid strong foundations for the collegial relationships that grew in the early 1990s and were so fruitful in developing the early childhood field in subsequent years.

Brenda Bushouse (2008) uses the concepts of 'convergence' and 'divergence' in her account of how New Zealand became a world leader in early childhood education. She names Anne Meade as playing 'pivotal roles' (p. 17) in this policy journey. Within the teaching of early childhood studies at Victoria, Anne Meade was also to play a highly influential role.

In late 1989, Meade approached Professor Gerald Grace about an advertised Victoria University vacancy, expressing interest in applying to join the Education Department if the advertised position could include a

---

6   Once the lecture was given, Grace, who sat in on the lecture, urged Dalli to publish it. The lecture eventually appeared in *Early Childhood Education and Care*, a leading journal in the field (see Dalli 1990).

7   The *Before Five* policies stipulated that centres needed to be chartered if they were to qualify for higher funding. Charters were contracts between early childhood centres and government and had to show evidence that the centre's policies exceeded the minimum requirements set by early childhood regulations.

focus on early childhood education. Meade's approach can be likened to Fate dealing a winning hand to Grace's plans to expand early childhood studies. At the time Grace was spearheading the development of a new Master of Education programme and he was keen to position the degree as having a strong policy orientation, which he saw as befitting the university of the capital city. Anne Meade was completing a two-year secondment to the Prime Minister's Office. She had worked there during the intense period when *Tomorrow's Schools* (Department of Education 1988a) was finalised; in 1988 she had held the additional responsibility of leading the working group on early childhood education that produced *Education to be More* (the Meade Report). Most of the recommendations of this report became policy when *Before Five* (Department of Education 1988c) was launched in January 1989. Anne's previous permanent position had been as a Regional Senior Education Officer (ECE) in the old government Department of Education. While she was on secondment, her permanent job was disestablished.

Responding to Anne Meade's interest, Gerald Grace said that the successful applicant would need to teach a compulsory paper in education policy as well as a Masters course that fitted their special expertise. That was not a problem for Meade who had been 'living' education policy for two years. Her eventual appointment as senior lecturer in the Education Department at the end of 1989 meant that in 1990 Anne Meade taught much of the core master's level course on education policy with John Barrington. In the same year, she and Carmen Dalli joined forces to teach a new 300-level paper called Early Childhood Education, and by 1991 Meade and Dalli also jointly taught the first master's level paper in early childhood policy entitled Early Childhood Care and Education.

The difference in the title of the two courses is interesting to comment on as it mirrors a common debate in the early 1990s. In a policy context where responsibility for childcare services and those considered 'pre-school' services (kindergartens and playcentres) had been integrated, many argued that it was now politically useful to use the term 'early childhood education' as automatically inclusive of care. The opposing position was that to do so was to render invisible the care component of early childhood work, and that this held the danger that this work would become undervalued. Meade and Dalli discussed these positions at length – that they ended up using both terms in course titles reflects the lively debate of the time.

By launching these two courses at the beginning of the 1990s, Victoria University became a leader amongst New Zealand universities. The focus of the courses complemented the more vocationally oriented courses in the three-year Diploma programmes that had been established in colleges of education when integrated training for all early childhood teachers began in 1988 (see May, elsewhere in this volume). While many of these colleges of education were later to amalgamate with universities and thus offer early childhood courses within their diploma programmes, in 1990 no New Zealand university had as yet introduced early childhood studies as part of their BA or MEd programmes.

The context for this focus on early childhood education was optimal: the significant policy changes made it obvious that political interest in the sector was high and that the government of the day valued early education. Beyond transferring the administration of childcare services from the Department of Social Welfare to Education, in the late 1980s the government's investments in early education included:

1. merging all training courses into a Diploma of Teaching (ECE) programme that was the equivalent of a Diploma of Teaching for primary teachers;

2. commissioning a working group on early childhood care and education as part of the education reforms (Department of Education 1988b);

3. taking bold steps to reform early childhood education policy in *Before Five* (Department of Education 1988c) and to increase funding markedly;

4. announcing a staged increase in the proportion of qualified teachers in all licensed services where parents were not present.

These government policies made New Zealand a world leader in early childhood education. The polices were applauded by a wide range of organisations (women's groups, unions, early childhood providers), as they had been sought for many years by advocates for improved quality in the provision of early education (Dalli 1990). As Meade (1990) argued at the time, the wider education reforms provided the opportunity for early education advocates to get a 'foot in the door' during a period when increased state support were against the odds (see also Wells 1991). The pattern in the state sector reforms in the 1980s had been to have *less* state involvement and funding, yet the early childhood education sector gained *more* of both. However some of the gains were short-lived – following the election of the National government in late 1990 there was a period of 'divergence' and the early childhood policies were eroded (Dalli 1993, Meade and Dalli 1991, Mitchell 2005).

The optimal time for establishing early childhood education courses at tertiary level was 1990. Gerald Grace, Anne Meade and Carmen Dalli seized the opportunity, and did so.

Establishing a research agenda: The Competent Children study

With so many significant changes, the time was ripe for sowing the seeds for a research agenda. For Dalli, the priority was to enrol in her doctoral study, for which she had been unable to find a supervisor until Anne Meade's arrival on the staff of the Education Department.

For Meade, the priority was to start filling the research gaps that her recent policy work had revealed as crucial to sound policy advice for quality early childhood provision. In 1990–1991 Meade teamed up with Cathy Wylie at the New Zealand Council for Educational Research (NZCER) to write a proposal for a longitudinal study of the effects of early childhood education. Gerald Grace had now returned to England to take up another Chair at Durham University. In talking with the new professor of education, Hugh Lauder, a much more ambitious proposal was developed for a two-cohort longitudinal study. The Ministry of Education was excited by the joint proposal, and the Competent Children and Smithfield projects were funded and launched. The main base for the initial phase of both projects was the prefabricated buildings on Kelburn Parade where the Education Department was housed at the time.

As we write, the vision of studying a sample of children for a dozen years or more through to the end of their secondary schooling has been realised (Wylie et al. 2008), although the original plan, that the Competent Children project team would replicate the Smithfield project, had to be abandoned. The Smithfield project had a 'bumpy passage', and its 'captain' went overseas, never to return; the project stopped soon after. The Competent Children project, on the other hand, has benefited from a stable team who continued to study the sample every two years for well over a decade. At the time of writing NZCER is halfway through gathering data from the young people in the sample as they turn twenty. The longitudinal project reports have been very influential, because the results show that high quality early education has enduring effects on students, even after eleven years (Wylie and Hodgen 2007).

The Education Department, despite its poor housing in prefabricated buildings at the top of Kelburn Parade, was an ideal home for the Competent Children project in its formative years. During class sessions of the new 300-level paper Early Childhood Education, Anne Meade, working with Anne Kerslake-Hendricks, a researcher for the project, asked early childhood students to pilot some of the instruments that the two Annes had developed with Cathy Wylie and Jacky Burgon at NZCER. Some of those instruments have withstood the test of time, with the quality rating scale being adapted and used again and again in numerous evaluation projects in New Zealand contexts. It was a significant start to an early childhood research agenda within Victoria, even though the project moved to NZCER when Anne Meade became its Director in late 1991.

The early 1990s: A time of divergence

Meade's departure to NZCER was unexpected. Yet the clear expectation after her departure was that now that the position had been established, replacing it would be a straightforward process.

However, in a move that mirrored the change of fortunes for government early childhood policy at the start of the 1990s (Dalli 1993, May 2001), a staff meeting advertised as a forum to discuss the vacant early childhood position swiftly emerged as a lobbying session to appoint a policy scholar, with a prepared proposal to this effect tabled by a number of senior staff. The final decision to advertise a generic policy position, as opposed to an early childhood one, was bitterly contested by Dalli, who had not been informed of the alternative proposal ahead of the meeting. The politics of the decision rankled within the early childhood world and resulted in some strong letters to the then professor of education, Hugh Lauder, and the university council, urging swift action to redress the decision. This included a submission from Anne Meade and another from Kathie Irwin, at the time lecturing in Māori education within the department. Irwin, herself trying to build the area of Māori scholarship, knew only too well the importance of creating a strong nucleus of scholars from which a discipline might grow; her history of involvement within Kōhanga Reo also made her a strong supporter of early childhood studies. In the event, the generic policy position was unable to be advertised due to budgetary constraints within the university. Some months later, the position was converted into part funding for the foundational Chair of teacher education, set up after the establishment of a new Faculty of Education with staff from Wellington College of Education and Victoria's Education Department.[8] The position seemed lost to early childhood studies.

The mid-1990s: A new convergence emerges

However, out of the ashes of the loss of the senior lectureship, a new initiative soon arose that reinvigorated plans for the expansion of early childhood studies, this time within the new Faculty of Education.

Mergers between tertiary institutions were common in the early 1990s. In Wellington, the issue of closer relationships between Victoria University and the Wellington College of Education (WCE) had been on and off the agenda a number of times; the decision to set up a conjoint Faculty of Education in 1992 was based around the teaching of a new four-year BEd teacher education programme aimed at primary, secondary and early childhood teacher trainees.

As this development gained momentum, Tony Holmes from WCE approached Carmen Dalli with the idea of setting up a Centre for Early Childhood Studies that, within the context of the newly established faculty, would be jointly supported by Victoria and the College. Recently returned from an international study visit to a number of early childhood teacher training institutions and research centres, Holmes could see the potential of such a centre for enhancing the scholarly base of early childhood teacher education and for establishing a space that could act as a clearing house or library to support early childhood research; he was also keen for the centre to be a resource for the whole early childhood community. As there was already a strong presence of early childhood people at the WCE site, it was agreed that it would be advantageous to locate the Centre at Victoria, which would also be more centrally located for the broad early childhood community. Dalli was enthusiastic; by then she was immersed in fierce politics around the development of early childhood unit standards to be placed on the New Zealand Qualifications Authority (NZQA) framework,[9] and in co-leading (with Linda Mitchell) a national

8   Planning and resource committee papers, November 1992. Institute for Early Childhood Studies archives.

9   Lobbying centred on ensuring that any early childhood qualification registered on the NZQA framework would be sufficiently robust to maintain the sector goal of lifting the professional profile of the early childhood sector.

working group to develop an early childhood code of ethics for Aotearoa New Zealand. A Centre for Early Childhood Studies would be a base for advocacy and research. It would also provide a specific early childhood space on the Kelburn campus for staff and students. During 1993 Holmes and Dalli formally gained support for the proposal from colleagues at the two institutions, from individuals, and from community early childhood organisations, including NZCER, now headed by Anne Meade. Graeme Oldershaw, principal of the College, and Lynne Bruce, head of early childhood teacher education at WCE, were key supporters of the proposal, which was approved by the Faculty Board in November 1993 subject to consideration by the Faculty Planning and Resource Committee. On the recommendation of the Vice-Chancellor, Les Holborow, the Centre was later renamed as an Institute to distinguish it from the early childhood education and care centres on campus.

With the Centre/Institute approved, lobbying for a senior early childhood appointee was again possible. The appointment of Adrienne Alton-Lee as the foundation professor of teacher education in the new faculty provided an unexpected ally. From the start Alton-Lee was keen to support early childhood initiatives. Working with Dalli and Holmes, and with the support of Lynne Bruce and Graeme Oldershaw, by March 1994 Alton-Lee was spearheading a proposal for a professorial appointment in early childhood teacher education through the university's systems. The final case for the Chair was argued on the basis of the policy context that made New Zealand a world leader in early childhood education; Victoria's past recognition of this in establishing a lectureship in early childhood education, which had attracted to the position someone of Dr Meade's standing, and the associated research kudos of having initiated the *Competent Children* project; the need to support the new BEd and MEd developments; and the need to reinstate academic and professional support for the work of Dalli, who had now transferred to the field of early childhood within the department.[10] It was proposed that one of two new lectureships created to support the BEd should be upgraded to a Chair in early childhood teacher education and advertised for an initial term of five years; the College's pledge to provide the additional funding necessary to upgrade the position from a lectureship to a Chair put the final seal on the proposal. The professorial position was advertised in October that year and interviews held a month later.

---

10 Proposal dated 28 April 1994; archival papers at the Institute for Early Childhood Studies.

The arrival of the professor: Growth and development

The new professor of early childhood teacher education, Helen May, was chosen from an excellent field of national and international applicants. With a history of union activism and negotiation behind her, a reputation as a staunch feminist, and her recent experience of co-leading the development of New Zealand's first early childhood curriculum document, *Te Whāriki* (Ministry of Education 1996), May took up her inaugural chair at Victoria in mid-1995. Her arrival had an immediate and pervasive impact on early childhood studies at Victoria, and on its resourcing.

One of the conditions of the professorial appointment had been that the new professor would be the director of the nascent Institute for Early Childhood Studies. With characteristic astuteness, May had negotiated a seeding grant as part of her employment package that enabled the Institute to start building what became an excellent collection of early childhood resources. She also brought with her a substantial archival collection of historical materials accumulated during her time at Waikato University. These materials soon transformed 89 Kelburn Parade, which Dalli had managed to secure as the first premises of the Institute, from a squatter's space to a mecca for early childhood students and staff alike. The resourcing of the Institute was a far cry from the un-won battles with the library in the late 1980s over the purchase of early childhood journals and books. It became an open home to the early childhood community and regularly attracted visitors from both national and international early childhood venues.

A decade of consolidation: Visibility, collaboration and early childhood professionalisation

Between 1995 and 2005, with the professor of early childhood teacher education as the director of the Institute, and, from 2001, Head of the School of Education, the Institute became the public face of early childhood education at Victoria.

Central to the increased visibility were the early childhood teacher education programmes developed collaboratively by the early childhood staff across Victoria and WCE. Collaboration meant that courses were often jointly planned and taught by staff across the institutions, with joint staff meetings held at regular intervals. May's chapter in this volume recounts the story of the development of the early childhood teacher education qualifications, including the design of a stand-alone three-year degree programme separate from the four-year BEd degree initiated when the joint Faculty of Education was established in 1992. As professor of early childhood education, May led these developments, working with the early childhood team at WCE who were under Lynne Bruce's leadership. Bruce and May worked closely together, deliberately putting the professionalisation of the early childhood workforce ahead of institutional considerations. This collaboration meant that the early childhood three-year BEd (Teaching) Early Childhood degree survived as a jointly awarded qualification even when the working relationships of the two institutions became strained to the point where the Faculty arrangements were dissolved. A four-year conjoint degree programme for early childhood teachers, the BA/BTeach (ECE), developed in 2003, was similarly collaboratively planned and jointly awarded. The new degree was designed to reflect the increasingly multidisciplinary focus of early childhood studies and, in line with the project of professionalising the early childhood sector, was further motivated by the need to ensure that early childhood graduates had a programme that would make them eligible for the same employment conditions as their primary and secondary counterparts.[11]

Meanwhile, early childhood studies also grew in profile within the BA programme, as four courses developed for the BEd programmes were also able to be offered within the generic BA degree. Furthermore, the early childhood studies major that formed part of the new four-year conjoint BA/BTeach (ECE) was made available as a stand-alone 'major' within the BA programme.

At the postgraduate level, significant developments occurred as more students, including early childhood staff from WCE, undertook early childhood papers and developed masterate theses focused on early childhood. Doctoral projects likewise grew in numbers and in 2000 the Institute instigated a series of PhD lunchtime seminars for early childhood doctoral students, with the idea of providing a supportive structure for senior students.

The public visibility of early childhood studies at Victoria was further aided through the publication of the Institute's two Occasional Publications series. The first of these was initiated in 1996, with Dalli as founding editor; a second series was launched in 2003, edited by Val Podmore, who

---

11 Proposal approved by VUW academic committee on 20 February 2003.

had joined the Institute staff in 1999. The publications proved extremely popular, with a broad early childhood readership nationally as well as internationally. Eighteen papers were published in the first series and five in the second series. Additionally, the Institute hosted a number of public seminars, including three national seminars collaboratively organised with the Children's Issues Centre at the University of Otago. The publications and seminars raised the public profile of early childhood studies and of the Institute and drew numerous visitors, who were able to use the resources of the Institute, archival and contemporary, by private arrangement.

As the teaching programmes and other activities of the Institute increased, so too did the number of early childhood staff. Four years after its establishment, in 1999, when the Institute and the position of professor were first reviewed, there were six early childhood staff at Victoria: May and Dalli had been joined by Sally Peters, Sophie Alcock, Sarah Te One and Val Podmore. When Peters later returned to a position at Waikato University and Sophie Alcock took up a position at the Ministry of Education, they were replaced by Judith Loveridge and Margaret Brennan.

The 1999 review noted that: "The Institute has achieved a significant reputation within the international early childhood community since its inception, partly because of the quality of the staff and its publications." It recommended that the Institute "continue as an Institute carrying out its current range of activities and that it stays as a special case. . . thus not being required to attract substantive external funding *in the medium term*" (our italics).

Concluding reflections

Ten years have passed since that first review of the Institute. The intervening years have wrought numerous changes, not least the merger in 2005 between Victoria University and the Wellington College of Education. Early childhood staff at both institutions welcomed the merger and saw it as an opportunity to further strengthen the field of early childhood studies at Victoria by bringing two strong early childhood teams closer together.

In the year before the merger, and as a separate exercise, the university conducted a review of all its research centres and institutes, with the aim of rationalising their terms of reference and bringing these in line with the university's strategic plan. The review clarified the research role of institutes and singled out teaching functions as the purview of schools. For the Institute for Early Childhood Studies, this meant separating its programme responsibilities from its functions, and a redefined future direction focused more strongly on research. The notification of the outcome of the second review, a decade on from the establishment of the Institute, stated:

> . . . the sub-committee has recognized the important work of the Institute for Early Childhood Studies and has therefore decided to *confirm it as one of VUW's research centres*. In so doing, the sub-committee recommends that the Institute address the task of seeking externally funded research projects.[12]

Clearly, the "medium term" noted by the first review team had run its course. As we write, the Institute for Early Childhood Studies, headed by Dalli, is now part of the Jessie Hetherington Centre for Educational Research. The overarching focus of the Jessie Hetherington Centre is on research and development to enhance theoretical and evidence-based educational policy and practice from early childhood to higher education, nationally and internationally.

Five years on from the merger of the institutions, the teaching of early childhood education at Victoria is firmly established and is carried out by around twenty staff located across the three schools of the Victoria University Faculty of Education. Responsibility for early childhood teacher education programmes and all other early childhood courses rests with an associate dean of early childhood studies, Sue Cherrington, previously the Head of the School of Early Teacher Education at WCE.

In 2010 the arrangements for the teaching of early childhood education at Victoria are clearly much larger in scope and scale than the humble beginnings of the late 1980s. This is to be celebrated, for certainly it indicates a 'coming of age' for early childhood education both as a scholarly field and as an area of professional practice.

At the same time, the new arrangements are also a departure from the traditional way of 'doing early childhood education' which as an area has thrived best when it has 'protected its borders' from, for example, the trickle-down effect of primary education.[13] To some extent, it is a

---

12 Letter from Vice-Chancellor, dated 22 August 2005.

13 The case of the development of the early childhood curriculum, *Te Whāriki*, is one example of this. See Carr & May (2000).

new experiment, a sally into the "border crossings" (Giroux 2005) characteristic of the post-modern, changing and uncertain times in which we live. Our travel through new borders will no doubt provide new convergences as well as divergences. After all, as Jerome Bruner (1996) once said, "education is a risky business", and early childhood education is no exception.

References

Bell, M. (2004). The pioneers of parents' centre: movers and shakers for change in the philosophies and practices of childbirth and parent education in New Zealand. PhD Thesis. Victoria University of Wellington.

Bruner, J. (1996). What we have learned about early learning. *European Early Childhood Education Research Journal*. 4, 1. pp. 5-16.

Bushouse, B. (2008). The 20 hours free early childhood education programme: A USA perspective. *New Zealand Annual Review of Education, 18:2008*, pp.143-158.

Carr, M. & May, H. (2000). Te Whāriki: curriculum voices. In H. Penn (Ed.). *Early childhood services: theory, policy and practice*. Buckingham: Open University Press. pp. 53-73.

Collinge, J. (2000). Hugh Crawford Dixon Somerset, 1895–1968. In V. O'Sullivan (Ed.). *Eminent Victorians: great teachers and scholars from Victoria's first 100 years*. Wellington. Victoria University of Wellington: Dunmore Press. pp. 147-154.

Dalli, C. (1990). Early childhood education in New Zealand: current issues and policy developments. *Early Child Development and Care*. 64. pp. 61-70.

Dalli, C. (1993). Is Cinderella back among the cinders? A review of early childhood education in the early 1990s. *New Zealand Annual Review of Education*. 3. pp. 223-252.

Gardner, D.E.M. (1969) *Susan Isaacs: The first biography*. London: Methuen.

Giroux, H. (2005). *Border crossings: cultural workers and the politics of education*. New York and London: Routledge.

Department of Education. (1988a). *Tomorrow's schools*. Wellington: Government Printer.

Department of Education. (1988b). *Education to be more*. Wellington: Department of Education.

Department of Education (1988c). *Before five: early childhood care and education in New Zealand*. Wellington: Government Printer.

May, H. (1992). Marie Bell: Working for Women, Working for Change, an Interview with Helen May, *Te Timitanga*, 10(2), pp. 3-35.

May, H. & Mitchell, J. (n.d. a) (Eds.). *A celebration of early childhood. Vol. 1*. Hamilton Teachers' College: Centre of Early Childhood.

May, H. & Mitchell, J. (n.d. b) (Eds.). *A celebration of early childhood. Vol. 2*. Hamilton: Waikato University Department of Early Childhood Studies.

May, H. (2001). *Politics in the playground*. Wellington: Bridget Williams Books & NZCER.

Meade, A. (1990). Women and young children gain a foot in the door. *Women's Studies Journal*. 6, 1/2.

Meade, A., & Dalli, C. (1991). Review of the early childhood sector. *New Zealand Annual Review of Education*. 1. pp. 113-132.

Ministry of Education (1996). *Te Whāriki: He Whāriki Mātauranga: early childhood curriculum*. Wellington: Learning Media Ltd.

Ministry of Education (2002). *Pathways to the future: a 10 year strategic plan for early childhood education. Ngā Huarahi Arataki*. Wellington: Ministry of Education.

Mitchell, L. (2005). Policy shifts in early childhood education: past lessons, new direction. In J. Codd and K. Sullivan (Eds.). *Education policy directions in Aotearoa New Zealand*. Southbank, Vic.: Thomson Learning Australia.

Morris, B. (1967). *Understanding children*. Palmerston North: A.H. & A.W. Reed.

Moss, P. (2007). Leading the second wave: New Zealand in an international context. Presentation at the Travelling pathways to the future. Early Childhood Education Symposium. Wellington: Ministry of Education, 2-3 May 2007.

Wells, C. (1991). The impact of change – against the odds. Keynote address. In M. Gold, L. Foote & A.B. Smith (Eds) *Proceedings of the 5th Early Childhood Convention, Dunedin, 8–12 September*. pp. 115-127.

Wylie, C. & Hodgen, E. (2007). *Continuing contributions of early childhood education to young children's competency levels*. Wellington: Ministry of Education.

Wylie, C., Hodgen, E., Hipkins, R. & Vaughan, K. (2008). *Competent learners on the edge of adulthood. A summary of key findings from the Competent Learners@16 project*. Wellington: Ministry of Education, http://www.nzcer.org.nz/default. php?products_id=2430.

Reframing Some Windows on Early Childhood Education: An Unlikely Career

Helen May

Introduction

Early childhood education in the 21st century is an integral aspect of education studies at universities in New Zealand, due mainly to the mergers of the six colleges of education into co-located universities between 1991 and 2007. From 1974, when the kindergarten colleges in each of the four main cities were moved into their nearby teachers' colleges, the colleges became the architects of early childhood pedagogy, although some of the people and pedagogy also had roots in the Playcentre movement (May 1997a). In 1988 the nature of this pedagogy was transformed with the introduction of a three-year qualification that integrated care and education, was inclusive of children from birth to school age, and produced graduates who could be employed in either kindergarten or childcare. This brought some staff into colleges of education whose experiences in the politics and pedagogy of childcare challenged the orthodoxy of older programmes.

Prior to the start of the mergers, the presence of early childhood education as a field of study in university education departments was limited. Appointments and interests were framed around child development that significantly excluded early childhood pedagogy and politics as relevant to any study of education. My inaugural address in 1997 as the foundation professor of early childhood education at Victoria University (May 1997b) traversed this story, and did note some exceptions. In 1967 Beverley Morris was appointed to a position of Lecturer in Child Development and Family Relations in the Department of University Extension at Victoria. The position resulted from advocacy by Gwen Somerset, who combined her work within Playcentre and adult education with a close connection to the Department of Education, in which her husband Crawford was Associate Professor (McDonald 2000). Beverley's roots were also in Playcentre and her energies forged across the divides of Playcentre, kindergarten and childcare (May 1989). Although she did not teach in the Department of Education she maintained close links to it. In 1974 Anne Smith was employed by the University of Otago to teach child development, and as a childcare user became a lone academic voice in support of quality childcare services (Smith 1978).

Conversely, what was taught as early childhood education in the colleges was also limited. Its pedagogy was shaped by the areas of play in which activities such as jigsaws, dough, water, carpentry, blocks etc., had been exalted into subjects. Encroaching across the activities of play were the traditional primary school subjects, taught as seemingly simpler versions by often outcast staff from primary programmes. Broader and deeper considerations of the pedagogy, sociology and politics of early childhood education were largely absent. While a passion for early childhood education was strongly embedded amongst early childhood staff in colleges, research and scholarship was not part of the job. Many of the staff did not have degrees. That is not the case now at Victoria University, with a raft of masters and doctoral degrees in the field of early childhood awarded and/or underway. This transformation began long before the 2007 merger.

This book is published in recognition of the demise of the Department of Education at Victoria University. Three years after the merger with the Wellington College of Education it was restructured out of existence; so too was the large Department of Early Childhood in the College, as well as the physical presence of the joint Institute for Early Childhood Studies (IECS) that from 1995 linked the two. The academic presence and place of both early childhood and education were mainstreamed into a different configuration. The controversy and consequences of these decisions is not part of the commentary of this chapter. Rather, this is an autobiographical story concerning the reframing of early education during three windows of time at Victoria University when I was:

• a junior school teacher and an undergraduate student in the late 1960s;

• the crèche supervisor and a postgraduate student in the late 1970s and early 1980s; and

- the foundation Professor of Early Childhood Education from 1995 to 2005.

Each window of 'education' at Victoria University provides a snapshot of an unexpected career progression in the practice, then politics, and later scholarship of early education. From the early 1980s, I became engaged in a scholarly quest to:

- document the history and politics of early childhood care and education in New Zealand;

- support advocacy and policy development in the early childhood sector through historical analysis;

- construct 'early years' history and politics as a core component of teacher education programmes;

- create new theoretical spaces for the 'early years' history of education in university contexts; and

- position 'new world' frames of 'early years' history as integral to the stories of its 'old world' origins.

The 'education' window of 1995–2005 at Victoria University was hugely productive in realising this quest with six books completed and/ or seeded. It is timely to reconsider and reframe this historical journey, which included a long interlude at the University of Waikato and is still underway at the University of Otago, and to acknowledge the place and people of Victoria University in shaping both the story and its teller. Other authors in this volume will traverse broader aspects of Victoria's early childhood story. My personal journey was not a solo campaign and these stories will likely weave across each other.

Junior school teacher

I first enrolled at Victoria University in 1968 as a student, not of education but of anthropology. I was the new entrant teacher at Berhampore School in my third year of teaching. These were the days of developmental free play, long since lost, coloured cuisenaire mathematics rods, also relegated, and the new *Ready to Read* books, now out of print. Apart from loosely defined 'suggestions' for teaching reading and mathematics, there was considerable freedom to determine what to teach. On a whim we would walk around the streets, visit the park or build a 'boat', as a group of boys did one week, outside the classroom window.

Berhampore new entrant class 1968.

Like many student teachers I started a degree while at teachers college. I avoided doing Education One at Canterbury University as was the norm, and opted for a new Pacific and Asian History paper that made my mind soar. Thus began the pattern of combining teaching the young and university study, although it was many years before the scholarly interests of these separate domains coalesced. I left Canterbury in 1967 to study anthropology at Auckland University. These dual interests were considered somewhat unusual, particularly for a junior school teacher. An inspector warned that academic qualifications were wasted teaching juniors, although teaching young children was a good preparation for motherhood! Interestingly, the headmaster at Berhampore School was supportive of academic study and allowed me to attend a lunchtime lecture as well as leave early one afternoon a week. Anthropology, unlike education, was not timetabled for the attendance of teachers.

The study of anthropology had been established by Jan Pouwer at Victoria University in 1967, to where I relocated in 1968. Pouwer was a Dutch scholar imbued with the radical ethos of European structuralist scholarship. We were immersed in the writings of Lévi-Strauss, Bourdieu, Gramsci, Foucault and Althusser long before any education department ventured down these pathways; we grappled with the ideas of Marx, Hegel, Heidegger, and Marcuse. This was heady and provided new theoretical frames for the big questions about society, culture, power, and people. Yet I made few intellectual links with the early school pedagogy that surrounded me at work, issues of culture in my class of mainly Pacific immigrant children, or the politics of gender and junior school teachers. The intellectual furore of anthropology was too exciting. We were in the midst of something extraordinary. Academic staff and students from other disciplines came to classes that often ended in debate and argument. Pouwer would sometimes give the lectern to those who disagreed or tell us to destroy our earlier notes because he had changed his mind. He made us think – if we dared – but not about education! These were separate worlds.

Crèche worker – supervisor

In 1975 I re-enrolled at Victoria after several years teaching in English infant schools, then a position with five-year-olds at Brooklyn School and the birth of my first child. My naïve intention was to take a year's maternity leave and then return to teaching, but there was no available childcare for infants. The exception was the Victoria University crèche. Over the next nine years the crèche became a home for my children, a workplace for me, and the unlikely trajectory towards an academic career.

Helen May and Maureen Locke at the 'baby' crèche 67 Fairlie Terrace.

I completed my degree in anthropology, including a history minor. Jan Pouwer was still pushing boundaries and in 1975 introduced ANTH 203: Dialectical Approaches into the anthropology major. The arguments raged and the mind soared again. In ANTH 305: Society and Culture in South East Asia, Peter Webster transported our imaginations to grapple with the cultural politics of caste and power in India and the Himalayas. This was breathtaking.

From being a teacher of young children I became a part-time childcare worker at the crèche. The disparity in salary and status between teaching and childcare work was hugely anomalous but I was largely unaware of the burgeoning political demands of childcare advocates (May 1985, Smith and Swain 1988). My son loved the crèche; I enjoyed the work and the company of student mothers, and was stimulated by the study.

At the end of 1976 Jan Pouwer returned to Europe. Students who had intended to continue with postgraduate studies were bereft and the Department of Anthropology was intent on less radical scholarship. This caused my shift to education studies. After the birth of another child I enrolled for a Diploma in Education Studies (for graduates) that included five undergraduate papers and two years teaching experience. Thus began my association with the Victoria University Department of Education. First-year education had its irritations after the small-scale intellectual hothouse of anthropology. EDUC112: Human Development, while of some interest, was not enthralling and I did not process beyond stage one. I was fortunate that EDUC 111: Education and Society was fronted by Jim Collinge and Jack Shallcrass. This was a revelation. The texts were Paulo Freire's *Pedagogy of the Oppressed* (1972) and Ivan Illich's *Deschooling Society* (1971). With my anthropology toolkit, and the inspired teaching of Collinge and Shallcrass I began to reflect on the politics of schooling and teaching.

EDUC 221: Educational Thought was a course on radical education. We read Chris Wainwright's New Zealand exposé, *The Degree Merchants* (1977), an attack on the business of education, and we analysed the progression and politics of our own education. We continued to trawl through critiques of Western and colonial education systems; we read the works of the Tanzanian political leader Julius Nyerere, and collected money in class for a tape recorder to be taken to Tanzania by Phil Amos, a renegade past Minister of Education. Shallcrass's EDUC 324: Education in New Zealand opened the mind further. This was timetabled in the graveyard slot of Fridays, 4–6pm, in Shallcrass's large study in the Hunter building. The class became the social highlight of the week. There were about fifteen students, one of whom, Sue Middleton, another crèche parent, became a friend. The course was misnamed because we were free to study whatever we chose and at each session would report to the group on our reading and thinking. There were neither essays nor exams, just talk, and a final session with Shallcrass when he asked, "What grade do you think you are worth?" This was radical education in practice. I determined to read the philosophical works of Karl Popper, who as a refugee from Vienna spent the war years at Canterbury University. *The Open Society and its Enemies* (1945) had huge ideas that I struggled to connect to the issues of education – but not early education, the focus of my work. There was still a divide.

In 1978 I was appointed the Co-ordinating Supervisor of the Victoria University crèche and for five years seamlessly combined a new career, motherhood and study. I enrolled for a Bachelor in Education Studies comprising five postgraduate papers and five years' teaching experience. There was a flurry when I requested that my work in childcare be counted as the required teaching experience. This had not been done before. For many people childcare was not 'education' and we were childcare workers and not teachers. I finally had met Beverley Morris, who was also an advisor to the crèche. I also met Sonja Davies, who had been campaigning for government support for childcare over many years. She determined to start a union for childcare workers and I became part of that endeavour (May 2003). Through these political forays I met Anne Meade and Anne Smith, fellow scholars in early childhood education, as well as long time leaders and activists such as Marie Bell (then in the Department of Education), Mary Purdy, Val Burns and Pam Cubey from Wellington College of Education and Lynne Bruce, a Kindergarten Teachers' Association activist. The job as crèche supervisor thrust me into the midst of the thriving politics of early childhood and feminism; it started to dawn that this story was silent in the politics of education I was studying in the Department of Education. My study, however, was still gripping, particularly as I included a postgraduate paper in anthropology with Peter Webster, as well as more scholarly journeys with Jack Shallcrass. This time I read the works of Jean Paul Sartre, and with Jim Collinge was able to consider Sartre's philosophy of individual freedom in the context of education. In the course on sociology run by the newly appointed lecturer Ken Stevens I also sought to link what I had read in anthropology to education. These were clumsy thoughts, but an effort to cross the divides of work and study.

In 1982 I embarked on a master's thesis on the politics of childcare, intending to draw together the theory I was reading and the politics I was immersed in, and also to position childcare within the realm of interest of an education department. Jack Shallcrass was my supervisor, but also recruited to the task was Cathy Wylie, then in the Department of Anthropology and also a past student of Jan Pouwer. The thesis revealed a previously silent historical and political story of childcare, and formed the basis of the book *Mind That Child* (May 1985).

More broadly I was intent on positioning early childhood education, beyond its child development considerations, as a field of study in education at university. My friend Sue Middleton had been appointed as the first woman in the Department of Education at the University of Waikato. In the late 1970s, Jane Kroger and Lise Bird were appointed to Victoria, although they were not the first women appointees (in 1948 Betty Odell had been appointed a junior lecturer in child development). The interests of Kroger and Bird were primarily developmental. This became an issue in 1983 when I wanted to start a doctorate. Determined to keep exploring the politics of childcare, I intended to write an oral history analysis of the broader contexts of the lives of women as mothers, workers and wives. Jack Shallcrass was planning retirement. The proposal was passed around other staff in the department, who indicated that a thesis on motherhood had little do to with education excepting a study with a developmental focus. Instead, I became a student of the Department of Anthropology and would have been supervised by Cathy Wylie if her fixed term position had not ended. She too was en route to a career in education. The Department of Education still recognised me as 'one of their own' with a three-year James McIntosh Postgraduate Scholarship in Education which, with the Sarah-Ann Rhodes Research Fellowship, allowed full-time study. I also shifted to Hamilton to live with Crispin Gardiner, a Reader in Physics at the University of Waikato and long-time political advocate for childcare.

My academic home was now the Department of Education at Waikato University, where Sue Middleton facilitated space and support. I met Kay Morris-Matthews, another postgraduate student; together we shared many lowly piecemeal academic jobs. Apart from study I continued my advocacy work in childcare, and within a three-month window in 1986 had another child, got divorced and remarried. I had previously visited Jan Pouwer several times in the Netherlands and he came to stay on one occasion in Hamilton. He was intrigued that two of his foundation anthropology students were working in education. He was also insightful in assisting me to see the theoretical frameworks emerging from the data of the thesis. Dialectical approaches were again to the fore. The doctorate was awarded by Victoria University in 1988. My links with Victoria were by then so slight I did not go to graduation. The thesis was later published as a book called *Minding Children, Managing Men* (May 1992).

Professor of early childhood

Dominion 23/8/95

Creche worker returns as professor

By COLIN PATTERSON

TWELVE years after finishing her job as supervisor of the Victoria University creche, Helen May has returned to the university as New Zealand's first professor of early childhood teacher education.

The education of young children has been a long-time interest for Dr May. She had to make use of childcare for three children in the late 1970s and early 1980s while she was a student, and supervised the creche.

After nearly 20 years of working, researching and writing in the field, Dr May fears that policy changes aimed at achieving greater competition in childcare are resulting in the erosion of quality, while fee levels are making quality unaffordable for many.

"Parents are no longer being assured of quality childcare for their children. Competition is also discouraging agencies from working together."

A change that particularly upsets her is the Government's push to make kindergartens charge fees. "Kindergartens are being required to sell quality to get funding. They are being told to pull back their level of affordability to that of other providers. However, their teachers are better paid and they provide better ...

Helen May, New Zealand's first professor of early childhood teacher education

quality for children. Overseas research clearly shows learning outcomes for children are related to the quality of care they receive."

Some policy aspects do receive Dr May's approval, however. She says that after having visited Britain and America, she was aware New Zealand had the advantage in getting funding directly to centres. She also welcomes the diversity of childcare services available here. The training of childcare workers at a tertiary level, especially through the Bachelor of Education course at Victoria and the Wellington College of Education, is an initiative she keenly supports.

Dr May has also become the first director of the Institute for Early Childhood Studies, established by Victoria and Wellington College of Education to promote research in early-childhood teaching.

Among her priorities for the next 12 months is the completion of a book on the history of childcare in New Zealand. She is also working with a former colleague on a history of teachers' ideas, and plans to set up an archive on early childhood education that would be accessible to professionals and researchers.

Before her latest appointment Dr May chaired the department of early childhood studies at Waikato University. She was a main contributor to the development of the first national curriculum for early childhood education in 1993 and is a board member of the Council for Education Research.

She was also the first national president of the Early Childhood Workers' Union.

In Wellington's *Dominion* newspaper (23 October 1995) the headline read, 'Crèche Worker Returns as Professor'. There had been a twelve-year break in my employment at Victoria University and the difference in status of these positions was newsworthy, but the professorial position at Victoria was also groundbreaking for other reasons. It was the first professorial chair in early childhood in New Zealand, and part of an international trend amongst universities to recognise the forefront position of early childhood education in education policy initiatives. It was also unique as a joint position with Wellington College of Education, a long-term partner with Victoria in delivering a four-year Bachelor of Education that subsumed a three-year Diploma of Teaching taught by the College. The new position was situated in a joint Institute of Early Childhood Studies (IECS), housed in a grand villa set amidst beautiful gardens, with panoramic Wellington views. The professorship and the IECS were the result of a campaign led initially by Carmen Dalli, a lecturer with early childhood interests at Victoria, and Tony Holmes, a lecturer in early childhood teacher education at the College. They gained the support of Lynne Bruce, Director of Early Childhood, and Graeme Oldershaw, Principal of the College, as well as Adrienne Alton-Lee, Dean of the Faculty of Education at the University. Convincing the University Council was more difficult. It was helpful though that Marie Bell was a Council member.

Carmen Dalli's ire had been raised after the departure of Anne Meade from the Department of Education in 1992. Anne's term at Victoria as the first academic appointment in early childhood education had been short and energetic. She came directly from the Prime Minister's Office in 1990 after the heady politics of *Education to be More* (ECCE Working Group 1988) and *Before Five* (Department of Education 1988) (Meade 1990). Anne, with Carmen, was the architect of an early childhood political and pedagogical presence in the Department of Education's course offerings. Carmen continued with the task but was incensed when the replacement position for Anne was captured by other interests. The professorship and the IECS were the eventual consequence and I was the fortunate beneficiary.

Quite apart from these politics I had, since 1987, been in the midst of a transformation in early childhood studies at Hamilton Teachers College and, after its merger with the University of Waikato in 1991, became the Head of the first Department of Early Childhood Education in a New Zealand university. In 1987, I met a scholarly soul mate – kindergarten teacher Margaret Carr, also recently appointed to Hamilton Teachers College. When the three-year early childhood qualification was introduced, in something akin to a coup, we took the lead, abandoned the ethos of the existing kindergarten qualification and created a qualification with strong political, pedagogical and bicultural underpinnings. The result was a stand-alone early childhood degree outside the realm of primary teaching influence (Carr, May and Mitchell 1991). I established a paper on the history and philosophy of early childhood that combined my scholarly interests and political endeavours. This course became the catalyst for a raft of books still in progress (May 1997, 2001, 2003, 2005, 2009, Middleton and May 1997).

Lynne Bruce and Helen May dancing at the opening of the Institute for Early Childhood Studies, with Pacific staff from the Wellington Aoga Amata, 1995.

The theoretical and political reframing of early childhood education in the university was the forerunner of work embarked on during 1991–1992 when Margaret and I led the development, under contract to the Ministry of Education, of a national early childhood curriculum later known as *Te Whāriki* (Ministry of Education 1993, 1996, Carr and May 1993). Realising that teacher education was a key to any successful implementation of *Te Whāriki*, we again restructured the Waikato degree qualification to demonstrate the pedagogical possibilities of curriculum papers shaped around the new language of belonging, well-being, communication, exploration and contribution. It was also imperative that *Te Whāriki* be a springboard for new research questions regarding pedagogy and practice. Forging an early childhood research presence in universities was crucial. Margaret's own doctoral thesis on technological practice (Carr 1997) was the first of a stream. It was necessary too that *Te Whāriki* receive international scrutiny and critique. We embarked on our first journeys in 1991 – Margaret to the UK and I to the US – when the development of the curriculum was still underway. We had no inkling of the subsequent, and still ongoing, international acclaim for *Te Whāriki* as a curriculum document (Nuttall 2003).

At Victoria University in 1995 there was a jointly taught Bachelor of Education degree, but only a few early childhood students from the College were enrolled in it. The education papers in the degree included both primary and early childhood students. This was not a happy situation and on arrival in 1995 my task was apparently to create a better place for early childhood within the existing degree. This was a flawed approach and subsequently, following the lessons of Waikato and with the support of early childhood staff at Wellington College of Education, I proposed a stand-alone early childhood degree. When the colleges of education, including Wellington College of Education, dramatically pulled out of four-year degrees with universities to offer their own three-year degrees, Lynne Bruce and I determined that early childhood would not be a casualty. Our new proposal was another first; a jointly awarded Bachelor of Education (Early Childhood) by Wellington College of Education and Victoria University. Due to the staff's priority commitment to early childhood matters over university–college loyalties, the degree qualification and the IECS became the significant connection between a squabbling university and college. This became more acute when the College established its own postgraduate qualifications and withdrew financial support for the professorial position. The University determinedly gave strong support to both the position and the work of the IECS with the College. The Department of Early Childhood at the College was similarly committed in its support for the degree and the IECS.

Amidst these inter-institutional turmoils the IECS forged its own agendas. With Margaret Carr at the University of Waikato and Val Podmore at the New Zealand Council for Educational Research, we engaged in collaborative research projects to develop new frameworks for assessment and evaluation for early childhood in relation to *Te Whāriki* (Carr 1998, Podmore and May 1998, Carr, May and Podmore 1999, 2002). Many early childhood staff from the College were upgrading their qualifications to master's level and Carmen Dalli launched a popular series of Occasional Publications to disseminate this work. There also began a drift of students to undertake doctoral level qualifications at the Institute. This gathered momentum after Carmen completed her doctorate (Dalli 1999) and Val Podmore was appointed to the IECS in 1999. The IECS built up a large array of resources and archives and became a regular stopover for international scholars. A highlight for the IECS was when Marie Bell, aged 82 years, received her doctorate in 2004. For some years Marie had incongruously worked as a tutor at the IECS while also being a member of the University Council. When first approached about supervising her doctoral studies I cautiously asked, "Marie, are you sure that you want to do a doctorate?" silently adding "at your age!" The stern reply was, "I always wanted to be Dr Bell." And so she became (Bell 2004). Her daily presence at the IECS over some years was a privilege.

In these heady times I was still was immersed in early childhood history and policy. I had ready access to the nearby national archival collections at home, and overseas travel allowed me to trawl though significant collections and libraries and keep abreast of current international policy developments. Research and teaching were entwined. The students were always the first to comment on my research finds and this fuelled the quest for further journeys. In the new degree underway in 1998, I established EDUC 153: Discovery of Early Childhood, named after the title of the book started at Waikato (May 1997a), as well as EDUC 253: Early Years Debates, a course intended to foster debate about controversial issues in early years education. Later, BA students could enrol in both courses as part of a new major in early childhood studies. 'Discovery' was taught in various forms: for BA students at Victoria, teacher education students at the College, and Diploma students in Whanganui, a city whose own rich history in education provided a different pathway of discovery. In the early twentieth century Emily Blennerhassett showcased the possibilities of Montessori methods at the Central Infant School. Along the Whanganui River there were 19th century missionary schools including the foundling home of Sister Suzanne Aubert at Jerusalem, and at Pipiriki School in the 1940s Sylvia Ashton-Warner first wrote about the troubles of her Māori infant room.

Sally Peters, Carmen Dalli, Sophie Alcock and Helen May; Institute of Early Childhood Studies staff in 1998.

Newly graduated Dr Marie Bell with Carmen Dalli and Helen May, 2004.

Another journey was the development in 2004 of a Māori pathway for 'Discovery' for the College's Whāriki Papatipu students who were kaiako (educators) in Kohanga Reo around Te Awaikairangi (Hutt Valley). They gave the first reaction to my research on early 19th century missionary infant schools for young Māori children, a hitherto untold story enmeshed in the uncomfortable language of 'heathenism', 'savagery' and 'cannibalism', and the surprising facts of educational innovation and the precociousness of very young Māori scholars (May 2005). Māori leader and kaumatua, Kara Puketapu launched 'Discovery' for the Whāriki Papatipu students at the Pukeatua Kokiri Centre in Wainuiomata. His beginning story was the 1984 Te Māori exhibition in New York and its showcasing of the power of ancestral taonga. My story began in the 18th-century Age of Enlightenment, as curious European explorers wondered about land riches in the Antipodes. And so the discovery of these entwined stories began. Kuia Nanny Jean Puketapu watched and guided her kaiako and the lecturer on this journey. In 2004, the year before the merger with Victoria University, Wellington College of Education honoured Nanny Jean with a Diploma of Teaching, recognising her founding role within Kohanga Reo and the support of the first cohort of students through the Whāriki Papatipu programme.

In 2001 Carmen Dalli took over the helm of the IECS while I became Head of the School of Education. The IECS remained my home and for three years, with the forbearance of administrative staff in Scott House, the School was run from the Institute's second location in a suite of rooms in Murphy Block. When the College sought to re-establish a formal partnership with the University, the work of the IECS was showcased as a model of collaboration.

In 2002 Jack Shallcrass turned eighty and a one-day seminar was hosted with Wellington College of Education. Present were three professors of education who were previously Jack's students: Cedric Hall, Sue Middleton and myself. Sue and I presented a montage of images reminding the audience of a time when being a student of education was hugely exciting and devoid of course outlines, Blackboard, study guides, or the language of objectives and outcomes. We wondered whether the culture of accountability then pervading universities gave students the freedom to think and explore as Jack had allowed us.

The merger story will remain outside this chapter. My shift to the University of Otago in 2005 was unexpected but opportune. The possibility

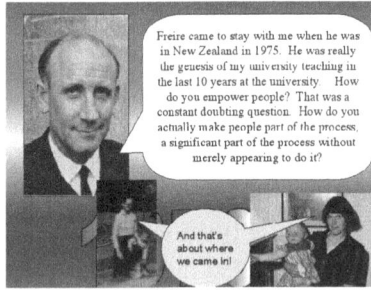

Introductory slides for a presentation by Sue Middleton and Helen May (designed by Sue Middleton) for Jack Shallcrass: 80th Birthday Seminar, August 4, 2002, Victoria University of Wellington.

was seeded in a dramatic setting on Carmen Dalli's beloved island of Malta. It was the night before the 2004 European Early Childhood Research Association Conference and Carmen was hosting several New Zealanders for dinner. It was close to midnight and hot, with children still playing on the streets of the hill castle town of Medina. I was sitting next to Anne Smith, who mentioned a professorial position at Otago as the Head of the Faculty of Education and encouraged me to apply. I was dismissive of the idea. I had recently passed on the Head of School role to Kay Morris-Matthews, who herself had an interesting to route to Victoria via both women's studies and education. I had determined to focus more fully on early childhood.

But there were temptations in Anne's suggestion despite the likely scenario of another merger. My husband, Crispin Gardiner, had a research partnership with physicists at the University of Otago. From a personal perspective, to be the Dean of the University of Otago College of Education (eventually established in 2007) was an unlikely pre-retirement job for a junior school teacher who had wanted to study anthropology. The appointment was also evidence that early years education, being the entire portfolio of my research and practice, was now accepted and mainstreamed into the university discipline of education. I was ambivalent about such mainstreaming, having fought to create separate spaces and places for early childhood within other universities, which had not been sustained. At Waikato University the once Department of Early Childhood was later amalgamated into a Department of Professional Studies; and at Victoria University there was not only the loss of the professorial chair after I left, but the later demise of the Department of Early Childhood Teacher Education and the dismantling of the separate IECS and its resources. The small size of early childhood programmes at Otago has precluded any stand-alone structures. Nonetheless, at each of these universities early childhood qualifications are strongly positioned in terms of numbers and pedagogy, and the programmes continue to be strengthened by new scholarship emerging from the doctoral scholars and graduates who now staff the university 'colleges' of education.

My formal links as a professor at Victoria concluded as they began, at the start of my third Victoria experience. In 1995 I was accompanied and handed over to Victoria by early childhood staff from Waikato, led by kaumatua Fred Kana. In 2005, IECS staff and colleagues from Victoria similarly travelled south and handed me to Otago. The threads of this support from both Waikato and Victoria remain with me and I am still publishing work seeded at both institutions. *School Beginnings: A Nineteenth Century Colonial Story* (May 2005) reconnected me to my junior school origins when I was first a student at Victoria. Its sequel, *New Beginnings: A Twentieth Century Story of Early Schooling*, is inching towards completion.

These personal snapshots of time are written in 2009 as a tribute to 'education' at Victoria University and the role it played in creating and supporting an unlikely university career in early childhood as a student, a crèche worker, and a professor.

References

Bell, M. (2004). Pioneers of parents' centre: movers and shakers for change in the philosophies and practices of childbirth and parent education in New Zealand. PhD Thesis. Victoria University of Wellington.

Carr, M. (1997). Technological practice in early childhood as a dispositional milieu. PhD Thesis. University of Waikato.

_____(1998). *Assessing children's experiences in early childhood: final report to the Ministry of Education: part one*. Wellington: Ministry of Education Research Division.

Carr, M. & May, H. (1993). Choosing a model: reflecting on the development process of Te Whāriki, national early childhood curriculum guidelines in New Zealand. *International Journal of Early Years Education*. 1, 3. pp. 7-22.

Carr, M., May, H. & Mitchell, J., (1991). The development of an integrated early childhood training programme. In M. Gold, L. Foote and A. Smith, (Eds.). Fifth Early Childhood Convention papers. Dunedin. pp. 376-393.

Carr, M., May, H. & Podmore, V. (1999). *Evaluation in early childhood: final report to the Ministry of Education*. Wellington: NZCER.

_____(2002). Learning and teaching stories: action research on evaluation in early childhood in Aotearoa–New Zealand. *European Early Childhood Research Journal*. 11, 1. pp.115-126.

Dalli, C. (1999). Starting childcare before three: narratives of experience from a tri-partite focus. PhD Thesis. Victoria University of Wellington.

Department of Education (1988). *Before five: early childhood care and education in New Zealand*. Wellington: Government Printer.

Early Childhood Care and Education Working Group (1998). *Education to be more*. Wellington: Department of Education.

May, H. (1985). *Mind that child: childcare as a social and political issue in New Zealand*. Wellington: BlackBerry Press.

_____(1989). The early postwar years for women: an interview with Beverley Morris. *Women's Studies Journal*. 5, 2. pp. 61-75.

_____(1992). *Minding children, managing men: conflict and compromise in the lives of postwar pakeha women*. Wellington: Bridget Williams Books.

_____(1997a). *The discovery of early childhood: the development of services for the care and education of very young children*. Auckland & Wellington: Auckland University Press & NZCER.

_____(1997b). *'Discoveries', triumphs, trials and 'talk' of early childhood teacher education: inaugural address.* Institute for Early Childhood Studies, Victoria University of Wellington.

_____(2001). *Politics in the playground: the world of early childhood in postwar New Zealand.* Wellington: Bridget Williams Books with NZCER.

_____(2003). *Concerning women considering children: battles of the Childcare Association, 1963–2003.* Wellington: Te Tari Puna Ora o Aotearoa-NZCA.

_____(2005). *School beginnings: a nineteenth century colonial story.* Wellington: NZCER.

_____(2009). *Politics in the playground: the world of early childhood in New Zealand,* 2nd Ed. Dunedin: University of Otago Press.

McDonald, G. (2000). Gwendolen Lucy Somerset 1894–1988, (Ed.). V. O'Sullivan, *Eminent Victorians: great teachers and scholars from Victoria's first 100 years.* Victoria University of Wellington, Stout Research Centre. pp. 155-164.

Meade, A. (1990). Women and children gain a foot in the door. *New Zealand Women's Studies Journal.* 6, 1/2. pp. 96-111.

Middleton, S. & May, H. (1997). *Teachers talk teaching 1915–1995: early childhood, school, teachers' colleges.* Palmerston North: Dunmore Press.

Ministry of Education (1993). *Te Whāriki: draft guidelines for developmentally appropriate programmes in early childhood services.* Wellington: Learning Media.

_____(1996). *Te Whāriki: He Whāriki mātauranga mo nga mokopuna o Aotearoa, early childhood curriculum.* Wellington: Learning Media.

Nuttall, J. (2003). *Weaving Te Whāriki: Aotearoa New Zealand's early childhood curriculum document in theory and practice.* Wellington: NZCER.

Podmore, V. & May, H. (1998). *Evaluating early childhood programmes using Te Whāriki: final report on phases one and two to the Ministry of Education.* Wellington: NZCER.

Smith, A. (1978). The case for quality day care in New Zealand: liberation of children and parents. In B. O'Rourke and J. Clough (Eds.). *Early childhood in New Zealand.* Auckland: Heinemann Educational Books. pp. 248-252.

Smith, A. & Swain, D. (1988). *Childcare in New Zealand: people, programmes politics.* Wellington: Allen & Unwin & Port Nicholson.

RURAL EDUCATION

An Open Learning Matrix to Sustain Education in Rural New Zealand

Ken Stevens

New Zealand is one of the most physically isolated countries in the world, where a small population lives in a variety of remote locations beyond the main cities. Agriculture, fishing, forestry and horticulture have traditionally been prominent in New Zealand's rural economy, so the education of the children of those who work in these important sectors is nationally important. In this isolated country rural schools, distance education and, recently, e-learning, have contributed to the way of life of people who live beyond the main centres.

As the New Zealand economy has changed, the structure and organisation of rural education in this country has adapted to sustain communities located beyond major urban centres. Technological changes in rural education over the last two decades have enhanced the relationship between the urban centre and the rural periphery (Nash 1980) and encouraged the study of internet-based communities (Brown 2004, Lai 2005). This chapter describes the move from educational provision in small rural schools throughout the country to increasingly sophisticated electronic teaching and learning networks that have brought new opportunities to rural New Zealanders.

Rural education in community schools

As New Zealand society and its economy has changed and become increasingly urbanised, the viability of some schools in rural communities has been questioned. Almost two decades ago the 1991 *Report of the Economic and Educational Viability of Small Schools Review* (hereafter, the Report) was published amid media speculation about the future of rural schools in this country. The "educational viability" of a small school proved difficult for the review to establish. The Report defined a small school as educationally viable "if pupils in it are taught an appropriate curriculum to a reasonable standard in an environment which enhances achievement and social development". An appropriate curriculum was "one which follows the official syllabuses and associated guidelines developed by the Department of Education before 1 October 1989 and the Ministry of Education since 1 October 1989". The 1991 review addressed a key issue in New Zealand education that is common in other parts of the world: how can small schools in rural communities provide education that is of comparable quality to what is available in larger institutions in urban areas? The Report noted that secondary level students in rural schools might lack the range of subject areas available to their urban counterparts despite the availability of distance education. A policy issue facing the New Zealand government – and governments in other countries – is justifying the provision of curriculum resources and the appointment of specialist teachers in rural schools in which there are very small enrolments, particularly at the senior high school level.

The economic viability of small schools, it was argued in the Report, depended on the level of resources that a government was prepared to use to "purchase educational services from schools." In determining the economic viability of small schools, the Report noted that there are no published reports addressing the issue of whether economies of scale exist in New Zealand schools, but that "it is assumed in the funding formula for operational grants that economies of scale do exist". It was pointed out, however, that:

> Population density in large part influences the size of schools; consequently, accepting that a school is required in an area of low population density usually means that the costs involved will be higher than in a more densely populated area. (the Report, p. 25)

The Report noted that there is no New Zealand research on the relationship between school size and educational effectiveness and that "it has yet to be demonstrated that pupil achievement suffers because of the size of a school" in spite of the acknowledgment that it is often thought that rural students "tend to achieve at a lower level than their urban counterparts". It acknowledged the popular belief that smallness in itself may seem an undesirable characteristic in a school by many people, but pointed to research that suggests such an idea is unfounded in relation to small rural schools overseas (Bell and Sigsworth 1987).

A major issue to emerge from the review, in addition to its consideration of educational, economic and community relationships, was conflict between availability and choice:

> It is important to note that at present the Education Act 1989 provides the entitlement to free enrolment and free education at any state school. This entitlement creates obligations on the institutions and on the system as those with the entitlement exercise their choice. There is a tension between choice and entitlement. (the Report, p. 32)

Where a small school was considered to be "non-viable" a variety of "alternative possibilities" were outlined: amalgamation (or merging) with another institution, consolidation with other schools, closure, relocation of the school to another site, use of the Correspondence School, and increasing transport and boarding assistance to enable pupils to attend schools in other communities. The review recommended that "the provision of senior secondary school education in New Zealand (particularly in rural areas) be reassessed with a view to developing more appropriate and efficient structures for expanding learning and training possibilities" (p. 55). It also recommended that "any examination of the viability of schools in rural areas take note of their contributions to their communities and to the overall life of New Zealand" (p. 54).

An important insight into rural adult education that has implications for New Zealand agriculture can be found in Ken Moore's *Learning on the Farm*, following a survey of 110 farmers in the South Island over a three month period in 1988, which aimed to discover how they learned to farm and the methods they used to stay up to date with developments in agriculture. In New Zealand, these are important questions which link the major national industry and the education system. In spite of the ready availability of farming and management expertise Moore found few people entered New Zealand farming with any formal training for the job. Most farmers were reported to rely on other farmers for advice. Moore found a direct relationship between the length of schooling farmers received and the extent to which management practices were used, or, more commonly, not used. New Zealand is an exporter of agricultural expertise and it is surprising, therefore, that in a country that relies so heavily on farming for its national income and in which such expertise is readily available, most farmers were found to be little influenced by agricultural education and training. A problem in the further education and training of New

Zealand farmers that Moore found was the low level of formal education many have received and the difficulties subsequently experienced "at the more symbolic or formal operational stages". He found, for example, that there was a gap in understanding between scientists (and scientific language) and farmers who were the agricultural practitioners. The role of the polytechnics in educating the farming community was the subject of some discussion and Moore concluded that these institutions, practically all of which are located in urban areas, need to "explore ways to better serve rural areas, particularly in the provision of farm related training". *Learning on the Farm* concluded with the prediction:

> It is likely that farm productivity will drop until a higher proportion of farmers receive better education and training. If this better trained group of farmers fails to emerge, the likely trend will be to fewer, larger farms, managed by essentially business-trained people overseeing a stockman/ tractor driver group who provide the manual labour. (Moore 1990, p. 77)

Unless science, management and farming can communicate more satisfactorily, the future of rural communities may be challenged.

Distance education – collaboration between the centre and regions

The New Zealand Correspondence School has had a role in the education of many New Zealanders, including those in rural communities. It is the largest school in the country, with a student enrolment of over 20,000, and it is one of New Zealand's best known educational institutions. The Correspondence School has several important functions, including the provision of education for people in remote locations, the delivery of courses to students attending other secondary schools who cannot have classroom tuition provided on a regular basis because of lack of available staff or lack of numbers to constitute a class, the provision of adult education and the provision of second-chance education. Many New Zealanders have continued their education overseas through the Correspondence School while travelling and others have been able to receive lessons from it at home or while in hospital or prison. The Correspondence School's many functions meet a wide variety of educational needs in New Zealand, including those of early childhood education and a range of specialised areas, like English as a second language. It is a unique, multi-purpose national school with a diverse enrolment.

An important supportive role of the New Zealand Correspondence School has been the provision of extended curriculum options for rural students, particularly at the secondary level, who attend local schools but for whom access to specialised subjects in traditional, face-to-face classrooms is not possible. Some students of the New Zealand Correspondence School maintain daily attendance at local community schools while they are concurrently enrolled with this national, centrally located institution. The Correspondence School has therefore become an integral part of the academic life of many schools throughout the country, providing distance education for students in a very wide variety of educational settings. Following restructuring in 2007 the school adopted a more regionally focused approach to the provision of education. The internet now gives it new ways of providing learning opportunities throughout the country, although its name reflects its origins that pre-date the cyber world. The Correspondence School is moving many of its courses online, which will further extend its educational base, both within New Zealand and beyond.

The Open Polytechnic of New Zealand (TOPNZ), like the Correspondence School, is a unique institution with a special niche in the education of New Zealanders. As its name suggests, it provides a large range of post-secondary courses for New Zealanders, primarily, but not exclusively, of an applied, technological nature. The Open Polytechnic has for many years provided New Zealanders with access to courses as diverse as agriculture, business, technology and applied science, while also preparing students for such occupations as real estate, tourism, quantity surveying and many others. Like the Correspondence School, TOPNZ provides access to a wide range of courses for New Zealanders who are in employment and who wish to study part time to enhance their careers, and it is also moving many of its courses online.

The New Zealand Correspondence School and the Open Polytechnic of New Zealand together provide open learning opportunities for New Zealanders from pre-school to degree level. Massey University has always had, and continues to have, a pre-eminent role in the provision of distance education degrees in New Zealand. However, the growth of information and communication technologies, an expanding range of educational software, and the increasing prominence of the internet in education has encouraged other New Zealand universities to consider the possibilities and the institutional advantages of open learning, something that has become an established dimension of academic life in most New Zealand universities.

The Correspondence School and the Open Polytechnic are centralised, open educational institutions that have successfully extended learning opportunities for New Zealanders, including those who live in rural communities. Today they face a challenge from a newer type of open educational institution, in the form of collaborative inter-school teaching and learning.

Open structures for school collaboration – e-learning

As New Zealand society became increasingly urbanised, rural families migrated to cities to take advantage of educational and job opportunities. Accordingly, student enrolment in many small rural schools declined. The provision of quality education in small communities that were distant from major centres of population became increasingly difficult to maintain, and rural educators and parents were motivated to explore new ways of accessing educational opportunities. Before the introduction of the internet in the New Zealand education system, a collaborative structure was developed that enabled twelve small Canterbury schools to explore new teaching and learning possibilities (Stevens and Moffatt 2003). Each participating school was provided with a dedicated phone line by Telecom New Zealand for the purpose of organising audio-graphic networking. Students in each of the schools that became sites in the network could hear one another and participate in learning using a graphic tablet that could be seen by students on other sites during a lesson. With this pre-internet technology, students on one site within the school network were able to join a class that was delivered from another place. Teachers taught beyond their own classrooms and students met peers through the audio-graphic network from other schools in the Canterbury region. This pre-internet initiative heralded a conceptual change in the nature of classrooms, schools and the work of both teachers and students (Tate 1993). Small rural schools in the region academically and administratively opened to one another for that part of the school day during which classes were either delivered or received. With the advent of computers in schools and the realisation of the internet's potential for teaching and learning, the audio-graphic network and the pioneering virtual classes within it were enhanced (Stevens 1994, 1995a, 1995b). Teachers were introduced to the idea of teaching beyond their classrooms to students in real time and students were able to access subjects that were not locally available from collaborating sites (Stevens 1999).

The development of the inter-school teaching and learning network was known as 'Cantatech' (The Canterbury Area Schools Technology Project). The project brought rural schools together to explore ways in which teaching and learning resources could be shared. Each school was able to provide its students with traditional face-to-face teaching on-site in core subjects – English, Mathematics and Science – as well as instruction in one or two specialised subjects such as French, Japanese, Economics or Agriculture. By collaborating in the teaching of specialist subjects between participating schools, senior students who wished to receive instruction in courses not locally available were able to access them from another site in the Cantatech network. By mutual consent, designated schools in the Cantatech network accepted responsibility for a particular area of the curriculum in which they had a qualified teacher, in return for access to specialist expertise from other schools in other subjects. Subsequently, the Cantatech network developed links to polytechnics and other educational organisations to further extend educational opportunities for rural students throughout the Canterbury region.

By collaborating in the appointment of specialist teachers to each Cantatech site it was possible to avoid duplication of human resources and encourage the development of an expanded range of shared appointments. Each school in the network was increasingly able to provide its senior students with access to an extended range of learning opportunities. It became a condition of appointment for teachers in the Cantatech schools that courses were to be provided in both the traditional, face-to-face way, on site, as well as to other parts of the network, using emerging technologies. The development of the Cantatech network brought about changes in the administrative and academic life of each participating school. Each school in the network had to academically and administratively interface with each of the other schools and work collaboratively in the interests of the broader, regional educational community, not just its originally designated local one. Because of the necessity of finding new solutions to the delivery of education to geographically isolated senior students, each school in the Cantatech network had to consider the potential role of new and emerging information technologies for delivery of the curriculum. Information technology became a means to enlarge local educational and, indirectly, vocational opportunities for young people.

Following the success of the Cantatech project and several similar initiatives in other rural areas of New Zealand, e-learning in schools became a national educational priority (Ministry of Education 2001, 2003). In 1998 the *National Information and Communications Technology Strategy* was published, containing four objectives. The first was to improve learning outcomes through the use of information technologies in schools for teaching and learning. The second was to increase the effectiveness and efficiency of teachers and schools by helping them to use these technologies. The third objective was to improve the quality of teaching and leadership in schools by helping teachers and principals to identify their technology needs and to develop the skills necessary to meet them. The final objective was to increase opportunities for schools, businesses and government to work together in developing an information technology-literate workforce (Ministry of Education 1998).

The national strategy developed several major initiatives. A resource centre was created to provide teachers and schools with a mechanism for the delivery of multimedia resources, including curriculum and administration resources, using the internet. The centre provided links to curriculum experts, bilingual discussion forums, databases, multimedia and a variety of other sites. Schools were encouraged to create their own websites and to have these placed in the online resource centre. A 'Computer Recycling Scheme' was initiated to enable more schools to obtain computers for student and teacher use, at low cost, when they were replaced in other organisations in the public and private sectors. The scheme was described as the "recycling and up-grading [of computers] in schools" (Ministry of Education 1998, p. 12).

Teacher professional development for implementation and planning was introduced during the first year of the national strategy. Principals and senior administrators in schools throughout New Zealand were provided with professional development opportunities in their local areas through meetings that focused on the use of information technologies for teaching and learning. Finally, 'Professional Development Schools' were initiated. Twenty-three schools, strategically selected from throughout New Zealand, were designated information technology professional development lead schools from late 1998. Their purpose was to assist the development of information technology in other schools within their local areas. Each lead school was chosen primarily for the technological expertise of its staff.

The development of virtual classes in rural New Zealand can be summed up as having origins in small schools in rural communities, an emphasis on collaborative teaching and learning and, from 1998, government involvement in e-learning. A range of initiatives to encourage online learning to complement existing educational structures and processes were promoted (Education Review Office 2005, Ministry of Education 2006).

From closed to open approaches to sustain rural schools

Since the introduction of inter-school electronic networks based on the internet, it has become possible to conceptualise New Zealand schools as open or closed. Traditionally, schools have appointed their own teachers, enrolled their own students and served designated districts, suburbs or towns. They have been assigned to teach particular age groups that reside in certain places and, as such, they are closed learning environments, not open to students from other places. Students in traditional schools are taught by teachers who are appointed to them. Since the introduction of the Internet, some schools, such as those in the Cantatech network, have become both academically and administratively open to other schools, sometimes being timetabled together so that classes can be shared for at least part of a school day. In an open educational environment schools can be considered as sites within teaching and learning networks.

The move from closed to open classes in rural New Zealand has contributed to the sustainability of education in small and often remote communities. The move from closed to open teaching and learning in rural New Zealand can be considered within a matrix of

(a) *organisational* changes that expanded school size and capacity;

(b) *technological* enhancement that changed ways knowledge could be accessed and shared;

(c) *pedagogical* adaptation to new inter-school relations as well as teacher –student interaction; and

(d) a *re-conceptualisation* of the meaning of rural education based on learning technologies and the internet.

Organisational, technological, pedagogical and conceptual changes together form a matrix of rural education and e-learning in New Zealand.

A Matrix of Rural Education and e-Learning in New Zealand

Technological	Pedagogical
Organisational	Conceptual

Organisational changes in the provision of education in rural New Zealand can be seen in the move from closed to open teaching and learning environments. The traditional rural school has been complemented and supported by the New Zealand Correspondence School for many years and, with the introduction of e-learning in school-district intranets, some rural schools have become sites in teaching and learning networks. A significant dimension of the organisational changes that have taken place in the provision of education in rural New Zealand has been teacher and student collaboration as traditional physical classrooms acquire a virtual dimension to include peers and colleagues from other places. It becomes difficult to discuss 'small' schools when institutions that have few students attending in person, on a daily basis, teach many students off-site. The range of curriculum options in small and physically isolated schools has been expanded through inter-school sharing of teachers and other resources. The organisational changes that have taken place in rural New Zealand education were made possible by the availability and introduction of emerging learning technologies, including the internet, leading to pedagogical challenges as teachers learnt to teach not just in schools, but between schools (Dorniden 2005). Organisational, technological and pedagogical changes in rural schools contributed to re-conceptualisation of the significance, in educational terms, of school size and location (Hawkes and Halverson 2002).

Technological changes have underpinned the transformation of rural schools in New Zealand, initially by enabling the Correspondence School to supplement teaching by enrolling students in areas of the curriculum not available on-site, and more recently by embracing internet-based e-learning. A feature of a growing number of rural schools in New Zealand is the interaction of traditional face-to-face instruction with virtual teaching and learning. The introduction of new technologies in rural schools was initiated by declining enrolments. As many rural schools declined in size, inter-school teaching and learning and the creation of intranets developed.

Pedagogical changes in rural New Zealand schools followed the introduction of intranets. Teaching across multiple sites simultaneously is a new skill that teachers in a growing number of rural schools have had to acquire. Teaching across multiple sites requires collaboration between teachers and the development of shared timetables if lessons are not to be repeated. Teachers have had to explore ways of engaging students across multiple sites as well as developing and sharing lessons with colleagues who were appointed to other schools.

Conceptually there have been several changes in rural New Zealand education. The Correspondence School and regional intranets together enable students in rural New Zealand to engage with teachers and learners in other places, both in real and delayed time. The significance of location and school size – as determined by the number of students who attend, in person, on a daily basis – has decreased, while the strength of electronic and pedagogical connections to other places has become increasingly important. An increasing number of schools in rural New Zealand have increased in size in terms of the curriculum they can provide both on-site and online.

Conclusion – sustaining rural education in New Zealand

Rural schools in New Zealand have been sustained by the development of open learning that draws on the interaction of technological, pedagogical, organisational and conceptual change. Small schools in rural New Zealand communities that are part of intranets have, in effect, become sites within expanding teaching and learning networks that are academically and administratively integrated. Conceptual, organisational, pedagogical and technological changes have collectively enhanced the educational capacities of participating sites, sustaining small schools while possibly making 'rural education' obsolete.

References

Bell, A. & Sigsworth, A. (1987). *The small rural primary school: a matter of quality.* Philadelphia: Falmer Press.
Brown, M. (2004). *The study of wired schools: a study of internet-using teachers.* Palmerston North: Massey University.

Education Review Office (2005). *E-learning in secondary schools*. Wellington: Education Review Office.

Dorniden, A. (2005). K-12 schools and online learning. In Howard, C., Boettcher, J.V., Justice, L., Schenk, K., Rogers, P.L and Berg, G.A. (Eds.). *Encyclopedia of distance learning*. Hershey, Idea Group Reference. pp. 1182-1188.

Hawkes, M. & Halverson, P. (2002). Technology facilitation in the rural school: an analysis of options. *Journal of Research in Rural Education*. 17, 3. pp. 162-170.

Lai, K.-W. (2005). *E-Learning communities: teaching and learning with the web*. Dunedin: Otago University Press.

Ministry of Education (2006). *Enabling the 21st century learner: an e-Learning action plan for schools 2006–2010*. Wellington: Learning Media.

Ministry of Education (2003). *Digital horizons – learning through ICT*. Wellington: Learning Media.

Ministry of Education (2001). *Information and communication technologies (ICT) strategy for schools 2002–2004*. Wellington: Learning Media.

Ministry of Education (1998). *Interactive education – an information and communication technologies strategy for schools*. Wellington: Ministry of Education.

Ministry of Education (1991). *Report of the economic and educational viability of small schools review*. Wellington: Ministry of Education (mimeo).

Moore, K. (1990). *Learning on the farm – the educational background and needs of New Zealand farmers*. Wellington: New Zealand Council for Educational Research.

Nash, R. (1980). *Schooling in rural societies*. London: Methuen.

Stevens, K.J. & Moffatt, C. (2003). From distance eEducation to telelearning – the organization of open classes at local, regional and national levels. In, J. Bradley (Ed.). *The open classroom – distance learning in and out of schools*. London & Sterling, VA: Kogan Page. pp. 171-180.

Stevens, K. (1999). Telecommunications technologies, telelearning and the development of virtual classes for rural New Zealanders. *Open Praxis*. 1. pp. 12-14.

_____(1995a). Geographic isolation and technological change: a new vision of teaching and learning in rural schools in New Zealand. *The Journal of Distance Learning*. 1, 1. pp. 3-38.

_____(1995b). The technological challenge to the notion of rurality in New Zealand education: repositioning the small school. *New Zealand Annual Review of Education*. 5. pp. 93-102.

_____(1994). Some applications of distance education technologies and pedagogies in rural schools in New Zealand. *Distance Education*. 15, 4. pp. 318-326.

Tate, O. (1993). *A vision of distance education in New Zealand*. Inaugural conference of Distance Education and Information and Communications Technology Providers, National Library of New Zealand, Wellington.

The Introduction of a Collaborative New Zealand Model to Sustain Rural Schools in Atlantic Canada[1]

Ken Stevens

The organisation of rural education in Atlantic Canada was directly influenced by developments in small schools in New Zealand that are outlined in the preceding chapter. In 1997 I was appointed to an Industry Canada-funded chair of Tele-Learning (e-learning) at Memorial University of Newfoundland from Victoria University of Wellington. Most schools in the Canadian province of Newfoundland and Labrador are located beyond major centres of population, and it was appropriate to focus research on the development of e-learning in and, subsequently, between them. The concept of teaching from one school to another was new and had not been tried, but one school board in Newfoundland and Labrador volunteered to explore its possibilities in a rural school district. Elements of the matrix that emerged in New Zealand of conceptual, organisational, technological and pedagogical change in rural schools were explored during the initial year of e-learning in rural Newfoundland and Labrador schools. Two senior New Zealand educators, both from rural schools, visited the Newfoundland and Labrador schools and took part in meetings with Canadian teachers that explored the implications of the internet-based teaching that linked classrooms during the initial year of the intranet.

It could be argued that a new type of rural education has subsequently developed in Canada over the last decade, based on acceptance of e-learning and virtual classrooms (Stevens and Stewart 2005). Within the new rural education, schools have become regional centres for the

1   An earlier version of this chapter was published in the *International Journal of Education and Development Using Information and Communication Technology* Vol. 2, Issue 4, 2006, pp. 119–127 as 'Rural Schools as Regional Centres of e-Learning and the Management of Digital Knowledge: The Case of Newfoundland and Labrador.' This extended version is reproduced with permission.

management of digital knowledge, through which they challenge notions of distance, isolation and rurality. It could be further argued that small schools in rural communities have become templates for other schools through their acceptance of modern educational technologies, collaborative teaching and learning, and the integration of on-site and online instruction. Schools that have traditionally been considered small in size, based on the number of students that attend in person on a daily basis, have become, to an increasing extent, large educational institutions when the number of students who attend classes virtually is considered.

Over the last decade the introduction of inter-school electronic networks has added a new dimension to education in Canada that is challenging teachers, learners and administrators. Schools in geographically isolated communities that have traditionally faced difficulty providing instruction to small numbers of senior students, particularly in specialised areas of the curriculum such as science and foreign languages, can now complement on-site classes with specialised online teaching and learning. Many rural Canadian schools have been transformed as virtual classes are integrated with traditional, physical learning spaces in a similar way to developments in New Zealand.

A decade of e-learning in small schools in rural communities

During the last decade, a pan-Canadian initiative to prepare people across the country for the Information Age (Information Highway Advisory Council 1997, Ertl and Plante 2004) has provided impetus for the classroom application of emerging technologies. In rural Atlantic Canada the introduction of the internet and internet-based technologies has had a transforming effect on the capacity of small schools to deliver programs (Healey and Stevens 2002, Stevens 2001, 1999a). In other developed countries with substantial rural populations to be educated there have also been major changes in the configuration of small schools in isolated communities. In New Zealand (Stevens 2000, 1999b), Finland (Tella 1995), Iceland (Stevens 2002), Russia (Stevens et al. 1999) and the USA (Dorniden 2005, Glick 2005, Schrum 2005) a variety of communication technologies have been engaged to promote educational opportunities for students and more efficient ways of organising and managing knowledge in collaborative electronic structures, which have implications for regional economies.

The rapid growth and educational application of the internet has led to a challenge to traditional ways of teaching and learning at a distance (Ben-Jacob et al. 2000) that were based on paper and the postal system. E-learning is internet-based and does not require the degree of central control that distance educators have traditionally employed within dedicated institutions. The growth of e-learning in schools has led to pedagogical changes and to the development of new ways of managing knowledge to enable these institutions to assume extended roles in the regions they serve.

In the last decade two e-learning developments have changed the nature of education in rural Newfoundland and Labrador: (a) the introduction of the opportunity to study online from schools located in remote communities, and (b) the possibility of enrolment in Advanced Placement (AP) courses from rural schools.

The opportunity to study online in rural Canadian schools

With the decline in the provincial fishing industry that has always been the main economic activity in Newfoundland and Labrador's coastal communities, rural schools have become steadily smaller in size, as shown in the following table.

Table 1: Number of Schools by School District 2000–01 to 2005–06*

School District	2000–01	2001–02	2002–03	2003–04	2004–05	2005–06
Labrador	19	19	19	16	16	16
Western	92	89	85	82	82	79
Nova Central	80	79	79	75	75	70
Eastern	140	134	129	127	125	124
Conseil scolaire francophone provincial	6	5	5	5	5	5
Total	337	326	317	305	303	294

* *Department of Education of Newfoundland and Labrador (2006) Education Statistics – Elementary–Secondary 2005–2006 School Information.*

As rural schools decline in physical size, their viability is often questioned by educational policy-makers. The introduction of e-learning in schools in Canada, as in other developed countries, has been particularly noticeable in rural communities and has been influenced by declining enrolments. The Department of Education of Newfoundland and Labrador (2006) distinguishes between urban and rural on the criterion that cities, towns and metropolitan areas with a population of over 5,000 are urban and all other settlements are rural. Table 2 shows that a large proportion of schools in three of the five provincial school districts of Newfoundland and Labrador are classified as rural.

Table 2: Urban and Rural Enrolment and Schools, by School District, 2005–06*

School District		Labrador	Western	Nova Central	Eastern	Conseil scolaire francophone provincial	Province
Urban	Schools	6	15	12	66	3	102
	% Schools	37.5	19.0	17.1	53.2	60.0	34.7
	Enrolment	2,968	5,685	4,766	30,789	83	44,291
	% Enrolment	68.7	39.7	34.0	70.1	40.9	57.7
Rural	Schools	10	64	58	58	2	192
	% Schools	62.5	81.0	82.9	46.8	40.0	65.3
	Enrolment	1,351	8,624	9,246	13,131	120	32,472
	% Enrolment	31.3	60.3	66.0	29.9	59.1	42.3
Total	Schools	16	79	70	124	6	294
	Enrolment	4,319	14,309	14,012	43,920	203	76,763

* Department of Education of Newfoundland and Labrador (2006) Education Statistics – Elementary–Secondary 2005–06 School Information.

The search for appropriate new educational structures for the delivery of education to students in rural Newfoundland and Labrador has led to the development of school district digital intranets, within which virtual classes have been organised. The electronic linking of eight sites within the Vista school district (now part of the Western School District) to collaborate in the teaching of Advanced Placement Biology, Chemistry, Mathematics and Physics created a series of open classes in rural Newfoundland that became known as the Vista School District Digital Intranet. The creation of the Vista School District Digital Intranet was an attempt to use information and communication technologies to provide geographically isolated students with extended educational and, indirectly, vocational opportunities. It involved changing a closed teaching and learning structure into an open one. Accordingly, administrative and academic adjustments had to be made in each participating site so that Advanced Placement classes could be taught. The Vista school district initiative challenged the notion that senior students in small schools have to leave home to complete their education at larger schools in urban areas. By participating in open classes in real (synchronous) time, combined with a measure of independent (asynchronous) learning, senior students were able to interact with one another through audio, video and electronic whiteboards. From time to time they also met for social occasions and to engage with their science teachers in person.

Advanced Placement courses for e-learners in rural Canadian schools

Advanced Placement (AP) courses enable senior students to begin undergraduate degrees, with part of their program completed from high school if their AP courses are passed at grade levels specified by the universities of their choice. AP web-based courses in Biology, Chemistry, Mathematics and Physics were developed by a four-person team in each subject area. A lead science teacher in each discipline was paired with a recent graduate in each of the disciplines of Biology, Chemistry, Mathematics and Physics who possessed advanced computer skills, including web-page design, Java and HTML. The lead teacher and the graduate assistant were advised from time to time by Faculty of Education specialists at Memorial University of Newfoundland in each curriculum area and, where possible, scientists from the Faculty of Science; however, most course development took place through interaction between the lead teachers and the graduate assistants. Although at times professors had different opinions as to the most appropriate approach to the design of the courses, this model enabled the four courses to be developed over a sixteen-week summer recess period in time for the new school year. Minimum specifications were adopted for computer hardware and network connectivity. All schools involved in the project had DirecPC satellite dishes installed to provide a high-speed downlink. In most rural communities in this part of Canada, digital telecommunications infrastructure does not enable schools to have a high-speed uplink to the internet. Appropriate software had to be identified and evaluated for both the development of the resources and the delivery of instruction within the intranet. FrontPage 98 was selected as the software package. Additional software was used for the development of images, animated graphics files and other dimensions of course development. These included SnagIt/32, GIF Construction Set, Real Video, and similar packages. Many software packages were evaluated and finally WebCT was selected. This package enabled the instructor to track student progress; it contained online testing and evaluation, private e-mail, a calendar feature, a public bulletin board for use by both instructor and student, and a link to lessons and chat rooms for communication between teacher and student. For real-time instruction, MeetingPoint and Microsoft NetMeeting were selected. This combination of software enabled a teacher to present real-time interactive instruction to multiple sites. An orientation session was provided for students in June, prior to the implementation of this project in September. Students had to learn how to communicate with each other and with their instructor using these new technologies before classes could begin.

In eight schools within the rural Vista school district of Newfoundland and Labrador, fifty-five students were enrolled in AP Biology, Chemistry, Mathematics and Physics courses. While AP courses are a well-established feature of senior secondary education in the United States and Canada, it was unusual for students to be able to enrol for instruction at this level in small schools in remote communities. The advanced nature of these courses requires highly qualified and experienced teachers who are often difficult to attract and retain in small schools in rural communities. Furthermore, small rural schools, because of their size, have few students who are able to undertake instruction at this level. This initiative was significant for rural Canadian education in that it was, as far as can be ascertained, the first time courses at this level were delivered to students who would otherwise not have had access to them because of the size and location of their schools. By introducing AP subjects to small schools in a remote region of Canada, a step was taken toward inclusion of rural people in the emerging knowledge economy. Several graduates of this program were subsequently able to enrol in science and engineering faculties at the local university with a small part of their post-secondary program already completed. Perhaps more importantly, they entered universities with the knowledge that they could successfully compete academically with students anywhere in North America.

From closed to open teaching and learning environments at the regional level

The major change for students in the first digital intranet in Newfoundland and Labrador was the opportunity to study advanced science subjects and mathematics as members of open classes from their small, remote communities. Students in the Vista School District Digital Intranet were frequently subject to scrutiny by their peers as they responded to one another through chat rooms, audio and video, as well as with their AP online teacher. The digital intranet provided students with access to multiple sites simultaneously, as well as the opportunity to work independently of a teacher for part of the day. It became increasingly apparent to both teachers and students that they needed to prepare for classes before going online if the open, synchronous, science classes were to succeed. In future, interaction will be both synchronous and asynchronous.

The advent of the digital intranet had implications for both students and teachers. Many students experienced difficulty expressing themselves and, in particular, asking questions in open electronic classes when they did not know their peers from other small communities. The organisation of social occasions for these students, so they could get to know their intranet classmates, helped overcome these inhibitions. The e-teachers had little to guide their practice in teaching at this level for the first time. Each of the four AP science subjects was taught in a different way. For example, the physics and mathematics teachers had little need for video in their interactions with students, but access to electronic whiteboards was critical so that the development of equations and calculations could be managed interactively. For the e-teacher of chemistry, experimental work posed a problem because of the dispersed locations of the students. Videos of experiments that were to be conducted in person, at designated sites and pre-arranged times, were found to be useful in preparing students for the laboratory component of the AP course.

In an evaluation of the Advanced Placement experiment, rural students commented:

I have been introduced to one of the best teachers I have ever had.

This is a significant comment, made by a student about an online teacher who was only known at a distance. The highly esteemed teacher would not have been encountered by this student had it not been for the AP online development. This comment illustrates the possibility of providing rural students with expertise from other than local sources.

Students in the first year of online AP courses in the rural Canadian network were critical of the technical and organisational problems that were encountered. One student noted:

> I think these courses are valuable, but there was much confusion early in the year.

Other members of the class were critical of the delivery of AP courses within the initial network:

> The intranet is unreliable when communicating between numerous sites. There are some slow connections.

> More use of video would help so that we can see the teacher.

The experience of working at post-secondary school level through AP courses was not, until this development, available to students in small, rural high schools. The intellectual challenge for university-bound students was considered to be useful. One student advised:

> If you are planning on doing post-secondary education, do one of these [AP] courses.

Another student reported at the end of the school year:

> This course has exceeded all my expectations – I believe I have passed.

In the process of developing e-teaching and e-learning within digital intranets in rural Newfoundland and Labrador, teachers, learners and administrators had to adapt to a new, electronic, educational structure. In the open teaching and learning environment of a digital intranet, participating institutions academically and administratively interfaced for that part of the school day during which classes were taught. This was, for teachers and administrators, a very different educational structure from the traditional and, by comparison, closed educational environment of the autonomous school with its own teachers and its own students. There was potential conflict between the schools' dual roles as autonomous educational institutions, serving designated areas, and sites within electronic teaching and learning networks that, in effect, began to serve a much larger region. Principals and teachers appointed to the closed, autonomous learning environments of traditional schools frequently discovered that the administration of the intranet scheme required the development of open structures, within which they were increasingly expected to collaborate with their peers located on a range of distant sites. Many discovered that the positions to which they were appointed in traditional (closed) schools became, in effect, locations within new (open) electronic schools.

The need for increased technical support (Asher 2005) for the new, open structure became increasingly urgent for teachers and students who were using information and communication technologies to teach and learn across dispersed sites. Both had to be provided with expert advice and instruction in the use of new applications. A particular problem that emerged was difficulty in securing and maintaining instructional design expertise in the preparation and upgrading of courses, although this issue is common in the development of online courses at high school level (Sweeney 2005). An essential aspect of the development of open electronic classes was the coordination of both hardware and software between schools. Without synchronised technology, schools cannot fully participate in electronic networks. However, the purchase of appropriate hardware and software was initially a matter of confusion for many principals, teachers and school boards, who had to seek expert advice and support. Many rural schools with open electronic classes realised that the successful administration of a network required shared local technical support. Unless adequate technical support systems could be established, electronically networked classes could, potentially, be curtailed by teachers who argued, with justification, that there was insufficient technical support for their investment in e-learning. While there were doubts by some teachers and administrators about the adequacy and robustness of the technology that was available, the solutions that were sought and the infrastructure that was implemented were at the regional rather than local school district level.

The changes that took place in the closed learning spaces of traditional rural schools in Newfoundland and Labrador with the introduction of a digital intranet and AP instruction online led to a ministerial inquiry into the implications of these developments for the future of rural education in the province. The provincial government, after a ministerial inquiry (Government of Newfoundland and Labrador 2000) expanded the linking of schools through the creation of the Centre for Distance Learning and Innovation (CDLI) within the Newfoundland and Labrador Department of Education. CDLI (http://www.cdli.ca/) develops and administers online learning that complements traditional classes in schools throughout the province. Since its inception it has considerably extended e-learning throughout Newfoundland and Labrador.

Pedagogy for e-learning

Pedagogy includes "the complexity of relational, personal, moral and emotional, aspects of teachers' everyday acting with children or young people they teach." (Van Manen 2002). Teaching in classrooms that are electronically linked to other sites requires different lesson preparation and delivery skills from teaching face to face. For teacher–student interaction in a new electronic structure to be effective, the strengths and weaknesses of the new regional environment have to be understood by everyone who participates. Audio-graphic networking has in the recent past provided schools participating in regional electronic networks with a simple and flexible way of accommodating the diverse needs of learners. Although open internet-based classrooms may not suit the needs of all students, they provide rural schools with choice in the way they can access educational and, in particular, curriculum opportunities. The student's need to concentrate on the audio lesson to fully participate in it when conducted in an open electronic class between several sites was noted by several participating schools in earlier research in New Zealand (Stevens 1994). Students cannot anticipate when they will be asked a question over the audio network, something that encourages preparation for classes conducted with teachers and peers who are not physically present (Stevens 1998).

Students often have more independence in managing their learning in open electronic classes, but most have to be assisted by teachers in the setting of goals, the meeting of deadlines and in evaluating their progress. Teachers are effective in open electronic classes if they can be flexible in the ways in which they enable students to participate in online lessons. Strategies and protocols for online teaching have to be developed between participating schools if all students are to be able to fully participate. The introduction of a rural school to an open electronic network considerably improves its resource base for both teachers and learners but does not solve all of its problems. A considerable measure of inter-institutional and intra-institutional cooperation is required to develop detailed and effective plans for collaboration. Two new educational professionals have emerged in Newfoundland and Labrador since the Ministerial Inquiry (Government of Newfoundland and Labrador 2000): e-teachers and m-teachers. E-teachers teach classes across a growing range of dispersed sites through the internet, administered by CDLI. These teachers were initially supported at each of the sites within their region by mediating teachers (m-teachers). M-teachers were usually traditional classroom teachers, providing instruction face-to-face in small schools in rural parts of the province. They liaised with e-teachers about issues on-site that e-learners faced in their courses. Subsequently m-teachers were replaced by m-teams through which on-site technical, pedagogical and personal support was provided. In some rural Newfoundland and Labrador high schools that receive e-learning through CDLI, the principal and all teachers are the m-team that support both e-teachers and their students.

There are several immediate pedagogical challenges to be considered for effective teaching in a digital intranet. Teaching face-to-face and online are different skills and teachers need to adapt their practice accordingly. This is fundamental to the success of e-teaching. Teachers have to learn to teach collaboratively with colleagues from multiple sites and have to judge when it is appropriate to teach online and when it is appropriate to teach students in traditional face-to-face ways. These judgments have to be defended on the basis of sound pedagogy.

Conclusion

The introduction of e-learning at the K-12 level has provided teachers, administrators and, most of all, students with extended teaching and learning options (Dell 2005, Hawkes and Halverson 2002). In Newfoundland and Labrador, as in New Zealand, a new type of rural education has emerged. An open model now challenges the closed model of schooling by questioning the need for appointing all teachers to schools, rather than to networks of schools. It questions the appropriateness of learners engaging solely with their peers within their own physical classrooms, and it questions the notion of the school as an autonomous institution. Awareness that the school is potentially a site within an extended electronic network, which can function at the regional rather than local level, has economic implications. The school district digital intranet's economic contribution to Atlantic Canada is its demonstration that local intellectual resources can be shared between sites, enabling collaborating institutions to provide opportunities for students that would not otherwise be available to them. By developing collaborative pedagogy between electronically integrated learning institutions, small schools in both Atlantic Canada and New Zealand have contributed to regional knowledge economies by providing templates for other sparsely populated areas of the world.

References

Asher, G. (2005). Inadequate infrastructure and the infusion of technology into K-12 education. In C. Howard, J.V. Boettcher, L. Justice, K. Schenk, P.L. Rogers & G.A. Berg, (Eds.). *Encyclopedia of distance learning.* Hershey, Idea Group Reference. pp. 1061-1063.

Ben-Jacob, M.G., Levin, D.S. & Ben-Jacob, T.K. (2000).The learning environment of the 21st century. *Educational Technology Review.* 13. pp. 8-12.

Dell, L.A.B. (2005). Connecting K-12 schools in higher education. In C. Howard, J.V. Boettcher, L. Justice, K. Schenk, P.L. Rogers & G.A. Berg (Eds.). *Encyclopedia of distance learning.* Hershey, Idea Group Reference. pp. 374-378.

Department of Education of Newfoundland and Labrador (2006). *Education statistics – elementary – secondary 2005-2006 school information.* http://www.ed.gov.nl.ca/edu/publications/k12/0506/SCH_05_2.PDF

Dorniden, A. (2005). K-12 schools and online learning. In C. Howard, J.V. Boettcher, L. Justice, K. Schenk, P.L. Rogers & G.A. Berg (Eds.). *Encyclopedia of distance learning.* Hershey, Idea Group Reference. pp. 1182-1188.

Ertl, H. & Plante, J. (2004). *Connectivity and Learning in Canada's Schools.* Ottawa, Statistics Canada, Government of Canada.

Glick, D.B. (2005). K-12 online learning policy. In C. Howard, J.V. Boettcher, L. Justice, K. Schenk, P.L. Rogers & G.A. Berg (Eds.). *Encyclopedia of distance learning.* Hershey, Idea Group Reference. pp. 1175-1181.

Government of Newfoundland and Labrador (2000). *Supporting learning: report on the ministerial panel on educational delivery in the classroom.* St John's, NL, Department of Education.

Hawkes, M. & Halverson, P. (2002).Technology facilitation in the rural school: an analysis of options. *Journal of Research in Rural Education.* 17, 3. pp. 162-170.

Healey D. & Stevens K. (2002). Student access to information technology and perceptions of future opportunities in two small Labrador communities. *Canadian Journal of Learning and Technology / La Revue Canadienne de l'Apprentissage et de la Technologie.* 28, 1. pp. 7-18.

Information Highway Advisory Council (1997). *Preparing Canada for a digital world.* Ottawa, Industry Canada.

Schrum, L. (2005). E-Learning and K-12. In C. Howard, J.V. Boettcher, L. Justice, K. Schenk, P.L. Rogers & G.A. Berg (Eds.). *Encyclopedia of distance learning.* Hershey, Idea Group Reference. pp. 737-742.

Stevens, K.J. & Stewart, D. (2005). *Cybercells – Learning in actual and virtual groups.* Melbourne: Thomson-Dunmore Press.

Stevens, K. (2002). Minnkandi heimur – Rafrænt net smárra skóla – Óvænt tengsl Íslenska menntanetsins við Nýja Sjáland og Kanada (Making the world smaller – the electronic networking of small schools – some unseen connections of the Icelandic educational network in New Zealand and Canada). *Skólavarðan*. 2, 2. pp. 22-24. [Icelandic translation by Karl Erlendsson]

_____(2001). The development of digital intranets for the enhancement of education in rural communities. *Journal of Interactive Instruction Development*. 13, 3. pp. 19-24.

_____(2000). Télé-enseignement et éducation en milieu rural en Nouvelle Zélande et à Terre Neuve. *Géocarrefour – Revue de Geographie de Lyon – Espaces Ruraux et Technologies de L'Information*. 75, 1. pp. 87-92.

_____(1999a). A new model for teaching in rural communities – the electronic organisation of classes as intranets. *Prism – Journal of the Newfoundland and Labrador Teachers' Association*. 6, 1. pp. 23-26.

_____(1999b). Telecommunications technologies, telelearning and the development of virtual classes for rural New Zealanders. *Open Praxis*. 1.

_____(1998). The management of intranets: some pedagogical issues in the development of telelearning. In A. Higgins (Ed.). *Best practice, research and diversity in open and distance learning*. Distance Education Association of New Zealand, Rotorua, New Zealand. pp. 279-286.

_____(1994). Some applications of distance education technologies and pedagogies in rural schools in New Zealand. *Distance Education*. 15, 4.

Stevens, K., Sandalov A., Sukhareva, N., Barry, M. & Piper, T. (1999). The development of open models for teaching physics to schools in dispersed locations in Russia and Canada. In V. Grementieri, A. Szucs & V.I. Trukhin (Eds.). *Information and communication technologies and human resources development: new opportunities for European co-operation*. European Distance Education Network, Budapest, Hungary, October 1999. pp. 148-154.

Sweeney, C. (2005). Critical barriers to technology in K-12 education. In C. Howard, J.V. Boettcher, L. Justice, K. Schenk, P.L. Rogers & G.A. Berg (Eds.). *Encyclopedia of distance learning*. Hershey, Idea Group Reference. pp. 481-482.

Van Manen, M. (2002). The pedagogical task of teaching. *Teaching and Teacher Education*. 18, 2. pp. 135-138.

Tella S. (1995). *Virtual school in a networking learning environment*. Helsinki, University of Helsinki, Department of Teacher Education.

HUMAN DEVELOPMENT, PSYCHOLOGY AND EDUCATION

Diversity, Development and Educational Psychology: Keeping Social Justice on the Agenda

Lise Bird Claiborne

The dissolution of education studies at Victoria University came quickly. Change is inevitable, yet perhaps what is surprising is that the department survived as a coherent grouping for so long. This chapter represents something of a personal journey about my experiences in education over nearly three decades of almost continual social change in Aotearoa, a journey both historical and autobiographical. It is also a tribute to some of the inspiring colleagues and students with whom I worked at Victoria.

Fortunately there is more theoretical credibility these days for an approach that includes authoethnographic detail, since the work of memory has become increasingly important in a world where much terror and joy has been experienced without testimony. Parallel to enormous social changes in Aotearoa, my work in the department changed from demarcated concerns about cognitive development, gender and motivation and big questions about educational structures and social justice, to a more passionately interconnected exploration of discourses around difference, diversity and development. The wider purpose of such a '4D' viewpoint is to consider possibilities for transformation in our lives, taking a wide-angle view of education, given support by collaborative research and teaching in diverse alliances. Each decade has seen considerable movement in the areas of diversity and social justice in education. In the years from 1979 to 2008, there were enormous changes in the whole landscape of education in New Zealand that were reflected in the department's programme of teaching and research. Taking a key narrative from human development, a chronological account of these trends is given below to illustrate this journey.

Feminism and the 1980s

I had been caught up by the second wave of the feminist movement that crashed onto Australian shores in the 1970s. There I had met two New Zealand women who, homesick but not intending to return, assured me that this country was far less matey and masculine than Australia. I was keen to find a place where my renewed interest in development and gender could blossom and I would not have to spend the rest of my days on laboratory studies or scaled tests.

When I arrived in the Department of Education at Victoria in 1979, I joined a staff of twelve, all but one of whom were Pākehā men. I understood that one professor considered that the appointment of two women to the department had been two too many; this ratcheted up my interest in feminism by several notches. Though I was only the second woman given a permanent appointment in the department (after Jane Kroger), earlier Fanaafi Ma'ia'i had been a lecturer who had made quite an impact there before returning to university work in Samoa; she helped to seed a concern with cultural matters that was to be so important in later decades.

I came to Victoria from postdoctoral work at the University of Wisconsin after earlier research in developmental psychology at Macquarie University and doctoral work in cognitive psychology at the Australian National University. Rather than follow the 'cognitive revolution', I had decided to return to work on childhood, focusing on metacognition and attributions about performance to add a socio-emotional side to the study of learning. From the 1970s there had been a lively debate about gender differences in attributions about learning: whether girls were less likely to think a recent personal success had been due to their own talents, for example, rather than effort or luck. I had read the work of John Nicholls, who had travelled from New Zealand to the US in the 1970s and become a leading researcher in achievement motivation, with an interest in groups of children differing by gender and ethnicity. Communications in those days were by post, and unreliable; only when I arrived in New Zealand did I realise that John was no longer here, and that in fact I was his replacement.[1] I was, however, impressed by the critically informed debates about education at the first New Zealand Association

---

1   Fortunately I was able to spend time with John at Purdue University on my first sabbatical, and kept in touch with him till his untimely death in 1994.

for Research in Education (NZARE) conference in Hamilton at the end of 1979; the bigger place given to cultural and gendered concerns convinced me that I had been right to move from psychology to education.

Academic life was very different in the 1980s, as it was a time when many women in their twenties, thirties and forties had decided to come to university despite leaving school much earlier. The ad eundem provisions that gave legal admittance to adults as 'mature entrants' were quite progressive internationally, though adults coming to study later often had to overcome the loss of confidence that so often attended their memories of failure at School Certificate, the dreaded gatekeeper Year 11 qualification. Many of these returning students were women with children – or men newly jobless from accident or redundancy – who headed to the first year Human Development course as their point of entry. As I understand the history,[2] this course had been on the books since Victoria's inception as a university, and was something of a flagship for the intertwining of education and care in the work of the department. This intertwining was evident in the fact that the university's sole lecturer in Nursing Studies, Bea Salmon, was based in the department. Apparently this conjunction of interests had long given the department the edge over psychology in covering the field of human development, including developmental psychology.

In the 1980s the university seemed to me more interwoven with the Wellington community than universities are today; coming to study at Victoria was a dominant activity for most women I was meeting in my local community (Brooklyn), and I was likely to be in the midst of or to overhear similar conversations about psychology, politics and feminism at a local café as at the university union. (This probably also reflects the very political environment that Wellington has always offered as the capital city.) As time went on, some students I had come to know took positions in government, non-governmental organisations or politics, influencing the policies and practices I was covering in my courses. When Gerald Grace took the Chair of Education in 1988, he turned the entire focus of the department towards educational policy, and asked me to concentrate on gender and education policy. This was, of course, right at the cusp of the *Tomorrow's Schools* changes, when the entire structure of education changed (New Zealand Department of Education 1988); to make some attempt to cover educational policy in this rapidly changing scene meant

---

2   I recall that this information came from Professor Reg Marsh.

that I sometimes called on former students working in government policy. Having been trained as a traditional academic, I felt quite nervous presenting information from oral sources in my classes; it felt as though I were simply passing on gossip, though most of the predictions proved to be accurate.[3]

I have never given up on psychology, particularly as New Zealand has long had lively intellectual input from feminist psychologists. The annual New Zealand Psychological Society conference was held at Victoria in 1981. As one of the programme directors for the conference, I worked to create a space for feminist work and presented some of my own Wellington-based work on boys' higher expectations of their performance (Bird 1981).

Throughout my career, a mainstay of my academic work has been the areas of developmental and educational psychology, particularly from a critical psychological perspective (e.g. Burman 2008).[4] This gave me the chance to consider many different areas of cognition of potential interest to feminist educators. I had the good fortune to co-supervise, with Geraldine McDonald, the doctoral thesis of Fay Panckhurst's (1989) Vygotskian-inspired work on young children's understanding of cartography. Though gender was not the focus of the research, I recall being fascinated by the different opportunities available culturally to girls and boys (e.g. the chance to navigate for a father in a driving job).

Because my training in psychology had emphasised the scientific foundations of the field,[5] during the 1980s I also became interested in the efforts of feminist educators to increase the numbers of girls studying science subjects and increasing the numbers of future women scientists.

---

3   In Aotearoa, oral sources are hugely important because change in a small country can happen far too quickly for written commentary (at least before the internet era).

4   I would like to pay tribute to the amazing students who took part in the postgraduate course on developmental and educational psychology that I ran for over twenty years. I learned a huge amount from students who have gone on to make their own contributions to the field; students such as Michael Carr-Gregg, Rita Chung, Ann Hendricks, Trevor McDonald, Bruce Nichols, Diane Mara, and many, many others; the work of few more will be mentioned below.

5   I felt comfortable in the 'scientist' identity even though I had experienced problems with the curriculum sequencing in my secondary education after my family migrated from the US to Australia. I had chosen psychology only after realising I did not (thankfully, in hindsight) have the prerequisites to become the globe-wandering, species-saving zoologist I had wanted to be.

There was a strong feminist influence on education and the labour market in general. For example, the 1984 Department of Labour campaign, 'Girls can do anything', was designed to get girls to take on a greater variety of jobs and economic roles. I joined CAWSE, a group of feminist educators interested in getting more girls into science, which included women science teachers and government scientists. Later I became a founding member of Women into Science Education (WISE). I spoke at the inaugural public meeting, presenting data from a study of high school students' drawings of scientists that had been collected by science teachers in the group. Most of these drawings showed only male scientists, though there were a couple of notable women: a witch mixing poison and a woman working in an illegal drug lab with a male 'hipi' (i.e., 'hippie') scientist. During those years four women in the WISE organising group (including Janet Davies, Robyn Baker, Ann Hodson and myself) created a curriculum resource celebrating famous New Zealand women in science (WISE 1989).

For some time I tried hard to bring social justice perspectives into what was then a rather positivist field of educational psychology. At the end of the 1980s, Deborah Willis and I received a Ministry of Education grant to study learning, motivation and assessment in Year 10 science. We spent a fascinating time attending classes as participant observers, learning a great deal about student culture and gaining a tremendous respect for the energy and creativity of the teachers involved. Like certain memories of my primary schooling, the lessons I observed have stayed with me more firmly than most of my own secondary school education. We did find some troubling gendered patterns in anticipated career choices, with many girls opting for more low-level professional choices in their preferred future (e.g., pharmacy assistant rather than chemist).

Several projects by thesis students in the 1980s indicated the swing of policy concerns of that time towards acknowledgement of feminist concerns. Andrea Scott's (1991) master's thesis explored the experiences of Year 10 girls in a co-educational school in trial girls-only science classes. While the quantitative achievements of the girls-only classes revealed few differences to those in mainstream co-ed classes, the transcripts of the classes were qualitatively different, with girls in the former classes expressing more enthusiasm about their study. In 1989, I began teaching Victoria's first course on gender and education. It seems hard to believe now, but at that time advocacy for girls' concerns in core education classes – such as happened in the first year 'education and society' course around that time – could be met with angry call-outs from boys. The third year Gender and Education course was quickly filled with women of strong opinion and men who were either supportive or determinedly sceptical. I remember the shouts of several women when a male student, a mathematics teacher, expressed his view that 'girls can't do maths'. It was not long, though, before I, like many feminist educators of that time, became disenamoured with a focus solely on gender that ignored the diversity among women and among men.

Interweaving feminist and cultural questions in the 1990s

In the 1990s the concerns about gender became more subtle, especially as the intersections of gender, class, culture and sexuality became important internationally. Perhaps a culmination of the work on the educational opportunities for girls came about the time of Helen Leahy's (1996) MEd thesis that recounted the history of the 'women and education' policies and structures at what is now the Ministry of Education. Since the Ministry's policy unit was disbanded in 1993, this thesis became an epitaph for an extraordinary series of educational achievements that opened many doors for girls and women in New Zealand, opportunities that are now so often taken for granted.

Indigenous issues were building in importance during the 1980s. Donna Awatere's (1984) wake-up call raised questions about the cultural inclusiveness of our teaching programmes. The sesquicentennial year of 1990 saw Pākehā struggling to put indigenous concerns at the front, not the margins, of university work. Some Māori students asked that the Treaty of Waitangi be emphasised in the initial curriculum statement for every course. Like many staff, I had keenly searched for some time for Māori writings to include in the curriculum for human development and educational psychology courses. There was a hunger amongst many Pākehā staff for more academic writing from Māori that could be included in course readings to direct the curriculum and concerns of students in education. It was hard, however, to find formal writing, and staff often relied on speech notes and more popular written accounts.[6] My own learning was greatly expanded through the opportunity to teach the Gender and Education course with Everdina Fuli (Ngati Porou, Ngati

---

6   Eventually I learned that Māori colleagues could be more up to date with recent changes in policy and educational change after a single hui than I was after weeks of academic work tracking down obscure documents.

Kahungunu, Te Whakatohea, Nga Puhi, Tokelau, Tuvalu, Cook Islands), Kathie Irwin (Ngati Porou, Rakaipaaka, Ngati Kahungunu), Joanna Kidman (Te Arawa, Te Aupouri), Sarah Acland and Carol Hamilton. The attention paid to the aspirations of wahine toa (strong women) grounded the course in Aotearoa while still holding open a place for a great diversity of experiences of students in the course. While there was acknowledgement of the important place of Māori women as mothers, there was also recognition of greater acceptance of sexual diversity (e.g. same-sex relationships) in pre-colonial times.

This diversity opened a space for a range of amazing women to bring their knowledge to the course. Samoan students explored the cultural traditions of fa'afafine and the virginal taupo in traditional fa'a Samoa. Christian, Jewish and Muslim students talked about their differences and common experiences of subjugation in male-dominant cultures. I learned much about gender as a culturally constructed form of identity from Francesca Costa's (2005) masterate work telling the history of southern Italian women from the island of Stromboli who had migrated to a rather inhospitable pakeha New Zealand in the mid-20th century. This had surprising resonances with Sheur-er Tu's (1998) doctoral work on limited opportunities for women in Taiwan due to structural inequalities in the state examination system. These experiences led me to the foregrounding of fluid, complex intersections of difference as the new millennium rolled into view.

Intersections in the new millennium

In the late 1990s a conjunction of several staff held the promise of an exciting course on difference and diversity in education, taking work on gender and education further to read diversity into every aspect. The possibility emerged, in the reshaping and expansion of specialties in the Master of Education, to bring together both policy and practice concerns about gender and education with the queer pedagogies course run by Shane Town. Sadly, Shane's untimely death in 2000 and other complexities of the work situation meant that the full promise of the course was in jeopardy. The Difference and Diversity in Education course eventually emerged, however, with Shane as its kaitiaki.[7] The course examined social justice

---

7   I am borrowing this indigenous term referring to a spiritual mentor or guide because
     Shane's contribution continued in time as though he were still with us.

implications for education at the intersection of gender, sexuality, culture and disability (see Bird 2004). Many intersections in the course were embodied by Karl Pallotta-Endemann, who lectured to rapt students early in the 2000s on the complexities of fa'afafine (a third gender of boys brought up as girls) understandings within fa'a Samoa (Samoan cultural traditions).

The field of 'diversity' was becoming normative by the mid-1990s, though courses at that time tended to cover the triumvirate of class/race/ gender as separate topics, as illustrated in many textbook titles of that decade. For some time I had been interested in normative ideas about students' appearances and capacities, which stemmed from theoretical interest in Michel Foucault's (e.g. 1975) work on discourses around normalisation. For this reason I looked for a way to integrate disability perspectives with more commonly covered areas of difference and identity, though there were few models available. Politically in Aotearoa, there were emerging problems with the *Special Education 2000* policy (Ministry of Education 1998) well before the millennium. There were huge tensions between medical discourses, which constructed special education approaches using the language of diagnoses and syndromes, and the growing 'inclusion' movement, which attempted to focus more on the ecology of the classroom and supports for students with a diversity of learning strengths and gaps (see Moore et al. 1999). My teaching at Victoria had become similarly bifurcated between psychological approaches in development and more culturally oriented social justice views of education. There seemed to be an unworkable split between social justice implications, drawing on post-structural theories, and critical perspectives on the psychology of human development and educational psychology. Fortunately more theoretically sophisticated critical perspectives in psychology had finally become more visible internationally.

To go back a step in order to see psychology from a wider historical vantage, it has been interesting to see the rise, fall and second coming of educational psychology during my time at Victoria. Though educational psychology had been popular in the middle of the 20th century (e.g. Parkyn 1948), by the 1980s there was considerable neo-Marxist influence on educational critique in this country. The field of educational psychology, with its traditions of psychological testing (particularly for that class-mired topic, IQ testing), was seen as irrelevant, even repugnant, and many courses were removed from compulsory options for teacher trainees. The field was sometimes described as taking far too narrow a view of the individual student in an era that was seeing more holism ascribed to Māori viewpoints in development and learning (cf. Pere 1991). Four of my colleagues had, in differing ways, wider critical views linking educational psychology to pressing social problems such as truancy (David Galloway), what would now be called disability studies (David and Valerie Harvey) and student assessment (Cedric Hall). In recent times there has been a resurgence of interest in educational psychology, with greater interest in cognition rather than simply 'learning', perhaps connected to the popular interest in 'brain science' for its predictions about educational achievement. One of my research interests has been in educational psychologists' social constructions of students' selves (e.g. their capabilities) in an era of rapidly changing biotechnologies (Bird 2005, 2006a, 2006b).

I remain somewhat sceptical of promises that might be made about predictions for individual students based on empirical models that elide their own cultural and historical location. Over time I have maintained connections with feminist psychology colleagues asking critical post-structuralist questions about topics such as violence against women (e.g. Nicola Gavey and Mandy Morgan). The vision of a more local, critically oriented view of developmental psychology provided part of the impetus behind my involvement, with Wendy Drewery, in creating textbooks covering development over the entire human lifespan that were centred in the cultural complexities of this country (e.g. Bird and Drewery 2000, Claiborne and Drewery 2009). I was initially reluctant to get involved in textbook writing; however I was convinced by the arguments of editor Max Loveridge and University of Otago colleague John Morss that students needed to hear local knowledge about human development from voices based in Aotearoa. That is one reason that Wendy and I added contributions from a range of commentators speaking directly about their research on contemporary difficulties in development over a range of ages and research problems.

As I continued to struggle to bring together my split personality – psychology with a social justice flavour – in the late 1990s I learned much about the groundbreaking possibilities from an amazing conjunction of doctoral students who went far beyond universal stages in theorising human development. AnneMarie Tupuola's (1998) work on Samoan identity explored young women's own identity constructions that ranged from 'New Zealander' to 'Niu Sila Samoan'. Susan Watson (2000) took a post-modern look at identity questions for students in a girls-only secondary school, finding difficult issues encountered in the realms of racism and sexism, played out around appearance norms. Shane Town (1998) examined his own cultural positioning on developmental and social questions about the construction of sexuality and identity in Aotearoa, through young gay men's recollections of their often harrowing experiences of secondary school in rural New Zealand. All of these research projects put gender/sexuality concerns into new cultural and social configurations in the stories of young people's lives.

I was heavily involved in postgraduate administration from the mid-1990s, inspired by three Deans in particular: Professors Hugh Lauder, Adrienne Alton-Lee and Helen May. The combining of strengths across two educational institutions gave the Victoria education department much more visibility and also, as a key part of an entire faculty, much more clout than it had had as an often overlooked member of the former Arts Faculty. After 2000, I worked with thesis students committed to examining social change in their studies through examination of their own professional practice. Gillian Tasker (2001) examined examples of effective practice of professional development for teachers working to improve secondary students' understanding of HIV and AIDS. Later two women used reflection on their past professional experience in youth justice to rethink future practice around gender, development and psychology. Alison Sutherland (2006) interviewed a range of young women and men who had committed offences, to consider ways that educators might have contributed to their difficulties and could, alternatively, help to make changes in their lives. Shirley Roberson Grace, a former clinical psychologist working with young offenders in Australia, focused on young New Zealand men who had been incarcerated for violent offending, exploring both their own visions of masculinities, and the psychological discourses which maintain a certain kind of masculinity that has contradictory positions about violence (2008).[8] Again, these projects all focused in some way on the lives of young people of secondary school age, but also on the effectiveness of 'interventions' by teachers and psychologists working with young people. So, in effect, the developmental focus was on adult professionals' inter-

---

8   I should also mention here related masterate work by Fiona Beals exploring young women offenders in the justice system.

generational communication with young people. Looking at development in a setting of incarceration challenged many norms about success and resiliency. The topics of these theses also illustrate significant difficulties facing young people in Aotearoa in recent times.

Beyond the justice/science split

It is perhaps most difficult to see present times in any historical context. Yet it seemed that during 2006 there were emergent possibilities for work that would bring social justice perspectives to human development and educational psychology into a fruitful interweaving. The Difference and Diversity course went '3D', as we strove to question the universal, normative models of developmental psychology (the third 'D') with the voices (and silences) of difference. After the arrival of counselling lecturer Sue Cornforth in 2004, we shared postgraduate teaching on development and counselling to include discursive examples and exercises; through this work, students who were educators, counsellors, government trainers or administrators began to question and revise their current frameworks for professional practice. With the changed departmental structure of the College of Education in 2007, there was a clear separation between concerns about social justice and research knowledge in educational psychology and human development: staff with whom I had worked for some time had to choose between one of two teaching groups – educational policy or educational psychology. Though I could see that eventually the cross-currents between the two areas that I have discussed above – the result of considerable reflection on practice over some decades by so many people – would once again come together, I did not feel I had the time to wait.

I have always preferred the riskier rapids of ongoing debate to the smooth flow of more settled ideas, which perhaps reflects a generational position for those of us who came to politics in the 1980s. Enormous changes in New Zealand in the past few decades affected the Department of Education at Victoria University perhaps as much as any other place, as academics worked with students to make sense of the past and consider possibilities for a more socially just future. I am quite certain that work will continue.

References

Awatere, D. (1984). *Māori sovereignty*. Auckland: Broadsheet.

Bird, L. (1981). *Are there sex differences in children's expectations and attributions about memory?* Paper presented to the NZ Psychological Society conference, Victoria University of Wellington, August.

Bird, L. Claiborne (2004). A queer diversity: teaching difference as interrupting intersections. *Canadian Online Journal of Queer Studies in Education.* 1, 1. Retrieved at http://jqstudies.oise.utoronto.ca/ journal/viewissue.php?id=1

Bird, L. Claiborne (2005). Ditching dualisms: education professionals view the future of technology and disabilities. *Disability Studies Quarterly.* 25, 3. Online at http:// www.dsq-sds.org/2005_summer_toc.html

Bird, L. (2006a). Beyond readiness: New questions about cultural understandings and developmental appropriateness. In Joseph L. Kincheloe & Raymond A. Horn, Jr. (Eds.). and Shirley R. Steinberg (Assoc. Ed.) *The Praeger handbook of education and psychology.* Westport, CT: Praeger. pp. 428-438.

Bird, L. Claiborne (2006b). New ways of speaking about life beyond bodies. *New Zealand Journal of Disability Studies.* 12. pp.119-131.

Bird, L. & Drewery, W. (2000). *Human development in Aotearoa.* Sydney: McGraw-Hill.

Burman, E. (2008). *Deconstructing developmental psychology.* (2nd Ed.). London: Routledge.

Claiborne, L. & Drewery, W. (2009) *Human development: family, place, culture.* Sydney: McGraw-Hill.

Costa, F. (2005). Le strombolane (women of Stromboli): education and ethnic identity of women from southern Italian descent in New Zealand. MA Thesis. Victoria University of Wellington.

Department of Education (1988). *Tomorrow's schools: the reform of education administration in New Zealand.* Wellington: Government Printer.

Foucault, M. (1975). *The birth of the clinic: an archaeology of medical perception.* New York: Vintage. [French translation by A.M.S. Smith]

Grace, S. (2008). (Re) thinking young men's violence: a discursive critique of dominant constructions. PhD Thesis. Victoria University of Wellington.

Leahy, H.M. (1996). Focusing on a faultline: gender and education policy development in Aotearoa New Zealand, 1975 to 1995. MEd Thesis. Victoria University of Wellington.

Moore, D., Anderson, A., Timperley, H., Macfarlane, A. Glynn, T., Brown, and Thomson, C. (1999). *Caught between stories: special education in New Zealand.* Wellington: New Zealand Council for Educational Research.

Panckhurst, F. (1989). Acquisition of cartography in preschool children. PhD Thesis. Victoria University of Wellington.

Parkyn, G. (1948). *Children of high intelligence, a New Zealand study.* Wellington: New Zealand Council for Educational Research.

Pere, R.R. (1991). *Te wheke: a celebration of infinite wisdom.* Gisborne: Ao Ako Global Learning New Zealand.

Scott, A. (1991). A girls-only science class in a co-educational secondary school. MA Thesis. Victoria University of Wellington.

Sutherland, A. (2006). From classroom to prison cell: young offenders' perception of their school experience. PhD Thesis. Victoria University of Wellington.

Tasker, G. (2001). Students' experience in an HIV/AIDS-sexuality education programme: what they learnt and the implications for teaching and learning in health education. PhD Thesis. Victoria University of Wellington.

Town, S. (1998). Is it safe to come out now? Sexuality and the education of ten young gay men. PhD Thesis. Victoria University of Wellington.

Tu, S.-E. (1998). Women in higher education in Taiwan: opportunities and barriers. PhD Thesis. Victoria University of Wellington.

Tupuola, A. M. (1998). 'Adolescence': myth or reality for 'Samoan' women? Beyond the stage-like toward shifting boundaries and identities. PhD Thesis. Victoria University of Wellington.

Watson, S. (2000). Gender and choice: girls, single sex schooling and school choice. PhD Thesis. Victoria University of Wellington.

WISE (1989). *New Zealand scientists: pioneer women*. Wellington: Women into Science Education (WISE) and the Department of Scientific and Industrial Research.

Adolescent Identity Development: Implications for Teaching and Counselling

Jane Kroger

When I first arrived at Victoria University in July 1977, basic research on adolescent development in New Zealand was virtually non-existent. While early childhood had been a strong focus of both research interest and application prior to this time, attention to adolescent development arose only gradually through the 1970s, as training programmes for both school psychologists and school counsellors were implemented throughout the country. Over the next decades, the importance of adolescent development and its implications for teaching and counselling practice became more apparent. In this chapter, I will overview some of the basic research on adolescent development that was undertaken during the time of my tenure in the School of Education at Victoria University of Wellington (VUW), and then turn my attention more specifically to the issue of adolescent identity development and its implications for teaching and counselling. I will also comment on the role that the School of Education played in promoting an interest in adolescent development among New Zealand educators.

Research on adolescent development in New Zealand

While universities in New Zealand did offer courses on adolescent development from the early 1970s onwards, research in New Zealand on normative issues of adolescent development was very limited. The mid 1970s saw the publication of R.A.C. Stewart's two volume edited series, *Adolescence in New Zealand* (1976a, 1976b). These volumes were among the first works devoted to an understanding of adolescent development in the country. My own work on adolescent self-concept and relationships began in the 1980s (e.g. Kroger 1982, 1983, 1985), and my later work on identity is reviewed below. In the 1990s, New Zealand education researchers became more interested in such topics as adolescent suicide, drug and alcohol use, and other mental disorders and problem behaviours among adolescents. By this time, those who had participated in both the Christchurch and Dunedin longitudinal growth studies were now in their teens, and adolescent research data was published on these topics (e.g. Fergusson and Lynskey 1995, Fergusson, Lynskey and Horwood 1994, Feehan, McGee and Williams 1993, Feehan et al. 1994). However, research on more normative issues of adolescent development was rare; work by Paterson, Field and Pryor (1994), for example, was among the few studies to examine age changes in adolescents' perceptions of attachment to parents and peers. Work on adolescent development in minority group contexts was in its infancy (e.g. Tupuola 1993).

Adolescent identity development: the identity status model

During the 1970s, 1980s and 1990s, research on adolescent identity development was becoming a topic of great interest in the United States, as several new journals of adolescent development carried frequent work on issues related to adolescent identity formation. I became interested, in particular, in the work of James Marcia (1966, 1967, Marcia et al. 1993) who had expanded Erikson's 1968 model of identity development to describe different styles of the processes by which adolescents undertook (or not) the identity formation process. These styles of identity formation became the focus for my own research at VUW, as I explored patterns of identity development over time and events associated with the adolescent identity formation process.

Erikson's well-known volume *Identity, Youth and Crisis* (1968) was among the earliest theoretical works addressing the topic of adolescent identity and the identity formation process. Erikson defined identity in an interdisciplinary way. He believed that one's sense of identity was based on the interplay of one's biological givens, one's psychological needs, interests, and wishes within a social milieu. Thus, if all went well, identity provided one with a sense of sameness and continuity across time and place. Subjectively, there should be a feeling of well-being: "[Identity's] most obvious concomitants are a feeling of being at home in one's body, a sense of 'knowing where one is going', and an inner assuredness of anticipated recognition from those who count" (Erikson 1968, p. 165). Erikson (1968) described adolescence as the key time in which identity-defining decisions are usually made in the psychosocial task of "Identity vs. Role confusion". Such identity-defining decisions generally involved an adolescent's choice of a vocational direction and the adoption of social, spiritual, relational and sexual values.

Erikson (1968) described the identity formation process of adolescence as a slow process of ego growth, in which identifications of childhood become gradually replaced by a new configuration:

> Identity formation, finally, begins where the usefulness of identification ends. It arises from the selective repudiation and mutual assimilation of childhood identifications . . . in a new configuration, which in turn is dependent on the process by which a society identifies the young individual. (p. 159)

In Erikson's view, tentative crystallisations of identity occur during childhood; during adolescence, however, a new configuration of identity emerges in which these identifications of childhood are sifted, subordinated, and altered in order to produce a new identity structure.

Marcia (1966, 2007) elaborated Erikson's views of this process, and his identity status model has been a popular means of assessing the exploration and commitment dimensions of Erikson's identity formation concept. A recent search in the database Psycinfo, for example, revealed some 10,895 hits when the search terms "identity status and Marcia" were entered. Marcia (1966) described four different styles by which late adolescents and young adults undertake identity-defining decisions in vocational, ideological, relational and sexual domains:

1. Identity achievement refers to the construction of an identity following a time of exploration and evaluating alternative psychosocial roles and values on one's own terms.
2. The moratorium status captures the exploration process itself, as adolescents search and try to find meaningful roles and values that will serve as their framework for entering adult life.
3. The foreclosed identity status refers to the process of adopting an identity based on childhood identifications. Here, there is little or no meaningful adolescent exploration of identity-defining alternatives, but rather firm identity commitments are adopted based on parental values or those of significant others.
4. The diffuse identity status is characterised by little or no identity exploration and no attempt to make personally meaningful identity commitments.

Marcia's identity statuses are therefore observable phenomena linked to those underlying processes of ego growth described by Erikson. The initial identity formation process may begin either with diffusion, in which no significant identifications are made, or, more normatively, with foreclosure, in which tentative identifications with significant childhood figures occurs. These early positions (optimally, in Erikson's view) would then be followed by a time of identity exploration (moratorium) eventuating in the capacity to make identity-defining commitments. These commitments are based on a thoughtful integration of one's own interests and talents with the vocational and ideological offerings of one's surrounding social and cultural context (achievement). After an initial identity is formed, naturally occurring life cycle events will, in all probability, disequilibrate this identity configuration, necessitating one or more further identity re-formation processes further ahead in adult life (Erikson 1968, Stephen, Fraser and Marcia 1992).

My own work with Marcia's identity status model while in New Zealand explored developmental processes and events likely to be associated with identity status change during late adolescence. I undertook several longitudinal studies with students entering university and examined developmental patterns of change some two years later in both studies. In these studies, I was trying to learn more about the attachment patterns associated with youth who formed a sense of their own identity (i.e. became identity-achieved) compared with those who did not (i.e. remained foreclosed or diffuse). I found that late adolescents who were not securely attached to their parents at the beginning of my studies tended not to forge their own identities some two years later (Kroger and Haslett 1988, Kroger 1995). From additional retrospective studies, colleagues and I learned that when key demographic variables were held constant (age group, marital and parental status, and level of education), different patterns of identity development were associated with various lifestyle choices (Kroger and Haslett 1991). From this same work, we learned that exposure to new contexts and internal feelings of change were strongly linked with movement into moratorium and achievement statuses during late adolescence and young adulthood (Kroger and Green 1996).

Others have consistently found a number of interesting developmental patterns while undertaking research into adolescent identity status. For example, in a number of western countries, studies have continually found that large percentages of youths have not constructed a sense of their own identities as they complete their university educations. From identity status distributions found in some ten studies of identity status change, approximately 50 per cent of individuals remained in foreclosed or diffuse identity status as they left university and entered young adulthood. Given that adolescence is the time in which individuals are most directly engaged with the identity formation process (Erikson 1968), such results were surprising. They were even more surprising when one considers that university environments provide the types of conditions generally supportive of the late adolescent identity formation task (exposure to new people and ideas, tolerance for diversity, support for exploration of different identity-defining alternatives). Reasons for this phenomenon are likely diverse. They may be related to individual personality factors such as degree of openness to new experiences, degree of identification with parents and parenting, and the range of identity alternatives to which one is exposed, as well as social expectations and supports in the immediate interpersonal environment (Yoder 2000). Among individuals who do move from foreclosure positions, progress to moratorium and eventual identity achievement has been most common.

Implications of the identity theory for education

A number of researchers have suggested ways in which educational settings and curricula can be organised to facilitate identity development during adolescence. Marcia (1986) has commented generally on the importance within educational contexts of not forcing occupational or major life choices early. While such practices may be expedient as an institutional practice, the results are likely to be psychologically costly for maximising identity development. Indeed Hummel and Roselli (1983) found that among high school seniors, experiencing and working through crises in beliefs and values were more closely associated with successful academic achievement and the formation of identity than were making specific commitments to a career or ideology alone. Marcia (1986) noted further some problems with accelerated training professional programs at the tertiary level of education.

> In highly technological societies, the danger is that the education of persons becomes confused with the manufacture of products. Training becomes synonymous with education. If we want the most fully human professionals, then we must allow time for the study and exploration of ideas and values. (p. 29)

Again, research has supported this notion. In long-term, longitudinal research on gifted children, Zuo (2005) found a strong correlation between identity formation and adult achievement. These and related findings suggest the importance of a clearly established identity to life accomplishment. In the arena of career development, Vondracek and Skorikov (1997) have demonstrated the positive identity outcomes for students who were encouraged and supported in exploring and participating in a wide range of possible activities (both school and leisure).

Dryer (1994) has synthesised researches on both cognitive and identity development to describe examples of identity-enhancing curricula. He acknowledges how difficult it is for many schools to let their curricula be coordinated by theory; however, given the reality of student development, a school that takes advantage of what is known about how youth think and feel is far more likely to be a vital and effective one than a school that does not. Employing identity theory does not lower academic standards: rather, integrating identity theory with teaching practice has the potential to add a critical student-based dimension to the educational work of a well-trained faculty.

Dryer (1994) continued by noting how the work of Marcia (1966, Marcia et al. 1993) is based on the dimensions of exploration and commitment. This model of identity formation is highly compatible with approaches to intellectual development such as that of Piaget (1972), who stressed that knowledge equals activity, to analytical reasoning (e.g. Flavell 1977), to moral reasoning (Gilligan 1982, Kohlberg 1984), and to intellectual and ethical commitment (e.g. Kitchener 1984). While cognitive development in adolescence involves the capacity for abstract reasoning and hypothetical thinking, identity development is based on the capacity to imagine alternative identity possibilities and the ability to make commitments to future moral values and goals.

What would be the format of an identity-enhancing curriculum? Dreyer (1994) suggested that it would begin with the student feeling that his or her schoolwork represented a real investment of his or her talents and feelings. Assignments that offered students an opportunity to choose tasks that were in some way personally expressive and meaningful (as well as fun) would enable them to have a genuine sense of ownership of their work. A curriculum based on identity theory would facilitate the exploration of new ideas as well as possibilities for new behaviours and engagements; such a curriculum also would foster commitments to oneself, to a whole person able to develop and express personal talents and interests in the contexts of work, family life, friendship networks, neighbourhood and community settings.

> An effective educational curriculum based on identity theory thus is more than a set of cognitive lessons and skill practices. It offers chances to take risks, learn from one's mistakes, and be surrounded by sensitive people who care not only about the subject matter at hand but also about each student and his or her ability to act in a confident and wilful fashion (Dreyer 1994, p. 128).

In sum, an identity-enhancing curriculum fosters exploration, responsible choice, and self-determination by students. It promotes perspective-taking and inter-generational learning. It promotes the student's understanding of time and historical context. And an identity-enhancing curriculum promotes self-acceptance in a supportive interpersonal context.

Implications of identity statuses for counselling adolescents in educational settings

Marcia (1986, 1994) has written extensively on the implications of the identity statuses, and identity development more generally, in a counselling context. Identity development in a counselling context means participating with another person in the exploration process – of current difficulties, solutions tried and now abandoned, and of new alternatives. A difficult task for any individual is to make real-life commitments to untested new directions, and the relationship to the counsellor, in a protected and nurturing situation, is essential for the adolescent to begin new explorations.

Marcia (1986) also notes the importance of targeting individuals in specific identity statuses with appropriate interventions; awareness of an adolescent's likely identity status should enable more effective forms of intervention to be made. At the same time, such interventions should be undertaken only with the willingness and consent of the adolescents themselves. Adolescent foreclosures rarely come to the attention of counselling agents unless there has been some disruption in their lives. They are generally staying out of trouble, dependable, and free from serious psychopathology. Their identity choices have been made based upon identifications with significant others, and their steadfast commitments have been undertaken at the cost of avoiding personal growth. One of two approaches might be undertaken with foreclosures. The counsellor may adopt a crisis intervention strategy and assist the student to reinstitute the same coping mechanisms that were present before the crisis occurred. A second alternative would be to use the crisis situation as a time of opportunity to try to facilitate entry into a moratorium period. However, the counsellor should proceed only gradually and carefully, in order to deal with the adolescent's legitimate resistance in relinquishing the internalised parental values and standards that have been used to form a sense of self and self-esteem. Too hasty an approach may leave the adolescent feeling very depressed and possibly suicidal.

Marcia (1986, 1994) suggests that adolescents in a moratorium position are the most likely of all the identity statuses to seek counselling assistance. In the throes of this developmentally important task, those in a moratorium process need an active and supportive listener, but NOT someone who will attempt to take a position or 'rescue' the individual from alternatives under consideration. If that happens, the counsellor's usefulness ends, for the adolescent's conflicts then become external rather than internal, and the struggle elevates to one between adolescent and counsellor rather than within the adolescent herself. A Rogerian approach of active listening may best be employed with those struggling with important identity-defining issues. The moratorium process involves loss, and all loss is painful. However, in the case of identity development and reformulation, the pain is meaningful and important to further development.

Adolescents who are identity achieved are likely to seek assistance only in obtaining further information around specific issues, but unlikely to seek deeper counselling or therapeutic assistance (Marcia 1986, 1994). The identity diffuse are unlikely to seek counselling assistance. It is often concerned parents or teachers who seek assistance to deal with a youth who seems just to be 'wasting his time' or 'not living up to her potential'. There may be a range of reasons for adolescent diffusion and hence a range of adjustment difficulties and approaches that are appropriate. Some identity diffuse youth may require remedial work and more in depth psychotherapy than is appropriate in a school counselling context. Other 'playboy' or 'playgirl' diffusions may need assistance to recognise the consequences of their action (or inaction); the hope here would be that enough concern could be generated to help engage such youths in productive direction planning. In sum, counselling intervention work with individuals in specific identity statuses should be targeted in different ways to free those 'stuck' or 'struggling' in a developmental process so that they might move once again (Marcia 1994).

Contributions of the School of Education to adolescent identity development within New Zealand education.

The Victoria University School of Education generously facilitated my research and applied interests in the area of adolescent identity development. In 1992, I received financial and practical support from the School of Education, the Department of Continuing Education at VUW, the John Ilott Charitable Trust, the Roy MacKenzie Foundation and the Canadian Embassy to bring a number of international adolescent identity researchers to New Zealand to host a series of meetings devoted to an understanding of adolescent identity development, for educators, counsellors, university researchers, and the general public. For the general public sessions in both Auckland and Wellington, a lecture, 'The family's role in adolescent identity development' by Professor Harold Grotevant, University of Minnesota, proved very popular, and he also gave several radio interviews to raise the importance of this issue. Other popular meetings were 'Adolescent identity and mental health', a day-long meeting for school counsellors and educators, and 'Researches on adolescent identity formation', a day-long seminar for a research-oriented audience. Through this week-long series of meetings and events, the School of Education was instrumental in raising the importance of research on adolescence and its applications within the New Zealand context. I later edited a book, *Discussions on ego identity*, from the contributions and conversations of researchers during their time in the School of Education (Kroger 1993).

In conclusion: looking back

I left the School of Education in 1996 to further my teaching and research interests in Europe. My eighteen years with the School provided me with many important opportunities to contribute to university and community programs in education and human development. Those years also provided an important foundation to my research interests on adolescence and young adulthood that have continued in subsequent years. Despite my current geographic distance, I have returned to the

School of Education on several occasions for periods of sabbatical leave, both to renew friendships and to remain in contact with the new generation of researchers undertaking studies of adolescent life 'downunder'. I am pleased to contribute to this volume and to help leave a record of the important contributions that the School of Education has made to the field of education in New Zealand.

References

Dryer, P.H. (1994). Designing curricular identity interventions for secondary schools. In S.L. Archer (Ed.). *Interventions for adolescent identity development*. Newbury Park, CA: Sage, Inc. pp. 121-140.

Erikson, E.H. (1968). *Identity, youth and crisis*. New York: W.W. Norton.

Feehan, M., McGee, R. & Williams, S. M. (1993). Mental health disorders from age 15 to 18 years. *Journal of the American Academy of Child & Adolescent Psychiatry*. 32. pp. 1118-1126.

Feehan, M., Stanton, W., McGee, R. & Silva, P.A. (1994). A longitudinal study of birth order, help seeking and psychopathology. *British Journal of Clinical Psychology*. 33. pp. 143-150.

Fergusson, D.M., & Lynsky, M.T. (1995). Childhood circumstances, adolescent adjustment, and suicide in a New Zealand birth cohort. *Journal of the American Academy of Child & Adolescent Psychiatry*. 34. pp. 612-622.

Fergusson, D.M., Lynsky, M.T. & Horwood, L.J. (1994). Childhood exposure to alcohol and adolescent drinking patterns. *Addiction*. 89. pp. 1007-1016.

Flavell, J.H. (1977). *Cognitive development*. Englewood Cliffs, NJ: Prentice-Hall.

Gilligan, C. (1982). *In a different voice*. Cambridge, M.A.: Harvard University Press.

Hummel, R. & Roselli, L.L. (1983). Identity status and academic achievement in female adolescents. *Adolescence*. 18. pp. 17-27.

Kitchener, K.S. (1984). A longitudinal study of moral and ego development in young adults. *Journal of Youth and Adolescence*. 13. pp. 197-211.

Kohlberg, L. (1984). *The psychology of moral development: The nature and validity of moral stages*. New York: Harper & Row.

Kroger, J. (1982). Relationships during adolescence: A developmental study of New Zealand youths. *New Zealand Journal of Educational Studies*. 17. pp. 119-127.

_____ (1983). I knew who I was when I got up this morning: the transitions of adolescence. *SET Research Information for Teachers*. 1. Item 13.

_____ (1985). Relationships during adolescence: A cross-national comparison of New Zealand and United States teenagers. *Journal of Adolescence*. 8. pp. 47-56.

_____ (1993). (Ed.). *Discussions on ego identity*. Hillsdale, NJ: Lawrence Erlbaum Associates.

_____ (1995). The differentiation of firm and developmental foreclosure identity statuses: A longitudinal study. *Journal of Adolescent Research*. 10. pp. 317-337.

_____ (1993). *Discussions on ego identity*. Hillsdale, NJ: Lawrence Erlbaum Associates.

Kroger, J. & Green, K. (1996). Events associated with identity status change. *Journal of Adolescence*. 19. pp. 477-490.

Kroger, J. & Haslett, S.J. (1988). Separation-individuation and ego identity status in late adolescence: A two-year longitudinal study. *Journal of Youth and Adolescence*. 17. pp. 59-79.

Kroger, J. and Haslett, S.J. (1991). A comparison of ego identity status transition pathways and change rates across five identity domains. *International Journal of Aging and Human Development*. 32. pp. 303-330.

Marcia, J.E. (1966). Development and validation of ego identity status. *Journal of Personality and Social Psychology*. 3. pp. 551-558.

Marcia, J.E. (1967). Ego identity status: relationship to change in self-esteem, "general maladjustment," and authoritarianism. *Journal of Personality*. 35. pp. 118-133.

Marcia, J.E. (1986). Clinical implications of the identity status approach within psychosocial developmental theory. *Cadernos de Consulta Psicólogica*. 2. pp. 23-34.

Marcia, J.E. (1994). Identity and psychotherapy. In S. L. Archer (Ed.). *Interventions for adolescent identity development*. Newbury Park, CA: Sage, Inc. pp. 29-46.

Marcia, J.E. (2007). Theory and measure: the identity status interview. In Watzlawik, M. & Born, A. (Eds.). *Capturing identity: quantitative and qualitative methods*. Lanham, MD.: University Press of America. pp. 1-15.

Marcia, J.E., Waterman, A.S., Matteson, D.R., Archer, S.L. and Orlofsky, J.L. (1993). *Ego identity: A handbook for psychosocial research*. New York: Springer-Verlag.

Paterson, J.E., Field, J. & Pryor, J. (1994). Adolescents' perceptions of their attachment relationships with their mothers, fathers, and friends. *Journal of Youth and Adolescence*. 23. pp. 579-600.

Piaget, J. (1972). Intellectual evolution from adolescence to adulthood. *Human Development*. 15. pp. 1-12.

Stephen, J., Fraser, E. & Marcia, J.E. (1992). Moratorium-achievement (MAMA) cycles in lifespan identity development: value orientations and reasoning system correlates. *Journal of Adolescence*. 15. pp. 283-300.

Stewart, R.A.C. (1976a). *Adolescence in New Zealand, volume 1: basic developmental influences*. Auckland: Heinemann Educational Books.

Stewart, R.A.C. (1976b). *Adolescence in New Zealand, volume 2: wider perspectives*. Auckland: Heinemann Educational Books.

Tupuola, A.M. (1993). Critical analysis of adolescent development – A Samoan women's perspective. M.A. thesis, Victoria University of Wellington.

Vondracek, F.W. & Skorikov, V.B. (1997). Leisure, school, and work activity preferences and their role in vocational identity development. *The Career Development Quarterly*. 45. pp. 322-340.

Yoder, A. (2000). Barriers to ego identity status formation: A contextual qualification of Marcia's identity status paradigm. *Journal of Adolescence*. 6. pp. 271-284.

Zuo, L. (2005). Gifted children's identity formation: Influential factors and significance. In A. Columbus (Ed.). *Advances in psychology research, vol. 35*. Hauppauge, NY: Nova Science Publishers. pp. 51-94.

A Capital Contribution: People, Proclivities and Programmes

Lex McDonald

Many cities throughout the world have universities that nourish the life-blood and soul of the community. Frequently the intellectual, social, cultural and economic qualities of a city are defined by the university and indeed, some cities are renowned for their university. Although the role of a university has been debated for many years, it is recognised by many that it functions with higher-order personal, social and intellectual skills to develop and expand knowledge and creative thinking. In doing so, the university's task is to work on local and international problems and concerns. Victoria University of Wellington (VUW) is no exception, and one of its former units, the School of Education Studies (SEDS) (previously known as the School of Education and the Education Department or Department of Education), has made a capital contribution to the university and community's success.[1] From its early beginnings the teaching of education at the University was an important aspect of VUW life and throughout the life of SEDS many colourful, energetic and innovative personnel have worked to create a high profile for the discipline. In this chapter, brief comments are made about the contributions of a sample of past and present staff and a snapshot is provided of some SEDS developments.

Victoria University College, established in 1897, was a constituent of the University of New Zealand and its inaugural classes were in Latin, English, mathematics, jurisprudence, French and physics. Prior to this, in the late 1880s, the Wellington Education Board had called for the establishment of a Chair of Psychology and Education in the proposed University College, and, immediately following the establishment of

---

1   I will refer to the unit as SEDS to provide a consistency of naming.

the University, the New Zealand Educational Institute proposed a Chair in Pedagogy, but funds were not available. In 1905 William Gray, the Principal of the Wellington Teachers' College (WCE), gave education lectures for the BA and seven years later, J.S. Tennant, the Principal of WCE at that time, became the first Professor in Education, although he still retained his position as principal. A fully autonomous University School of Education, independent of WCE, was established in 1927. In 1933, it was proposed that the University should assume responsibility for teacher training and establish a specialist degree, but the government did not support this proposal. Subsequently, liaison between the two institutions occurred mainly in the form of student enrolment in approved degree/professional qualification programmes. It was not until the 1990s that formal institutional arrangements were put in place, again with the formation of the ill-fated VUW–WCE conjoint faculty. In 2005, a formal merger occurred between the College of Education and the School of Education Studies and a Faculty of Education was established.

There have been many lively scholars in SEDS who have contributed to maintaining the high profile of the discipline, raising our consciousness about different issues and contributing to the community good. For example, Crawford Somerset, of 'Littledene' fame,[2] who joined the University Education Department in 1947, was considered one of the founding fathers of sociology in New Zealand. Colin Bailey, a professor appointed in 1946, highlighted the importance of education in developing countries, educational history and philosophy, and Māori education issues. The works of Professor Rollo Arnold outlined important aspects of New Zealand social history, while Jack Shallcrass, a nationally well-known public commentator, highlighted the works of the critical theorist Paulo Freire to a generation of students. Arthur Fieldhouse was a pioneer in the development of standardised achievement tests. Geraldine McDonald did not join the University until later in her life but had a very distinguished background as a teacher, researcher, and advocate for Māori involvement in early childhood centres. She assisted with the development of the Master of Education for the Wellington College of Education. Professor Helen May is known nationally and internationally for her promotion of early childhood education issues, whilst Professor Kay Morris-Mathews

---

2   Somerset's 1938 sociological study of the small rural town of Oxford, North Canterbury (which he dubbed 'Littledene') is still regarded as a significant and groundbreaking piece of scholarship.

has numerous publications on the history of New Zealand education, with particular reference to women's roles.

The above commentary has identified a range of individuals from the past who have contributed significantly. There are of course many people who previously worked for SEDS who are currently employed by VUW and who have already made, and continue to make, a significant contribution. I have chosen five people who have had a noteworthy involvement in SEDS, each having a significant impact within and outside the University. Undoubtedly, others could have been included in this discussion.

Professor Deborah Willis became Pro Vice-Chancellor and Dean of the Faculty of Humanities and Social Sciences at VUW in 2004. She trained initially as a teacher and was awarded an undergraduate and master's degree in education and psychology from the University of Canterbury before completing her doctorate in 1990 at Victoria University. Her involvement with SEDS spanned a period of over ten years, as a lecturer specialising in the areas of curriculum, assessment and evaluation. In 1998, Deborah became Director of the VUW Teaching Development Centre and four years later was appointed Assistant Vice-Chancellor (Academic) with responsibility for academic policy and all aspects of teaching and learning quality. On two occasions during her university career, Deborah worked in the Pacific (Cook Islands and Vanuatu) undertaking teaching and research. Her work on the National Tertiary Teaching Excellence Committee and as Chair of the Teaching Matters Forum is well known. Deborah was one of the younger set of SEDS staff in the 1990s who broadened the base of expertise and experience – many of this new generation of academics being women. From a national perspective, she made significant contributions in the areas of linking teaching practice to theory, integrating research on learning and curriculum assessment, and the impact of policy and published works on aspects of tertiary education. I had the privilege of working with Deborah on a number of projects and she always impressed with her willingness to work hard, her perceptive abilities and her very professional response to all tasks. She exudes friendliness, which has made her a very popular academic here and overseas. She is very capable of working within the complexity of the bureaucracy of universities and allied agencies as well as being able to provide valuable teaching assistance in a small Pacific Island school. Not too proud to ever stop learning, Deborah once commented to me "Teaching these teachers has actually made me think about some of those theories." One of her startling personal findings from working in the Pacific was that effective teaching can certainly proceed without an abundance of resources!

Dr Don Brown, currently Director of the Resource Teachers: Learning and Behaviour (RTLB) programme, has had a most distinguished career in education and has been recognised as a leader in his field, both nationally and internationally. He began work as a teacher but then became an educational psychologist, working in Wellington and in the UK for a number of years. Don's BA and BA (Hons) study was undertaken in SEDS between 1956 and 1966. From 1975 to 1978 he was the Director of Clinical Training in the Psychology Department of Victoria University and was responsible for an integrated training programme for clinical and educational psychologists. This was the beginning of his interest in an ecological and applied approach to psychology and education. Following this, Don was appointed Chief Psychologist for the New Zealand Department of Education, and remained in this position until 1985 when he became its Director of Special Education. As their employee, he represented the Department and government on numerous committees, boards, and national and international agencies, and at conferences and meetings. He has been involved in many special education agencies such as the Autism Association, IHC (New Zealand Society for the Intellectually Handicapped), CCS (Crippled Children's Society), the Royal Foundation for the Blind and the NZ Federation for the Deaf. Following the closure of the Department in 1989, Don became a consultant, researcher and lecturer in a variety of settings, including SEDS. During this time, he was responsible for a programme of teacher training for secondary school teachers that commanded considerable excitement – it was an innovative programme with considerable time devoted to pedagogical aspects and this had a significant impact upon the trainees' performance in the classroom. In 1999, he became the Director of the RTLB programme within SEDS.

Don's achievements are recognised for many reasons. Firstly, he is a 'walk-the-talk' professional – he has expertise in integrating theory with practice and this has proved invaluable for training teachers, psychologists and RTLB. Secondly, he is an innovator – for example, he changed the practice of educational psychology in New Zealand and pioneered a secondary-education training programme. Thirdly, many educators will think of him as one who has advanced cooperative learning in New Zealand. Fourthly, he has always had a keen interest in community involvement and promoted the rights of parents and their involvement in educational decision-making, especially the facilitation of the interaction between educational agencies and parents of students with special teaching needs. Don has demonstrated strong leadership and has concerned himself with key ethical and moral issues in education. For example, during his time at the New Zealand Department of Education, he revitalised special education, moving the education sector towards accepting a more inclusive orientation. His ideas changed the professional work of psychologists in education and he was responsible for a more reflective position on the role of psychometric assessments. Furthermore, Don ensured that corporal punishment was discontinued in schools under the control of the Department of Education and was responsible for development of the Draft Review of Special Education, which contained significant ideas for special education that were adopted as it moved into the new millennium. He certainly was the man for those times.

Associate Professor Carmen Dalli's current position reads like an entry in a *Who's Who*. She is Associate Professor/Reader in Education, Director of the Institute for Early Childhood Studies, and Associate Director of the Jessie Hetherington Centre for Educational Research. Carmen started her career in Malta as a primary school teacher, but quickly moved into a lecturing position at the University of Malta. She has worked in SEDS since 1986, initially on a part-time basis while working also at the New Zealand Department of Education. Following her full-time appointment to the then Education Department of VUW in 1988, she introduced the first early childhood courses at VUW with Dr Anne Meade and went on to take up a key role in establishing the Institute for Early Childhood Studies in 1994. She also became the foundation editor of the Occasional Publications Series of the Institute. Carmen was responsible for initiating discussions about the need for an early childhood code of ethics and this culminated in the adoption of a code in 1995. She played a significant role in establishing the four-year conjoint BA/BTeach (ECE) degree, which is jointly administered by Wellington College of Education and SEDS. Known nationally and internationally, she has given over twenty-seven keynote conference addresses or public addresses relating to early childhood education issues. Carmen has helped to welcome the first early childhood professor in New Zealand to SEDS; she was one of the 'new breed' of authoritative women in education who forged a working relationship with the 'old network' in the university environment; and, with some amusement now, she recalls the arrival of the first three SEDS personal computers to be shared by a staff of over twenty! Undoubtedly Carmen has been a significant force in transforming thinking about early childhood education at the tertiary level and in raising educators' consciousness about early childhood education issues. She is a most elegant person, sets and demands high standards, is a prolific researcher, and even has time to act as the honorary consul for Malta and practise her operatic singing in the corridors. She exudes style.

A few years back **Professor Wally Penetito's** elderly mother asked him what he was doing at university. He replied, "Teaching." In response, she peered at him quizzically and asked, "But isn't that what you have always done?" "Yes, mum," he replied, "but I hope I am getting better at it!" Wally has indeed got better at it. He started his career as a primary school teacher in 1960 and then over the years, alternating with study at university, he held numerous advisory, management and lecturing positions, taking a particular interest in Māori teacher education. Wally obtained his PhD from VUW in 2005. From 1994 to 1997 he worked part time in SEDS, being responsible for a Māori education paper, and in 1998 he was appointed as a full-time senior lecturer. From then until 2008, he was the Director and Co-Director of He Pārekereke: Institute for Research and Development in Māori and Pacific Education. In recognition of his work for Māori education, Wally was made an Honorary Fellow of the New Zealand Educational Institute in 1997. He has served on numerous public sector advisory committees for the Ministry of Education, the Education Review Office, the New Zealand Qualifications Authority and the Education Training and Support Agency. Wally has involved himself in many Māori education agencies, including being a lecturer and accreditation team member for Te Whare Wānanga o Awanuiārangi and Te Wānanga-o-Raukawa and has assisted with a review of the wānanga umbrella organisation, Te Tauihu o Ngā Wānanga. He helped establish Ngā Pae o te Māramatanga (the Māori Centre of Research Excellence) based at the University of Auckland. Wally has been a member of the World Indigenous Higher Education Consortium, presenting at the World Indigenous Peoples' Conferences on Education, and has internationalised Māori education issues. He has also played an important role for Treaty claims with the Crown as he has acted in the role of Ngāti Haua Iwi Liaison. He has always impressed his colleagues with his foresight, wit, patience, and understanding of Māori–Pākehā issues, and he has been an effective mentor for many students and staff members. Simply speaking, Wally has always been at the forefront of attempts to challenge and offer advice and guidance on how the education system can be responsive to Māori needs and aspirations. The following is the spirit of Wally to me:

Te Māori: My World

As I walk as an individual in the Pākehā world
I walk with my Māori world in my spiritual realm
Wherever I go I take my Māori world with me
I am never alone!
I walk with my wairua, my iwi, my hapu and my whānau
Being Māori is having a deep bond with my people whether it be physically or spiritually they will always be there, especially in times of sickness, unhappiness, at times of death or even happy times of celebration
For me, being Māori is being here for one another in our Māori world and in our Pākehā world also, I am never alone.
(Kelly Te Heuheu)

In 1964 a local lad from Moera in Lower Hutt, **Cedric Hall**, entered VUW and gained a BA majoring in psychology and education and then a BA (Hons) in educational psychology. After teaching secondary school mathematics for a brief period in Sydney, he then travelled to the UK and worked for a number of years at the National Foundation for Educational Research in London. His projects in this role centred on assessment and evaluation of assessment, particularly public examinations. It was during this time that Cedric enrolled in a PhD and, on his return to New Zealand, he became a lecturer and subsequently a senior lecturer in the School of Educational Studies (SEDS). From 1989 to 1997 Cedric was the Director of the University Teaching and Development Centre and worked with many academic staff to develop excellence in their teaching skills. In this role, he wrote extensively on issues relating to teaching and assessment. In 1997, he became a professor of education and was Head of School for SEDS until 2001. At the time of the merger between the College of Education and University in 2005, having long supported closer relations between the two, Cedric was appointed Deputy Dean of the new Faculty of Education and remained in this role until his retirement in 2007. Currently he continues to work part-time for SEDS on contract.

Cedric has had an immense influence upon the direction of SEDS and has developed particular expertise in a number of teaching areas including policy, assessment and evaluation, curriculum, educational psychology, human development, and research methods. He has had an ongoing interest in quality assurance in higher education, and assessment and evaluation at the secondary school and tertiary levels, and has written numerous chapters and articles about these issues, becoming a national and international spokesperson about standards-based assessment. He contributed significantly to the debate about NCEA assessment, strongly opposing, on both pedagogical and measurement grounds, the particular model of standards-based assessment developed for NCEA; he remains opposed to this model. Cedric has worked on numerous accreditation panels at the national level and has been an academic auditor for both New Zealand and Australian universities. In 1991–1992 he worked on the establishment of the Academic Audit Unit that was to serve all universities in New Zealand. In 2000 he was awarded a Significant Innovations in Teaching Award, essentially because of his work in developing one of the key courses (EDUC 114) in the Victoria Police Education Programme, a programme designed in conjunction with the Royal New Zealand Police College to ensure that police were broadly educated and prepared for further tertiary study of their choice. Although many will recall Cedric's academic expertise, students will certainly remember his very human qualities – he had understanding of their situation and demonstrated a deep consideration for each student. This empathic response and a championing of the students' cause has provided many staff with a model of behaviour to be emulated.

People can define an organisation, but another perspective that provides insight into the people who have worked for SEDS is to consider some programme developments. The three examples discussed below are a training programme for educational psychologists; the training of Resource Teacher Learning and Behaviour; and the development of the 'education and professional development' specialisation.

The training of educational psychologists

Following the Second World War there was an awakening of interest in students with special teaching needs. The ill-treatment these students had received, the growing power of parent groups, new research, and the rights movements of the 1970s all contributed to the awareness that action was needed to ensure equity of opportunity. Throughout the western world, there was a movement toward normalisation and mainstreaming, which meant that many more students with special needs would be located in regular schools and classes. One of the New Zealand government's responses was to increase the number of educational psychologists in training, and accordingly during the 1970s Victoria, along with Otago and Massey Universities, joined Auckland University as training venues. At VUW, training was administered jointly by the Education and Psychology Departments with Professor Reg Marsh and Don Brown leading figures in this development. There was a range of competencies required for certification as a qualified educational psychologist and at VUW the courses developed centred on counselling, remedial education, behavioural analysis, behavioural change, clinical psychology, physiology, psychology and education of the atypical. This inter-disciplinary training was for a period of three years and trainees qualified with an MA (Applied) in school psychology and a postgraduate Diploma of Educational Studies (Educational Psychology). Sadly, because the government slashed the number of psychologist trainee scholarships, in 1980 the programme at Victoria terminated. Some of those students who graduated are still practising as psychologists today, some returned to teaching, and some are using their skills in other positions. For example, Margaret Parkin holds a senior management position in the Ministry of Education, Dr Liz Jones is the Associate Dean (Academic) in the VUW Faculty of Education, Dr Lottie Thomson holds a key training position in the VUW Resource Teacher Learning and Behaviour programme and I am currently Head of the School of Educational Psychology and Pedagogy at VUW.

The training of Resource Teacher Learning and Behaviour

The School of Education Studies also acts to support the Resource Teacher Learning and Behaviour (RTLB) programme. This programme was established within a consortium of three universities, including the

University of Auckland and the University of Waikato, working together to provide training for a cadre of special education teachers, developed under a new policy (*Special Education 2000*). The training of RTLB is managed under a contract between the Ministry of Education and the University's contracting organisation, VicLink. The professional administration is under the wing of SEDS, where the staff have a community of academics with whom they can engage professionally. The school admits RTLB students to the master's programme.

The RTLB training was developed at VUW by Don Brown and Charlotte Thomson to meet the demands of a new paradigm for general and special education, one which embraces the aspirations of the new government policy of inclusive education. The emphasis is upon evidence-based, inclusive education. RTLB have changed the role of special educators from a deficit-based, functional limitation model of viewing students with special teaching needs, to one which draws upon advances in educational psychology, curriculum revisions and the experience of international and local special educational support personnel. Others in SEDS who have worked in the programme and assisted with its development are Liz Jones, Liz Manins, Mark Sweeny, Dick Grace, Carolyn Gould, Vonnie Jones, Lianne Kalivati and I. Dick Grace has ensured the development of the bicultural element of the programme, which comprised 25 per cent of the required study and practicum.

The programme has now been developed to the extent that it is internationally known, through conference presentations in a number of countries, publications in respected professional journals and the maintenance of a network of professional development activities by staff at the three contributing universities. The RTLB service has been reviewed by three agencies since its inception. School staff have rated the service as the most effective of the various special education agencies available to them. Some reviews have highlighted concerns about management of the service while others have pointed out the difference in quality of service between highly effective clusters of RTLB and those that are not functioning well. The RTLB programmes now follow a carefully documented procedural approach developed by the Ministry of Education, with input from the universities and school stakeholders, which recognises their collaborative problem-solving approach with schools, following an educational/ecological model. This official policy is not yet fully understood by some schools, where a deficit paradigm still dominates. The RTLB team have the potential to make a powerful contribution to the welfare and educational progress of a great many children who struggle with the curriculum.

The development of a professional development and training specialisation

I joined the University in 2002 with a particular interest in contemporary views on training and professional development. One of my mentors was Cedric Hall who I met as a new lecturer on the first day of my psychologist training in 1975. Over the years, we have cemented our friendship and have developed a number of common interests, one of them being skill and knowledge development for trainers and professional development facilitators. Fortunately, in the early years of the new millennium new course approval was relatively easily achieved and by 2003, we had arranged for three new postgraduate papers in this specialist area to be part of the course schedules.[3] Over the intervening period, a range of other people who had expertise in the area – Don Brown, Lottie Thomson, Liz Jones and Stephanie Doyle – became involved. The students had the option of taking four papers at the postgraduate diploma level (or certificate level for graduate papers), and these four papers centred on professional development and training foundations, motivation of participants, assessment and evaluation and a research paper in an area of the student's choice. In general terms, the modus operandi is to emphasise theory-to-practice links and to enable participants to contextualise the learning to their work environment. This programme was a particular success and continues today with high student enrolments. There have been several reasons for its success: it was a block course, which appealed to many participants (including a number from outside Wellington); there was no comparable specialisation in the Wellington region; it tapped into a market that was seeking to link training theory and practice; and all the lecturers had specialist research interests and practical experience in professional development and training.

---

3   Initially these papers were double coded; there were graduate and postgraduate options. The graduate option was for individuals without the academic qualification but with appropriate experience. The graduate option has now been withdrawn. A fourth paper (already existing) was also part of the specialisation – it was a research paper that would investigate some aspect of the participant's professional development/training work context.

Almost from the initial establishment of Victoria University, education as a discipline has had a key role. It has attracted many highly qualified people from all parts of the world and has contributed significantly to the local, national and international voice about the role and place of education in society. The School and its staff demonstrated their expertise in many and various ways but, as outlined above, there was always an emphasis upon acquiring, understanding and applying the education knowledge base. The capital contribution made by SEDS most certainly invited excellence, and provides a fine tradition upon which the new Faculty, formed from the merger of the 'old' university School and the 'old' Teachers College, can forge new and engaging plans.

EDUCATION MATTERS:
TEACHING AND PHILOSOPHIES

Reminiscences on Peace Education

Jim Collinge

In 1986 I started teaching a course entitled 'Peace Education' at the third-year level. At the time it was a Special Field course, that is a non-permanent course which was expected to run for only a couple of years; however, the course attracted 87 students in its first year, and 78 students in its second year, many more than any other third-year course in Education at that time. With the enthusiastic support of Gerald Grace, who had just taken up his position as Professor of Education, the course was put through as a permanent offering, and was taught, more or less continuously, until 2001. Subsequently an MEd course in Peace Education was also offered for a number of years. At the time these were the only courses on peace education being offered in a New Zealand university as part of a degree.

Writing this paper has enabled me to reflect, at some distance in time, on some of my thinking in teaching this course, and some of the influences on my ideas and practice. First, let me explain my reasons for offering such a course at that time. The mid 1980s, as will be explained below, was a time of considerable activity in peace education, both in New Zealand and abroad. I vividly remember Graeme Oldershaw, the Principal of Wellington Teachers' College at the time, saying on returning from a Principal's meeting that one of the main things that all the people at the meeting agreed on was that the colleges had to deal with peace education. I would be surprised if such a thing happened today. Secondly, there was a huge amount of extremely interesting literature being produced on the subject, literature not only about peace topics, but also reflecting imaginative views on education generally, which students would not otherwise have had contact with. This was a time when a lot of research was being done on the feelings of young people about living in a nuclear age. One of the findings of this research was that adults, both parents and teachers, were extremely reluctant to discuss such matters with them:

the American psychiatrist Robert Lifton (1982) coined the term 'nuclear numbness' for this attitude.

From the start, the course was always based on a broad definition of the meaning of peace. This is indicated by some of the people who were guest lecturers in the course over the years. In the earlier years I had speakers from the Women's International League for Peace and Freedom, who, with their many years of experience in the peace movement and their strong commitment to peace work, made a huge impact on the younger students. Alison Laurie from Gender and Women's Studies also lectured on her research on women peace activists in New Zealand, Jack Shallcrass gave us the benefit of his wide experience in a number of causes, and Don Brown lectured on Cooperative Learning. For the last two years of the course it was combined with Lise Claiborne's course on Diversity in Education. A particularly pleasing feature of the earlier years of the course was the number of students from Wellington College of Education who, as part of their work in the course, were able to prepare materials and units of work for use in their classrooms when they went on teaching practice.

In 1992 I was fortunate to be awarded a Fellowship from the Swedish Institute to work at the School of Education, University of Lund, with a great peace educator, Åke Bjerstedt, who ran a programme called Preparedness for Peace. As a result of this experience, I became involved with both the Peace Education Commission of the International Peace Research Association and the European Peace Research Association, thereby meeting peace educators from all parts of the world at a number of international conferences as well as gaining a forum for a number of my own publications.

As I said above, the 1980s was a time of activity and enthusiasm in peace education, but the history of formal interest in peace education in New Zealand schools can be traced back to 1929, when the New Zealand Educational Institute recommended that all teachers become active members of the League of Nations Union, read the League's magazine *Educational Survey*, and incorporate the work of the league into the school syllabus. In that year also, changes were made in the history and civics syllabus with an aim to "inculcate into the minds of the young . . . . a desire to promote peace among the nations" (Mulholland 1990, p. 10). Thirty years later New Zealand joined a decision to adopt the Declaration of the Rights of the Child, which in Principle 10 stated, "The child shall be brought up in a spirit of understanding, tolerance, friendship among peoples and universal brotherhood." Again, in 1978, at the First Special Session of the United Nations on Disarmament, an undertaking was given "to take steps to develop programmes of peace education at all levels."

A major step towards peace education was taken in 1975 when the New Zealand Foundation for Peace Studies was opened. This organisation has as one of its main aims the promotion of the study of peace in schools and tertiary institutions. In 1979 the Foundation published *Learning Peaceful Relationships*, a useful book for primary schools which has been reprinted many times. They followed this up in 1986, the United Nations Year of Peace, with a book for secondary schools, *Extending Peaceful Relationships*. Both of these books are extremely practical texts, full of stimulating activities for the classroom. A third volume was published in 1994, *A Volcano in my Tummy*, which has the aim of helping children to handle anger.

However, peace education, despite some initiatives, had very little place in New Zealand schools until the Labour government of 1984 renewed interest in the subject. Russell Marshall, Minister of Education, was clearly in support of it. He proposed that 'peace studies' should be introduced into the secondary school syllabus, a move which he said had a very practical aim – to teach adolescents to recognise and deal effectively with conflict. Russell Marshall was well aware of the opposition this move would generate in some quarters, opposition which he regarded to a large extent as being "confused or politically prejudiced" (Marshall 1985, p.17). Nevertheless he was determined to continue.

> If the result is less violence in the community, better industrial and race relations, improved relations between the sexes, between teacher and pupil, parent and child, then the idea will have paid its way. (Marshall 1985, p.18)

Within the Department of Education's Curriculum Unit two officers were given responsibility for development of peace education programmes in schools. A working party was set up to consult with teachers, parents, teachers' organisations, teachers college staff, and other interested people in workshops and meetings. These meetings resulted, in 1986, in a discussion document, *Peace Studies: Draft Guidelines*, with an update the following year. This was a period of intense activity in peace education, stimulated by the enthusiastic support of Russell Marshall.

It is instructive at this distance to look back on these activities. Very little support was given to the idea of peace studies being developed as a separate subject in the school curriculum. Marshall envisaged it as being "integrated into the present core curriculum, for example as part of the present history or social studies syllabi" (Marshall 1985, p.18). The authors of the draft guidelines agreed.

> Peace studies is not conceived as a separate subject to be added on to the present curriculum nor does it replace basic subjects. Rather it is a dimension which can be readily integrated into existing subjects and has cross-cultural implications. (*Peace Studies: Draft Guidelines* 1986, p. 3)

There are good educational as well as practical arguments for such an approach, but there is no doubt that many people involved in peace education were mainly concerned about counteracting those critics who expressed opposition to what they saw as a new time-wasting subject to be added to an already overfull curriculum. The more controversial aspects of peace education were also downplayed. Despite the enormous public interest in the nuclear issue at the time, nuclear matters had only a small place in the draft guidelines, the overwhelming emphasis being on conflict resolution, interpersonal relations and community issues.

Strong support came from the *Report of the Ministerial Committee of Enquiry into Violence* under Sir Clinton Roper. This excellent document, now sadly and inexplicably neglected, was the outcome of a high level of public concern about the incidence of violent crime. The committee undertook to advise the Minister of Justice on practical steps that could be taken to reduce the incidence of violence and violent crime in the community. In a substantial chapter ranging over numerous aspects of education, it was noted that hundreds of submissions mentioned the need for people to learn to resolve conflicts peacefully. The discussion document *Peace Studies: Draft Guidelines* was singled out for particular praise.

The Roper Report made two recommendations:

1. That all teachers at all levels be given opportunities to discuss and implement Peace Studies as soon as possible and that resources necessary to that end be made available.

2. That the public be informed of the true nature of Peace Studies, the title being ambiguous.

During this period a number of other significant publications were also produced. In particular the New Zealand branch of the International Physicians for the Prevention of Nuclear War commissioned an extremely useful series of Nuclear Issues Fact Sheets, which could be used in schools. They were published as a single volume in 1986. The Department of Education produced two information pamphlets, *Partners in Peacemaking* in 1988, which sought to explain peace studies, particularly for the benefit of parents, and in the following year *Writing a Peaceful Charter* which was sent to the new Boards of Trustees of Schools.

However, despite the care with which peace education was introduced and the support it received from such powerful bodies as the Roper Committee, the critics still came out in force. When Russell Marshall, in 1985, announced the government's intention to introduce peace studies in schools, some Opposition MPs attacked the proposal, referring to it as "antinuclear indoctrination", "brainwashing" and "sociological claptrap". One said that peace studies would "divide the country" and that the Socialist Unity Party was "forcing the Minister into the position of wanting to introduce peace studies into our schools." A group calling themselves the Coalition of Concerned Citizens sent out pamphlets all over the country expressing the view that the government was using education for political purposes. Peace studies, said one, was,

> being brought into the curriculum as a key element of Labour's political indoctrination. It is the Trojan Horse which Russell Marshall has allowed the peace movement to stable in our schools. It is a front for all kinds of propaganda – unilateral disarmament, radical feminism, liberalizing of sexual attitudes, promotion of Maori sovereignty and exercises designed to change children's values. (Coalition of Concerned Citizens 1987, p. 1)

The halcyon period of peace education in New Zealand was unfortunately a brief one. After the general election of 1987, Russell Marshall was removed as Minister of Education, and the country entered into a period of radical reform of education, which resulted in the Department of Education, including the Curriculum Development Unit, being replaced by a new Ministry of Education. Many of the people there who were most supportive of peace education moved on to other fields.

Nevertheless, peace education remains a sturdy plant in some quarters, often the result of private initiative. The Peace Foundation continues to provide excellent resources and strong support for peace education. Their Cool Schools peer mediation programme, which was developed in the early 1990s, is now a feature of schools all over the country. More recently the Foundation has introduced into New Zealand primary schools a splendid Canadian programme called Roots of Empathy (ROE), in which a local infant and parents visit a classroom every three weeks over the school year. A trained ROE instructor coaches the students to observe the baby's development and label the baby's feelings. In a very real sense, then, the baby is the teacher. With the guidance of the instructor, the children are helped to reflect on their own feelings and the feelings of others. The aim of the programme is for the emotional literacy taught to lay the foundation for more safe and caring classrooms, in which there is less likelihood of physical, psychological and emotional bullying and other violent behaviours. The programme is now operating in schools in Auckland, Wellington and Christchurch.

There are also possibilities within some of the New Zealand curriculum documents for the teacher who wishes to engage in peace education. *Te Whāriki*, the early childhood education curriculum, is probably unique among current official curriculum documents in New Zealand in its use of the word 'peaceful'. Young children, the document states, should have the opportunity to develop "a range of strategies for solving conflicts in peaceful ways, and a perception that peaceful ways are best." Throughout the programme, great emphasis is placed on inculcating attitudes and values that are very much in accord with the principles of peace education. Great emphasis is laid on giving children opportunities for cooperative ventures, for discussion and negotiation: "co-operative ventures, achievements and aspirations should be valued". Racism and sexism are to be actively countered through the development of intercultural understanding and positive judgments about gender and ethnic groups. When bias, prejudice and negative stereotyping are in evidence, adults are expected to challenge and discuss them.

Te Whāriki is a programme rich in opportunities for peace education. Of course it needs to be put into practice by teachers with the necessary sensitivity, training and skills. If this can be achieved then the programme, with its emphasis on cooperation, positive cultural understanding and peaceful resolution of conflict, would form a sound basis for peace education.

There are also several other areas of the school curriculum which offer valuable opportunities for peace education, such as Social Studies, Science and the Arts, but one particularly important area, I believe, is the Health and Physical Education curriculum, based as it is around the underlying concept of hauora, defined as a Māori philosophy of health, encompassing physical, mental, emotional, social and spiritual wellbeing. The socio-ecological strand in this curriculum can be seen almost as a programme for educating for peace, with its emphasis on students recognising the need for mutual care and shared responsibility between themselves, other people and society, respect for the rights of other people and a sense of social justice.

Peace is almost universally thought to be a good thing, but beyond that there is some debate as to what peace actually is. A traditional view of peace is usually associated with the absence of violent conflict. A nation is at peace when it is not actually at war. This is usually known as negative peace. Over the last few decades a wider definition of peace has gained some currency. Positive peace, which includes the absence of violent conflict, also includes a move towards a non-violent type of egalitarian, non-exploitative and non-suppressive type of cooperation between individuals, groups and nations. In other words the mere absence of fighting or overt conflict is not peace. Something more is required.

One of the key figures in the development of this broader notion of peace is Norwegian peace researcher Johann Galtung, who has coined the term 'structural violence' for inequalities and injustices that are built into the very structure of societies, which deprive individuals or groups of their potential for fulfillment and self expression and deny opportunities for development, but which may not necessarily lead to actual direct violence. In his fine book of 1996 *Peace by Peaceful Means*, Galtung has expanded this notion to include 'cultural violence', which he defines as those aspects of our culture which can be used to justify or legitimise direct or structural violence. Examples he gives are flags, anthems and military parades, the ubiquitous portrait of the leader, inflammatory speeches and posters.

Most peace educators would, I suggest, work within this wider definition of 'positive peace'. Peace education is not just concerned with issues of peace, war, defence, violence, and nuclear weapons, although these matters would be central in any programme. It must also include issues concerned with sexism and racism, social injustice, health, the environment, and importantly, human rights. As American peace educator Betty Reardon (1997) has pointed out, it is this concept of peace that is the foundational principle of the Universal Declaration of Human Rights.

Obviously what are involved here are issues of values and ethical decision-making processes, which should be much to the fore in our thinking about education today. I would also contend that peace educators should not shrink from dealing with controversial issues in these areas; they are among the most crucial questions that a school in a democracy can encourage its young citizens to think seriously about. As Paulo Freire constantly reiterated, the practice of freedom is "the means by which men and women deal critically and creatively with reality and discover how to participate in the transformation of their world" (Freire 1972, pp.13–14). At the heart of Freire's pedagogy is an insistence on a critical, interactive and cooperative approach to learning so that all the various issues arising from a generative theme are allowed to unfold. Issues of peace, war, violence in the community and family, nuclear power and nuclear weapons are today, as much as at any time, powerful generative themes for young people to study, not as recipients of a dogma, but as active participants in a search. As one writer on Freire has said, this approach transcends the bounds of 'technical peace education' and presents a challenge of 'morally imaginative peace education' which includes not only critical analysis but also the acceptance of feelings and the exercise of compassion (Rivage-Seul 1987).

Although peace education tends towards what might be termed a 'holistic world view' it is not intended to replace the traditional disciplines with some vague, woolly new subject, but rather it is thematic and integrated, concerned with interactions between the subjects rather than presenting a fragmented world view. Most peace educators, in my experience, would see their work as ranging across the curriculum, addressing peace issues in the framework of traditional school subjects. It is useful here to draw a distinction between explicit peace education, concerned with direct information about and discussions of war and peace, and implicit peace education which is concerned with the nurturing and acquisition of peaceful values and behaviour in a school environment which is oriented towards cooperation and dialogue.

The methods used in peace education should be in harmony with its principles; for example, students should be encouraged to work together cooperatively, procedures should be, as far as possible, democratic so that all students have an equal role, and the methods used should encourage active participation from learners rather than passive listening. These are, I believe, essential to the development of a thoughtful and critical approach to peace and related issues, an approach that is the very opposite of the indoctrination of which peace educators have so been often accused. In my third-year peace education course, rather than a predominant use of the lecture with its one-way communication, the emphasis was always placed on workshops, in which the students worked together in groups using the techniques and attitudes of cooperative learning. I found Don Brown and Charlotte Thomson's book *Cooperative Learning in New Zealand Schools* (2000) very useful here.

A central aim of peace educators is to help students develop techniques for the peaceful resolution of conflict and positive ways of dealing with anger. It has often been noted that conflict is frequently viewed negatively, whereas, it is, in fact, inevitable in any society, and can be, when properly handled, a creative and life-affirming force. The American peace educator Elise Boulding has pointed out the crucial fact that civil society depends on what she calls 'the peace of the negotiated social order', in which people negotiate a mutually acceptable solution. Because of the pejorative meaning that most people give to the word 'conflict' it is most commonly associated with winning and losing. Civil society would be impossible if people competed with each other all the time and did not find other ways of dealing with the conflicts of wants, interests and need that underlie all human interaction.

One concept which I have always placed at the heart of peace education is the development of imagination. In her book on the subject, philosopher Mary Warnock makes the case that the cultivation of imagination should be one of the chief aims of education, and yet it is one which is frequently neglected. Imagination, she writes,

> is a power in the human mind which is at work in our everyday perception of the world, and which is also at work in our thoughts about what is absent; which enables us to see the world, whether present or absent, as significant, and also to present this vision to others, for them to share or reject. (Warnock 1977, p. 196)

In Warnock's view, imagination is involved in all perception of the world, while remembering the past as well as envisaging the future. As a means of developing the imagination, the arts are of crucial importance, and, for her, no school curriculum which did not take education in the arts as seriously as education in other school subjects could possibly be complete or satisfactory.

One writer who has made a very clear connection between the arts, imagination and education for peace is the wonderful New York educator Maxine Greene. In her numerous books and articles, she has advanced the view that learning is always stimulated by a sense of future possibility, of what might be. Experiences with the arts can lead to a thoughtfulness, a sense of the unexpected, what she calls wide-awakeness. Imagination, she writes,

> opens us to visions of the possible rather than the predictable, it permits us, if we choose, to give our imagination free play, to look at things as if they could be otherwise. (Greene 1988, p. 495)

In her 1982 paper 'Education and Disarmament', Maxine Greene makes an explicit connection between education through the arts, education of the imagination and peace education. To her, peace education is a way of educating critical and self-reflecting men and women with commitments to value. An informed awareness of the arts,

> provides a heightened sense of place, a sense of being in the world . . . a sense of alternative realities, a recognition that things can be other than they are . . . . that is likely to overcome the abstractness as well as the passivity that is fostered by so many of the forces in our time. (Greene 1982, p. 132)

Education thus becomes a means of fostering value consciousness, a sensitivity to lacks and deficiencies in the world around, together with a willingness to take action to repair those deficiencies.

> It may be to develop the capacity to imagine a world that is truly just – a world in which bombings and torture and violations of human beings become personally offensive and intolerable to increasing numbers of people, a world in which, at last, there are moral constraints. (ibid p. 134)

In today's world I can imagine no more noble and crucial vision of education. Through peace education in which the development of imagination is a primary aim, our students (and ourselves of course) can, in Maxine Greene's words,

> be empowered to ponder new possibilities, alternatives to destruction and war . . . . to speak with their own voices, tell their own stories and, yes, to love the world. (ibid p. 136)

References

Boulding, E. (1987). Learning peace. In R. Vayrynen (Ed.). *The quest for peace*. London: Sage Publications. pp. 317-329.

Brown, D. & Thomson, C. (2000). *Cooperative learning in New Zealand schools*. Palmerston North: Dunmore Press.

Freire, P. (1970). *Pedagogy of the oppressed*. Harmondsworth: Penguin.

Galtung, J. (1996). *Peace by peaceful means*. Oslo: International Peace Research Institute.

Greene, M. (1982). Education and disarmament. *Teachers College Record*. 84, 1. pp. 128-136.

Greene, M. (1988). What happened to imagination? In K. Egan and D. Nadaner (Eds.). *Imagination and education*. New York: Teachers College Press. pp. 45-55.

Lifton, R.J. (1982). Beyond Nuclear Numbing. *Teachers College Record*. 84. 1. pp. 15-29.

Marshall, R. (1985). Peace studies: New Zealand. *PEP Talk* (Journal of the Peace Education Project, London). p. 8.

Mulholland, C. (1990). *Peace studies in primary, secondary and intermediate schools*. Wellington: PACDAC.

Peace Studies: Draft Guidelines (1986). Wellington: Department of Education.

Reardon, Betty A. (1997). Human rights as education for peace. In G.J. Andreopoulos and P. Claude (Eds.). *Human rights for the twenty-first century*, Philadelphia: University of Pennsylvania Press. pp. 21-34.

Report of the Ministerial Committee of Inquiry into Violence (1987). (Chair, Sir Clinton Roper), Wellington: Government Printer.

Rivage-Seul, M.K. (1987). Peace education: imagination and the pedagogy of the oppressed. *Harvard Education Review*. 57, 2.

Te Whariki (1993). Wellington: Learning Media, Ministry of Education.

Warnock, M. (1977). *Imagination*. London: Faber and Faber.

Learning to Read and a Half-Century of Research

G. Brian Thompson

Some changes in direction: 1940s to 1980s

Research in the Department of Education on learning to read was notable in the late 1940s and early 1950s. It was initiated by staff member Arthur Fieldhouse, who was influenced by the maxim "to be at once scientific and practical" to assist children with difficulties in learning to read (Fieldhouse 1988, pp. 35–36). The publications that ensued were ways of assessing children's progress in learning to read. The first was the Oral Word Reading Test (Fieldhouse 1952), for individual administration to children of seven to eleven years. This was the first test of reading attainment to be constructed in New Zealand with national norms. Some 7,500 children were administered the test in 1949 to establish those norms. The second publication (Fieldhouse 1957) was a description of procedures recommended to teachers to identify children with difficulties in learning to read. Fieldhouse maintained an interest in educational provisions for children with learning difficulties, to the extent that ten years beyond his retirement from a professorship in the Department of Education, he published a short history of these provisions in New Zealand, which included brief comment about his earlier research (Fieldhouse 1988, pp. 35–36). It is also worth mentioning that the late 1940s was an especially productive period for Master of Arts theses in Education that involved empirical research relating to reading (D.J. Coleman 1948, A.N. Forbes 1947/48, B. Sutton-Smith 1947/48).[1] Brian Sutton-Smith did not end his academic work with a master's thesis but progressed to a Victoria University PhD on children's games,[2] then to academic positions in the United States and recognition as an international leader in research on children's games, childlore, and play.

---

1   The theses are available in the W.J. Scott Library, Victoria University, although at the time of writing the Forbes thesis was yet to be catalogued.

2   Brian Sutton-Smith was awarded (1949–50) one of the first University of New Zealand doctoral fellowships.

From the mid 1960s there was a strong initiative for the New Zealand Council for Educational Research to construct nationally standardised assessment tools for teachers of reading (and other school subjects). This national organisation was now active in the area in which Arthur Fieldhouse had taken the initiative within the Department. In this changed situation, research on new assessment tools lost its importance within the Department, although it was not completely neglected. Professor Fieldhouse retired from the Department in 1977. In the following year I was appointed to the staff of the Department from Monash University (Melbourne).[3] At the time, Professor Marie Clay of the University of Auckland had been using her PhD thesis research of the 1960s to advocate assessment procedures involving teacher recording of children's oral reading responses to their reading books. This included the child's rate of self-correction of word errors. Unfortunately, I found that this procedure was without a satisfactory basis (Thompson 1981a, 1984), and this was confirmed by the results of independent empirical study (Share 1990).[4]

Toward an international contribution to theory and research

I was inclined toward research on the processes of learning to read,[5] taking an approach that emphasised: (a) revision of current theory or development of new theory; (b) empirical investigation with designed task comparisons or manipulations that test alternative theoretical

---

3   At Monash University I was a Senior Teaching Fellow in the Special Education group of the Faculty of Education. This group was headed by Professor Marie Neale, who was originally from New Zealand. My PhD thesis was conducted under her supervision (published in part in Thompson 1981b). Previously I had been employed as a psychologist in the Psychological Service of the New Zealand (Government) Department of Education.

4   Recently, in collaboration with an Australian colleague (McKay and Thompson 2009), we have shown the need to re-examine the commonly accepted assessment tools for a basic aspect of the reading process known to researchers and some teachers as 'phonological recoding' (the child's skill at attempting new print words by using the sounds that correspond to individual letters of the word).

5   My research in the 1980s included work on sex differences in processes of reading (Thompson 1987), and on selective promotion in schools that relates to sex differences in reading, favouring girls (Thompson 1983). At that time my research extended to work on the youth labour market and school participation (published in the *Journal of Industrial Relations*, *New Zealand Journal of Industrial Relations*, and *New Zealand Journal of Educational Studies*).

explanations; and (c) representative design for these empirical tests. In addition to obtaining the children's responses to reading and related tasks, this type of design involves determining the teaching environment experienced by the children, and determining their print environment (e.g., the vocabulary of their reading books; the letter and letter-sound patterns in that vocabulary).

The first opportunity to incorporate a determination of children's print environment into my research came by courtesy of Cedric Croft of the New Zealand Council for Educational Research. He provided an electronic database of the texts of reading books then in common use in the first three years of primary schooling in New Zealand. From these data, I determined vocabularies and frequency distributions of letters and letter combinations in different positions within words (Thompson 1985). There were subsequent analyses from newly published Year 1 reading books. The collection and coding of these several hundred reading texts was associated with PhD thesis work on modelling and computer simulation of a theory of children's initial learning of reading. This was conducted by Stephen Cassidy (1990, 1992), a staff member of the Computer Studies Department, for whom I shared supervision of his PhD.[6] These data on children's print environment have been invaluable in most of my research publications on the learning of beginning reading. Well-specified descriptions of classroom teaching approaches for reading have also been invaluable, and systematic in-classroom observation of both child responses and teacher practices was an important component of two cross-national studies (Connelly, Johnston and Thompson 1999, 2001, Thompson et al. 2008).

The first opportunity to incorporate contrasting teaching environments into my research came during my first university research and study leave in 1984, part of which was spent at the Department of Psychology, University College of London. This Department provided a postgraduate programme for the practice of educational psychology, a London equivalent of the Victoria University programme offered at that time by our Department of Education, under the leadership of Professor Reginald Marsh. The London Department had a young staff member with a strong research interest in the reading processes of children, Dr

---

6　This cross-disciplinary link ensued from a Victoria University practice of the time (initiated by the Vice Chancellor, Dr Ian Axford) in which new staff publications were listed in the weekly staff newsletter.

Margaret Snowling (subsequently to become an international leader in this area and a professor at the University of York). At her suggestion, I visited the University of St Andrews to make contact with Dr Rhona Johnston, whom I found had an interest in collaborating in cross-national research on the influences of explicit phonics teaching on the processes of children's reading. This led to several joint research studies (Johnston and Thompson 1989, Johnston et al. 1995, Thompson and Johnston 1993, 2000, 2007). I have also collaborated with Vincent Connelly, a PhD student of Rhona Johnston. Vincent conducted half his PhD thesis research fieldwork in New Zealand, in conjunction with the Victoria University Department of Education. The other half was conducted in Scotland (Connelly et al. 1999, 2001). More recently Dr Connelly, now at Oxford Brookes University, Oxford, UK, has collaborated in two other cross-national studies (Thompson et al. 2009, Thompson et al. 2008). One of these involved four samples of children across three countries: New Zealand, Scotland, and Australia. The two samples in Australia were the responsibility of Associate Professor Michael McKay, Australian Catholic University, Melbourne, with whom I had contact two decades earlier at Monash University.

Dr Claire Fletcher-Flinn, University of Auckland (but in 2008 appointed Associate Professor in the College of Education, University of Otago), was also a principal collaborator in these cross-national studies. In 1988 she was appointed from La Trobe University, Melbourne, to the position of Postdoctoral Fellow in my research programme in the Department at Victoria University. The position was later held by Dr David Cottrell, who was appointed from the University of New South Wales. The New Zealand University Grants Committee funding[7] of this position enabled a sustained research effort to test alternative theoretical explanations of the processes for learning to read at the beginning levels (Thompson, Cottrell and Fletcher-Flinn 1996, Thompson and Fletcher-Flinn 1993, Thompson, Fletcher-Flinn and Cottrell 1999). The alternatives tested included those derived from my development of new theory. Later, the theory was also tested in a comprehensive longitudinal case study of

7   Any other funding of the published research by the author and colleagues mentioned in this chapter was mainly from within the universities involved. The only other sources were travel grants from the British Council in New Zealand for Dr Rhona Johnston and myself, and UK research grants (Wellcome Trust, Medical Research Council and Carnegie Trust) that supported some of the research in the UK by Dr Johnston.

the cognitive processes of a preschool child with exceptionally advanced reading skills (Fletcher-Flinn and Thompson 2000, 2004).

The 'New Zealand anomaly' of learning to read

The most commonly accepted and well documented theory of how children learn to read printed words (Share 1995, pp. 160, 197) implies that the child at the beginning level (as well as having some experience of reading text) needs to be taught explicit phonics, that is, the use of explicit letter-sound correspondences to respond to successive letters of unfamiliar words (to 'sound out' the common sounds taught for the letters, e.g., 'ki' – 'o' – 'ti' for the unfamiliar word *cot*, and thereby infer the word sound 'cot'). This 'standard' theory does not explain how New Zealand populations of children commencing school in the 1980s and early 1990s were learning to read without using explicit phonics (Connelly et al. 1999, 2001, Thompson, Cottrell and Fletcher-Flinn 1996, pp. 211–212). In New Zealand since that time some teachers now teach the common sound for each letter to children in Year 1, but this is not necessarily accompanied by the inclusion of explicit phonics in their teaching.

Moreover, the standard theory does not explain results from a normal control sample in the studies by Fletcher-Flinn and Thompson (2004). These normal progress, eleven-year-old readers in New Zealand were found to have only 60 per cent accuracy in responding with the common sound for each of the sixteen letters which have sounds that cannot be readily inferred from the name of the letter. This compared with 50 per cent accuracy for a comparable sample of five-year-olds (Thompson, Fletcher-Flinn and Cottrell 1999). Neither sample was taught explicit phonics. Hence, the eleven-year-olds had underdeveloped explicit knowledge of sounds for individual letters, despite their normal progress in reading and satisfactory proficiency in reading sets of new words. This result is inconsistent with the standard theory, which implies that full explicit knowledge of letter sounds is required for normal reading development. How then did these children attain high accuracy in attempting to read new words? Clearly it was not because they were reading by remembering whole print words. They had not seen the sets of new words before. Other studies (e.g., Thompson and Johnston 2000) also had yielded results inconsistent with the standard theory. There are then three possible conclusions: (a) the standard theory remains valid but the

New Zealand children and their teaching environment are "an anomaly", as suggested by a notable overseas researcher; (b) the standard theory is valid for only some approaches to teaching reading; or (c) the standard theory needs replacement. This third conclusion has been the basis for much of our research effort.

The knowledge sources theory

I have for some time worked on developing the Knowledge Sources theory of learning to read (Thompson 1999, Thompson and Fletcher-Flinn 1993, 2006) and with colleagues tested it against research evidence (Thompson et al. 1996, Thompson, Fletcher-Flinn and Cottrell 1999, Thompson and Johnston 2000, Fletcher-Flinn and Thompson 2000, 2004, 2007). In this theory, at the beginning level of learning to read, when children have learnt to respond correctly to just a few print words, they implicitly acquire patterns of letter-sound correspondences that are common across subsets of those words (e.g., for initial *s*, *see*, *said*, *sit*; e.g., for final *t*, *cat*, *sit*, *got*, *went*). According to the theory these 'lexicalised' letter-sound correspondence patterns are then used, mainly non-consciously, to facilitate reading of new or unfamiliar words. As these new words become familiar, they become part of the updated vocabulary of reading words, which in turn implicitly provides updated patterns of letter-sound correspondences common to subsets of those words. This implicit lexicalised letter-sound knowledge facilitates learning of new reading vocabulary, and the new vocabulary facilitates the learning of new letter-sound knowledge. There is a continuing recursive relationship between the two sources of knowledge. In the standard theory there is no such recursive relationship at the beginning levels of learning to read. The taught explicit phonics letter-sound knowledge can only facilitate, and is not facilitated by, gains in reading vocabulary. In the standard theory (Share 1995, pp. 160, 197), at the beginning levels explicit phonics is the only source of knowledge of letter-sound correspondences for attempting new words. In contrast, in the Knowledge Sources theory, from the beginning reading levels there are potentially two knowledge sources for letter-sound correspondences. The explicit knowledge of letter-sound correspondences from phonics teaching is an optional knowledge source for learning to read. Knowledge of implicit lexicalised letter-sound correspondences is normally involved in learning to read, whether or not teaching of explicit phonics is provided.

My colleagues and I have described specific teaching implications of this theory (Thompson 1999, 2002, McKay, Fletcher-Flinn and Thompson 2004), and more descriptions for teachers are planned.

Empirical evidence for the Knowledge Sources theory was obtained from a series of studies, the design of which was critically dependent upon previously obtained data about the print environment of Year 1 children (Thompson et al. 1996). With these data from the children's reading books we were able to predict, on the basis of the theory, those letter-sound correspondences within new words that the children would and would not know. Moreover, with the child's expansion of reading vocabulary by particular words, we were also able to successfully predict those letter-sound correspondences that would be implicitly induced by the child from patterns in the child's updated reading vocabulary, and would be available when responding to new words, previously unseen. We provided the children with the means of learning the expanded reading vocabulary over a period of three weeks. The standard theory could not provide an explanation of the results.

Evidence for the two sources of knowledge of letter-sound correspondences

The distinctive characteristics of the two sources of knowledge of letter-sound correspondences were investigated as reading skills develop (Johnston and Thompson 1989, Johnston et al. 1995). Consistent with this distinction, children without explicit phonics were advantaged over those with such teaching, when required to decide which of each presented item (e.g., *well, wosp, help, mosh*) was a correctly spelt real word. Some (e.g., *wosp*) were homophonic misspellings of real words (e.g., *wasp*). The children with explicit phonics were particularly prone to accept these as correctly spelt real words. They apparently could not avoid focusing conscious attention on the word-sound obtained from their processing of explicit letter-sound correspondences. The children without this phonics teaching did not have these explicit sound associations to interfere with their conscious decisions about the words.

More recently, in the first study of its kind, we have presented evidence that the distinctive nature of the two sources of knowledge of letter-sound correspondences, which result from different types of teaching, is not only manifest during the school years but continues into adulthood

(Thompson et al. 2009). Matched samples of adults who were skilled readers were obtained in Scotland and New Zealand. The Scottish sample had their initial school years in regions of Scotland where explicit phonics was included in the teaching of reading. The New Zealand sample had their initial schooling in state primary schools in New Zealand, which at that time did not include any teaching of explicit phonics. The adult participants were presented with words they had not seen before. Some (e.g., *thild*) had 'rime' units (e.g., *-ild*) that exist in real familiar words but are consistently given a non-regular pronunciation (e.g., *child, mild, wild*). The postulated implicit lexicalised source of letter-sound correspondence knowledge includes these non-regular correspondences as well as the regular correspondences. The letter-sound knowledge from explicit phonics, if provided for the child, includes only the regular correspondences. Both samples gave a significant proportion of acceptable regular pronunciations for the new words. However, the adults who had received childhood explicit phonics teaching were much more likely to use regular letter-sound correspondences than those who had not. They were less likely to respond with non-regular pronunciations, which were exclusive to the knowledge source of implicit lexicalised letter-sound correspondences.

Compensatory learning of children without explicit phonics?

There are other considerations about the learning processes of children who have not received explicit phonics teaching. Because the standard theory implies that in such a teaching environment learning to read will be particularly difficult, it has been argued that beginning readers in this situation who do manage to reach a level of reading skill equal to those with explicit phonics teaching must be children who have engaged in some kind of compensatory learning. This was recently investigated (Thompson et al. 2008) with four samples of children making slower than average progress in learning to read in their second year at school. All samples were matched on their level of word accuracy in reading story texts. Two samples (in Scotland and Australia) were being taught, and using, explicit phonics, and two samples (in Australia and New Zealand) were not, receiving only text-centred teaching that on occasions included some listening to sounds within words of their reading texts. How did those children without explicit phonics manage to reach the same level of word accuracy in reading text as those with this teaching? When attempting new words, did the children without explicit phonics compensate by making more use of units larger than the letter, such as lexical 'rimes' (e.g., -un of the known words, run, fun, sun, for the new word, jun)? All the children showed a small positive influence of lexical rime units on their reading of new words,[8] but the extent of influence was not affected significantly by the type of teaching.

Alternatively, did the children without explicit phonics compensate by reading more slowly in order to read as accurately as the children with phonics teaching? In fact the converse was true. The samples of children with explicit phonics read story texts slower than the samples without. There are only two other published studies that provide any such comparisons. Both also showed a large reading speed disadvantage for those with explicit phonics teaching (Connelly et al. 2001, Elder 1970–71). What is the explanation of this finding? In our study it was found that the extent to which children sounded out letters of words did not explain the slower rate of reading of the children with the phonics teaching, although these were the children who did the most sounding out. It was concluded that the explanation lay with the differences in the teaching programmes and the ways the children responded to them. Although the teaching programmes with explicit phonics lessons provided scheduled time for the children to read texts, it was much less than that for the children in the programmes centred on text reading without explicit phonics. Hence, those children without the phonics received more practice at text reading, and with that extra practice achieved a faster rate of reading. This faster reading rate would have a multiplier effect. The samples without phonics on average read 46 per cent more words per unit of time in the assessment story texts than the sample with the highest level of explicit phonics. Hence, the children who received text-centred teaching obtained more exposures to and practice at reading words. This provided the means by which they managed to achieve word reading accuracy equal to the children with instruction in explicit phonics. But as a bonus, they gained a text reading speed that was not as slow as that of the children with the phonics teaching.

---

8   Regular pronunciations were the common acceptable responses for these new words, unlike those presented to the adult samples previously described. Those words were designed to provide response options between regular and non-regular pronunciations.

There is evidence from a major US review of empirical research (National Reading Panel 2000) that teaching of explicit phonics to children at the beginning levels facilitates learning to read isolated words, and especially those which are new words with regular pronunciations. In the review there were no studies for the beginning levels with adequate sample sizes that examined word accuracy of text reading, and none at all that examined speed of reading text (see Thompson et al. 2008, p. 508). Hence, that review as well as the standard theory provide only a partial account of the learning and teaching of beginning reading.

Uses of the research and theory

The teaching implications of our research results just described are transparent. The implications of our research results on the reading of skilled adults, however, need some elaboration. Our results have shown the continuing influence of the type of childhood teaching on the way in which adults attempt the reading of new words. This has a strong implication for cognitive scientists who construct theoretical models of the processes of skilled reading. These processes cannot be studied in full without knowledge of the type of teaching received in childhood. Our results also conflict with the idea that explicit phonics is an instructional heuristic, the processes of which are fully superseded as reading skill matures. Our research breaks new ground as the first to examine the influence of childhood teaching of explicit phonics on the processes of reading in adulthood. Hence, it adds a new dimension to the long-standing debate among educators about the merits of including explicit phonics in the teaching of reading in schools.

Our Knowledge Sources theory and associated research evidence has been used in the international literature for cognitive scientists (Jackson and Coltheart 2001, Ramus 2004), in reviews on the learning of reading (Byrne 2005, Ehri 2005), as well as research on learning Chinese as a second language (Wang, Liu and Perfetti 2004). In collaboration with Dr Fletcher-Flinn, and Japanese and New Zealand colleagues, we have applied the theory to research on how Japanese five-year-olds and second-language learners in New Zealand secondary schools learn the more complex components (*yo-on* kana) of the Japanese hiragana orthography (report in preparation for publication). I have contributed to books (Thompson and Nicholson 1999, Thompson, Tunmer and Nicholson

1993)[9] that have been used as set reading in university courses for teachers and educators in the United States, the United Kingdom, France and New Zealand. An encyclopaedia chapter (Thompson 1997), along with several articles by other authors, is being reproduced by the Indian National Council of Educational Research and Training, for distribution to teachers in the thirty-five states of India, to use in their programme of development of the teaching of reading at the beginning levels.

Our research[10] has made a significant contribution to knowledge about reading both overseas and within New Zealand (e.g., Ministry of Education 1999, pp. 10–11). In New Zealand it has provided teachers with a new theory, and associated empirical evidence, that is inclusive of their tradition of a text-centred approach to teaching reading.

Acknowledgements

The patience and care of all colleagues, other research contributors, and research assistants is acknowledged with gratitude. Several had the burden of coping with the serious illness or death of a close relative during the course of a project. The diligent work of the many secretarial, technical, computer support, and library staff is gratefully acknowledged. Without their services the research would not have been possible. We are indebted to the Test Library of the Department (School) of Education for the provision of tests and equipment, without which the research could not have proceeded. We acknowledge with gratitude the generous cooperation of the school authorities, school staff, the parents and the children in each of the projects.

---

9   The 1999 book also included a chapter on how children evaluate literature they read, contributed by Chanda Pinsent, then a master's student at the Department.

10 Other research has focused on the basic process of learning letters for reading. We have published case studies on children with normal reading attainment but a severe deficit in aspects of their identification of some letters (Fletcher-Flinn and Thompson 2007); also theory and research on how normally developing children learn 'abstract letter units' for reading (Thompson and Johnston 2007, Thompson et al. 2008, Study 2), and I have prepared the first literature review to appear on this topic (Thompson 2009).

References

Byrne, B. (2005). Theories of learning to read. In M.J. Snowling and C. Hulme (Eds.). *The science of reading: a handbook*. Oxford, UK: Blackwell. pp. 104-119.

Cassidy, S. (1990). When is a developmental model not a developmental model? *Cognitive Systems*. 2. pp. 329-344.

Cassidy, S. (1992). *A computer model of reading development*. PhD Thesis. Victoria University of Wellington, New Zealand.

Connelly, V., Johnston, R.S. & Thompson, G.B. (1999). The influence of instructional approaches on reading procedures. In G.B. Thompson and T. Nicholson (Eds.). *Learning to read: beyond phonics and whole language*. New York, NY: Teachers College Press. pp. 103-123.

Connelly, V., Johnston, R.S. & Thompson, G.B. (2001). The effects of phonics instruction on the reading comprehension of beginning readers. *Reading and Writing*. 14. pp. 423-457.

Ehri, L.C. (2005). Development of sight word reading: phases and findings. In M.J. Snowling and C. Hulme (Eds.). *The science of reading: a handbook*. Oxford, UK: Blackwell. pp. 104-119.

Elder, R.D. (1970–71). Oral reading achievement of Scottish and American children. *Elementary School Journal*. 71. pp. 216-230.

Fieldhouse, A.E. (1952). *Oral word reading test*. Wellington: New Zealand Council for Educational Research.

Fieldhouse, A.E. (1957). *How to conduct a reading survey*. Wellington: New Zealand Council for Educational Research.

Fieldhouse, A.E. (1988). *Educational provision in New Zealand for children with learning difficulties: an historical outline*. (Mimeographed) Wellington: New Zealand Council for Educational Research.

Fletcher-Flinn, C.M. & Thompson, G.B. (2000). Learning to read with underdeveloped phonemic awareness but lexicalized phonological recoding: a case study. *Cognition*. 74. pp. 177-208.

Fletcher-Flinn, C.M. & Thompson, G.B. (2004). A mechanism of implicit lexicalized phonological recoding used concurrently with underdeveloped explicit letter-sound skills in both precocious and normal reading development. *Cognition*. 90. pp. 303-335.

Fletcher-Flinn, C.M. & Thompson, G.B. (2007). Dissociation between deficits in explicit procedures and implicit processes in the visual-spatial and the phonological systems during reading acquisition. *Cognitive Neuropsychology*. 24. pp. 471-484.

Jackson, N.E. & Coltheart, M. (2001). *Routes to reading success and failure: toward an integrated cognitive psychology of atypical reading*. New York: Psychology Press.

Johnston, R.S. & Thompson, G.B. (1989). Is dependence on phonological information in children's reading a product of instructional approach? *Journal of Experimental Child Psychology*. 48. pp. 131-145.

Johnston, R.S. Thompson, G.B., Fletcher-Flinn, C.M. & Holligan, C. (1995). The function of phonology in the acquisition of reading: lexical and sentence processing. *Memory & Cognition*. 23. pp. 749-766.

McKay, M.F., Fletcher-Flinn, C.M. & Thompson, G.B. (2004). New theory for under-standing reading and reading disability. *Australian Journal of Learning Disabilities*. 9, 2. pp. 3-7.

McKay, M.F. & Thompson, G.B. (2009). Reading vocabulary influences in phonological recoding during the development of reading skill: a re-examination of theory and practice. *Reading and Writing*. 22. pp. 167-184.

Ministry of Education (1999). *Literary experts group: report to the Secretary of Education*. Wellington: Ministry of Education.

National Reading Panel (2000). *Teaching children to read. Reports of the subgroups*. Washington, DC: National Institute of Child Health and Human Development.

Ramus, F. (2004). The neural basis of reading acquisition. In M.S. Gazzaniga (Ed.). *The cognitive neurosciences* (3rd Ed.). Cambridge, MA: MIT Press. pp. 815-824.

Share, D.L. (1990). Self-correction rates in oral reading: indices of efficient reading or artefact of text difficulty? *Educational Psychology*. 10. pp. 181-186.

Share, D.L. (1995). Phonological recoding and self-teaching: *sine qua non* of reading acquisition. *Cognition*. 55. pp. 151-218.

Thompson, G.B. (1981a). Individual differences attributed to self-correction in reading. *British Journal of Educational Psychology*. 51. pp. 228-229.

_____(1981b). Semantic context and graphic processing in the acquisition of reading. *British Journal of Educational Psychology*. 51. pp. 291-300.

_____(1983). The sex differential of selective promotion in New Zealand primary schools: 1929–1981. *New Zealand Journal of Educational Studies*. 18. pp. 76-79.

_____(1984). Self-corrections and the reading process: an evaluation of evidence. *Journal of Research in Reading*. 7. pp. 53-61.

_____(1985). Orthographic structures: Grapheme patterns in child and adult texts. *Journal of Research in Reading*. 8. pp. 32-44.

_____(1987). Three studies of predicted gender differences in processes of word reading. *Journal of Educational Research*. 80. pp. 212-219.

_____(1997). The teaching of reading. In V. Edwards and D. Corson (Eds.). *Encyclopedia of language and education, vol. 2 – literacy*. Dordrecht, The Netherlands: Kluwer Academic. pp. 9-17.

_____(1999). The processes of learning to identify words. In G.B. Thompson and T. Nicholson (Eds.). *Learning to read: beyond phonics and whole language*. New York: Teachers College Press. pp. 25-54.

_____(2002). Teaching and the phonics debate: what can we learn? *New Zealand Annual Review of Education*. 11. pp. 161-178.

_____(2009). The long learning route to abstract letter units. *Cognitive Neuropsychology*. 26. pp. 50-69.

Thompson, G.B., Connelly, V., Fletcher-Flinn, C.M. & Hodson, S.J. (2009). The nature of skilled adult reading varies with type of instruction in childhood. *Memory & Cognition*.

Thompson, G.B., Cottrell, D.S. & Fletcher-Flinn, C.M. (1996). Sublexical orthographic-phonological relations early in the acquisition of reading: The knowledge sources account. *Journal of Experimental Child Psychology*. 62. pp. 190-222.

Thompson, G.B. & Fletcher-Flinn, C.M. (1993). A theory of knowledge sources and procedures for reading acquisition. In G.B. Thompson, W.E. Tunmer, and T. Nicholson (Eds.). *Reading acquisition processes*. Clevedon, UK: Multilingual Matters. pp. 20-73.

Thompson, G.B. & Fletcher-Flinn, C.M. (2006). Lexicalised implicit learning in reading acquisition: The knowledge sources theory. In C.M. Fletcher-Flinn & G.M. Haberman (Eds.). *Cognition and language: perspectives from New Zealand*. Bowen Hills, Queensland: Australian Academic Press. pp. 141-156.

Thompson, G.B., Fletcher-Flinn, C.M. & Cottrell, D.S. (1999). Learning correspondences between letters and phonemes without explicit instruction. *Applied Psycholinguistics*. 20. pp. 21-50.

Thompson, G.B. & Johnston, R.S. (1993). The effects of type of instruction on processes of reading acquisition. In G.B. Thompson, W.E. Tunmer and T. Nicholson (Eds.). *Reading acquisition processes*. Clevedon, UK: Multilingual Matters. pp. 74-90.

Thompson, G.B. & Johnston, R.S. (2000). Are nonword and other phonological deficits indicative of a failed reading process? *Reading and Writing*. 12. pp. 63-97.

Thompson, G.B. & Johnston, R.S. (2007). Visual and orthographic information in learning to read and the influence of phonics instruction. *Reading and Writing*. 20. pp. 859-884.

Thompson, G.B., McKay, M.F., Fletcher-Flinn, C.M., Connelly, V., Kaa, R.T. & Ewing, J. (2008). Do children who acquire word reading without explicit phonics employ compensatory learning? Issues of phonological recoding, lexical orthography, and fluency. *Reading and Writing*. 21. pp. 505-537.

Thompson, G.B. & Nicholson, T. (Eds.). (1999). *Learning to read: beyond phonics and whole language*. New York: Teachers College Press.

Thompson, G.B., Tunmer, W.E. & Nicholson, T. (1993). *Reading acquisition processes*. Clevedon, UK: Multilingual Matters.

Wang, M., Liu, Y. & Perfetti, C.A. (2004). The implicit and explicit learning of orthographic structure and function of a new writing system. *Scientific Studies of Reading*. 8. pp. 357-379.

Mathematics after Efficiency: An Agenda for Action

Jim Neyland

Introduction

Efficiency has a great strength and two paralysing weaknesses. It knows how well a thing *worked*, but it has no idea what the thing is *for*, and it cannot fathom what the thing *is*. It can proclaim for instance, as one well-regarded visiting British mathematics educator did some years ago, that it is more efficient than otherwise to teach division before multiplication. But it cannot figure out what division and multiplication are. It cannot determine their relative co-dependence as ideas. And it cannot assess their significance within mathematics more generally, or estimate the degree to which teaching division and multiplication in this way is in tune with the spirit of good education. Efficiency gives us darkly the rear vision only. It provides a retrospective calculation of proficiency, but is bewildered when asked to point the way ahead or decide on priorities. This is not a problem so long as efficiency takes its proper place, as secondary to other more important dimensions of mathematics teaching. The trouble is, because it panders to a recently felt instinct to tabulate and compare, efficiency suits our modern temper rather too well. Impressed by efficiency's technical apparatus we too easily forget its emptiness of meaning. In short, efficiency makes a poor overseer. It can put a price on relatively unimportant things, but it cannot determine the value of things because its perspective is necessarily deficient. It cannot, for instance, understand the cost education pays for efficiency's own success. This is efficiency's inherent limitation: it can measure the cost of achievement, yet it is unable to achieve the cost of measurement.

The efficiency movement has prevailed in New Zealand mathematics education for two decades, and it has effectively clouded over those larger horizons of qualitative distinction that ought to be our guide. How has mathematics fared under this regime? Unsurprisingly – one would not expect an efficient but mindless mathematics education to be a cause for celebration – it has suffered. In this essay I will briefly summarise how mathematics has suffered, and go on to propose an agenda for its rehabilitation. I will argue that, under efficiency, mathematics is losing its proper sense of orientation. It is becoming a precisely performed but empty ritual. What should we aspire to instead? I will argue that mathematics education should set its compasses towards four points. First, mathematics education space needs to be reinvigorated as a public space in which norms and priorities are created, ideals articulated, and social bonds formed. Second, mathematics education space needs to be understood as complex and emergent. Third, primacy needs to be given to the primordial ethical bond that exists between people. And finally, new horizons of significance need to be established for orienting mathematics teaching.

A word of clarification before I proceed. When I say that mathematics education is becoming empty ritual, I am not talking about the work of individual teachers or the learning in individual classrooms. Good teachers somehow manage to inculcate a love and understanding of mathematics despite the efficiency movement. I am talking instead about the government-run institution of mathematics education – aided and abetted by those training institutions and resource writers who unthinkingly acquiesce to its imperatives – that imposes upon teachers and students the bureaucratic cog wheels and pistons that relentlessly drive efficiency, and in the process drown out other, more beneficial orientations with their din.

The scientific management of mathematics education

The birth of the modern efficiency movement coincided with the birth of modern assessment. I have argued elsewhere that if one year and one place were to be chosen as the time and location of their birth they would be, respectively, 1980 and the United States (Neyland, 2007c). Freudenthal, founder of the Freudenthal Institute in the Netherlands, wrote about what he saw happening in United States mathematics at the time. He argued that "atomisation", "dividing into diminutive pieces", and the like, is "the most fashionable wisdom of instruction theory". Subjects are ground down to "powdered form" and "administered by spoonfuls". Indeed, mathematics seems to invite atomisation because it is "[i]solating, enumerating, exactly describing concepts and relations, growing them like cultures *in vitro*, and inoculating them by teaching – it is water to the mill of [these] pedagogues and general didacticians" (Freudenthal 1980, pp. 93–97). He went on to illustrate his point by making reference to a recently published text that systematically catalogued school mathematics into a list of 250,000 outcomes. This new fashion was eventually taken up in England and Wales – albeit in a less extreme form – and was the impetus behind their new outcomes-led curriculum: *Mathematics in the National Curriculum* (Department of Education and Science 1989). In this document school mathematics was divided into 296 statements of attainment organised into 14 parallel hierarchies, most having 10 levels. A few years later we in New Zealand introduced our own outcomes-led curriculum organised in levels, and supplemented this with Unit Standards and Achievement Standards.

But 'outcomes' and 'standards' were only the outward manifestation of what amounted to a new revolutionary movement in mathematics education. The decision to legislate into the heart of mathematics in an attempt to achieve unprecedented efficiencies requires four things. There needs to be an unambiguous statement of the outcomes that teachers, and in turn students, are to achieve. This, of course, is what is behind the outcomes-led curriculum and the proliferation of so-called standards. But it is not enough to set the outcomes that others must meet. The legislator needs to be confident that teachers and students will comply with these directives. In other words, there needs to be a theory of how legislators will initially establish and then maintain control over those who work in education. In contemporary scientific management the theory of control is a combination of Agency Theory, Public Choice Theory, New Public Management Theory, and Transaction-Cost Analysis Theory, and is founded on the belief that social relations are governed by a social contract. Simply put, the theory of control behind the efficiency movement stipulates that teachers will teach properly only because they are bound by a contract that rewards them financially if they follow authorised procedures and satisfy the governmentally stipulated outcome requirements. Because teachers are understood to be working to a set of contractual specifications, an audit agency is needed to monitor the degree of compliance. Finally, the system as a whole needs to be continually monitored and periodically recalibrated so that a state of maximal efficiency can be maintained. Accordingly detailed information needs constantly to be gathered about the condition of education space (Neyland 1994, 1998, 2000, 2004a, 2004c). Overall, what has emerged under scientific management is the situation where too much attention is given to the mathematics of education, and not enough to the education of mathematics.

A manufactured disorder in mathematics space

Modern scientific management is a trans-national phenomenon (Smyth 1995), and its leading characteristics rhyme with the disembedding dynamisms of globalisation. Giddens defines disembedding as the "lifting out of social relations from local contexts of interaction and their restructuring across indefinite spans of time-space" (1990, p. 21). In education the chief forms of disembedding are 'symbolic tokens' and 'expert systems'. Together these cause mathematics education to be progressively emptied of meaning. The former mode is evident in the way school mathematics under scientific management is increasingly losing its real value and assuming instead the exchange value of tradable standards. The process is now familiar. Complex mathematics space is rendered down into a sequence of atomistic units which are then stripped back until they resemble statements of outcomes. Subsequently these outcomes are foreshortened to so-called definitive performance criteria which ultimately substitute for what was formerly nuanced, contextualised and dynamic. Inevitably, and inexorably, the focus of attention shifts from the originally intended engagement with a layered and humanistic mathematics to its disembedded imitator, the ritualised demonstration of prescribed performance in exchange for tokens of credit. Needless to say this free-floating caricature-mathematics now bears little trace of its earlier situated, communally negotiated, and experientially grounded self.

This emptying of mathematical meaning is amplified by a corresponding emptying of ethical meaning from the relationship between teachers and students that attends the second disembedding dynamism of globalisation. Bauman (1992) argues that 'expert systems' result in the direct interpersonal encounter – which is fundamentally constitutive of the social bond – being emptied of its ethical significance and replaced by the performability criteria of technical accountability to centrally prescribed protocols. Expert systems, according to his award-winning analysis, are based on the conviction that doing things properly requires specialist knowledge held only by an elite few, and accordingly that these few ought to be in charge of the rest, who must adhere to the codes and standards they authorise.

Through this second mode of disembedding personal responsibility becomes separated from the interpersonal realm of ethical meaning and assumes the depleted form of the free-floating requirement to acquiesce to the demands of centrally stipulated procedures (Neyland 2004c, 2007a).

Ultimately what is at stake here is the crown of sovereignty over mathematics space. The leading manoeuvre in the battle for control is the concerted attempt by those who intend to assume authority to turn this space into a 'literary' space; that is, one which is fully legible, logical and enumerable, and able to be recounted in writing – which includes graphical and tabular representations – in meticulous detail. Literary mathematics space is presented as, in principle, containing nothing that might evade clear description. Nothing is constitutively ineffable, illegible or ambiguous. Nothing diminishes the central authority's capacity to fully domesticate and manage mathematics space. Any area of evident uncertainty or ambiguity is seen as being only temporarily so; it is seen as not yet legible, rather than as illegible. The fact that this space in reality is complex, locally emergent and diverse is passed over or denied. This leads to the fatal paradox of the efficiency movement. In an attempt to make mathematics space transparent and amenable to bureaucratic control, complex localised practices need to be overridden. But it is precisely these practices that provide a sense of orientation and meaning in education. The literalising of mathematics space results, therefore, not in teachers and students becoming better informed, purposefully motivated, and fully literate, but in them losing their former locally fashioned webs of meaning and sense of purpose. In other words, the engineering instinct to create a literary space causes those who work in it to become wrong-footed and illiterate.

For this reason, together with the debilitating consequences of the oft and loudly proclaimed mantra that only experts know best, what results from the drive for sovereignty is not a map of mathematics space – which conceivably could be helpful – but an artificially designed blueprint for the administration of that space. Mathematics territory is not charted, it is forced to conform to an imposed and predetermined overlay of outcomes, performance criteria and accountability protocols. There are two steps in the process of making mathematical space into one that is elite-ruled and artificially designed. First, the practice of mapping is normalised. Second, the expert elite take control of the process of mapping and turn the maps into blueprints. This occurred recently in mathematics through a kind of bloodless revolution that few appeared to notice. First, teachers were encouraged, as a supplementary step in lesson planning, to state the intended outcomes for each lesson. Second, once this practice was normalised, those in authority took effective control of the plans by specifying the outcomes centrally. The upshot of all this is the privatising of what was formally public education space. Public space is where norms and priorities are created, ideals articulated, and social bonds forged. Public space is communally shaped, emergent, situationally embedded and ethically oriented. But when public space is dismantled and colonised in the way just described, it becomes a privatised space characterised by extra-territorial protocols, codes and standards designed and administered by so-called experts. In summary, in an effort to achieve unprecedented efficiencies, those in authority dismantle the existing communally designed, emergent order and produce instead, not a new literary order, but an artificially designed, elite-ruled and privatised disorder. In a phrase, they create a manufactured disorder (Neyland 2006, 2007b).

An agenda for action

This, in broad and sobering terms, is the present condition of mathematics in New Zealand. Ideally things would be different. The rehabilitation of mathematics education space requires that efficiency be held in check and made subsidiary to other priorities. Among these are the following. First, mathematics education space – which has become in effect a privatised domain – needs to be reinvigorated as a public space in which practitioners themselves create norms and priorities, articulate ideals, and in the process strengthen social bonds. Second, mathematics education space needs to be understood, not as literary and designed, but as complex and emergent. Third, a new way of theorising the notion of social control needs to be understood and practised. This new way treats the ubiquitous code, protocol and standard as secondary phenomena which must be made answerable to something else which precedes them. Primacy needs to be given to the primordial ethical bond that exists between people. Fourth, the outcome statement and the performance criterion need to be accorded only a minor role in the organisation of mathematics. In their place, horizons of significance need to be recognised as both inescapable and better able to provide a sense of direction for mathematics teaching; and suitable horizons need to be brought into view.

The reinvigoration of public space, both within and outside the classroom, requires two things. First, within the classroom setting, it needs to be recognised that mathematics is neither structured nor unstructured, but nearly structured. It is neither wild nor tamed, but nearly tamed and forever untameable (Neyland 2004b). In line with this it needs to be recognised that frequently in scientifically managed mathematics, ideas are passed off as facts. A small example. Four thousand years ago, on clay tablets, Babylonian mathematics students learned to calculate the square root of two to the equivalent of six decimal places accuracy. But it took a further two-and-a-half thousand years before the idea of zero was invented (by the Hindus). Zero is an idea, but it is seldom taught as such. The difference is crucial. If ideas are misrepresented in this way, then mathematics teaching begins to emit the whiff of indoctrination, and it correspondingly loses something of its proper spirit. The difference is particularly marked at the point of justification. Ideas and facts are justified differently. Facts inhabit the realm of the true, and require proof. Ideas are not proved, they are justified by more interpersonal and humanistic processes such as those that involve the weighing up of pros and cons, persuading others about the soundness of metaphorical projections, criticism aimed at consensus, and an appeal to shared notions of elegance and utility (Neyland, 2009/ forthcoming). Importantly, the creation and evaluation of mathematical ideas occur in subjunctive education spaces which are increasingly being closed off and made indicative under the efficiency movement (Bruner 1986, Neyland 2008/forthcoming, Sumara and Davis 2007). Second, in the staffroom and local mathematics association, education ideals must be allowed to bump into one another, and in the process social bonds must be formed as imaginations are stretched in dialogue. Further, stories that sustain the education spirit need to be told and re-told, and constellations of meaning drawn out of catalytic situational events. It is this sort of localised, communal activity – not deference to the voice of authority – that a profession makes. And it is this that culminates in the crafting of true expertise – what Varela (1999) calls 'ethical know-how'.

Trembling legislators contemplate the prospect of an out-of-control disorder in education space. This is what lies behind their fixation on making this space comprehensible and predictable. But, as we saw earlier, their medicine worsens the illness; it produces a manufactured disorder. To some, this appears to leave the manager in a damned-if-you-do and damned-if-you-don't bind. In fact it betrays a limited understanding of the nature of education space. Education space is not complicated in the way that legislators believe; it only myopically resembles complicatedness. In reality it is complex and emergent (Davis, Sumara and Luce-Kapler 2000). In other words, education space, under the right conditions, is self-ordering, and does not require regimentation by self-appointed experts. What are these right conditions? I have argued elsewhere (for instance in Neyland 2004b, 2006) that the ingredients that lead to complex emergence are more or less the same as the six conditions that lead to the successful improvisation of a jazz combo: (a) an openness to complexity; (b) the paring back of structure to an optimally minimal level; (c) a willingness to play both inside and (d) outside that structure; (e) a focus on pursuing ideals; and (f) the nurturing and preservation of ethical know-how.

Within the realm of interpersonal responsibility an optimally minimal structure is one that accords primacy to the primordial ethical encounter between people. It is in this area, more than any other, that orthodox efficiency policy is found wanting. Orthodoxy gives primacy to the rule, code and protocol, when primacy ought to be accorded to the unmediated, empathic engagement of one person with another (Neyland 2004a). This idea runs so much against the grain of modern sensibility it is nearly unthinkable. Accordingly this assertion requires careful justification – I have attempted this in my recently completed book manuscript *If you don't strike oil, stop boring: rediscovering the spirit of education after scientific management*. It is not that codification and the like have no place; these things are necessary. The trouble occurs when they are allowed to escape a requirement to first be answerable to the primordial ethical encounter that precedes them (Ricoeur 1992). Whenever the train of codification leaves the tracks of trust, care and responsibility, the ethical relationship at the centre of education is eroded. The consequences are debilitating.

Finally, we need to become newly aware of the inescapability and necessity of horizons of significance. This is another notion that runs against the grain of efficiency thinking. What is an horizon of significance and why are they inescapable? I will illustrate this using an example. Last year approximately 200,000 mathematical theorems were proved; roughly two every working minute. These theorems, it hardly needs saying, are not equal in significance: some are trivial, others profound; some proofs are awkward, others elegant; some tack in place the final paling around an exhausted area of research, others throw open the window to the winds of change. How do we decide their relative significance? Is there a set of standards and criteria laid out for deciding such things? No. Such decisions are made on the basis of somewhat elusive horizons of significance without which we cannot decide. They are made on the basis of aesthetic, utilitarian and intuitively felt qualitative discriminations. Importantly, such decision-making is impossible to codify. Our ideas about what is good, useful, ideal and beautiful in both mathematics and education are of a different order from the realm of things that can be made precise. They cannot be reduced to a technical plane manipulable by a scientific manager. When mathematics space is oriented by horizons of significance – these are neither objective nor subjective, but inter-subjective – it is not regulated, it is animated; one could say, animated by the spirit Education.

The proposed agenda for action boils down to an agenda to bring to education a new spirit. There is nothing mystical or vague about the spirit of mathematics education. But, equally, it cannot be flattened down to the featureless, mean-spirited dimensions required by the efficiency movement. And it is possible to present a reasoned argument that outlines the dimensions of such a spirited education – *If you don't strike oil* contains such an argument. In summary, no one wants an inefficient and wasteful mathematics education, but what we have at the moment is an efficient and increasingly meaningless one. Educators did not choose the efficiency movement, it was visited upon them by an engineer who sought to fit the mathematics education cosmos into his head. But mathematics education, if these two words have any real meaning and character, aspires to exactly the opposite: to lift our collective heads into the enchanting mathematics cosmos. When history looks back on the efficiency movement I speculate that it will not judge approvingly its meticulousness in attempting to pixelate education space, but harshly for its timorousness, myopic vision, and diminished humanity.

References

Bauman, Z. (1992). *Intimations of postmodernity*. London: Routledge.
Bruner, J. (1986). *Actual minds, possible worlds*. Cambridge: Harvard University Press.
Davis, B., Sumara, D. & Luce-Kapler, R. (2000). *Engaging minds: learning and teaching in a complex world*. Mahwah: Lawrence Erlbaum Associates.
Department of Education and Science (1989). *Mathematics in the national curriculum*. London: Author.

Freudenthal, H. (1980). *Weeding and sowing: preface to a science of mathematics education*. London: Reidel Publishing Co.

Giddens, A. (1990). *The consequences of modernity*. Stanford: Stanford University Press.

Neyland, J. (1994). Problems with the proposed unit standard framework for mathematics. *New Zealand Mathematics Magazine*. 31, 1. pp. 1-9.

_____(1998). Outcomes-based mathematics education. In N. Ellerton (Eds.). *Issues in mathematics education: a contemporary perspective*. Perth: MASTEC, Edith Cowan University. pp. 60-75.

_____(2000). Testing public knowledge policy: the case of unit standards in mathematics. *New Zealand Mathematics Magazine*. 37, 3. pp. 21-28.

_____(2004a). An ethical critique of the paradigm case: the mathematics curriculum. In A-M. O'Neill, J. Clark & R. Openshaw (Eds.). *Reshaping culture, knowledge and learning: policy and content in the New Zealand curriculum framework*. Palmerston North: Dunmore Press. pp. 143-160.

_____(2004b). Playing outside: an introduction to the jazz metaphor in mathematics education. *Australian Senior Mathematics Journal*. 18, 2. pp. 8-16.

_____(2004c). Towards a postmodern ethics of mathematics education. In M. Walshaw (Eds.). *Mathematics education within the postmodern*. Greenwich, Connecticut: Information Age Publishing. pp. 55-73.

_____(2006). The literary curriculum and the denial of backgrounds. *Curriculum Matters*. pp. 63-80.

_____(2007a). Globalisation, ethics and mathematics education. In B. Atweh, A. Barton, M. Borba, N. Gough, C. Keitel, C. Vistro-Yu, and R. Vithal. (Eds.). *Internationalisation and globalisation in mathematics and science education*, Dordrecht: Springer. pp. 113-128.

_____(2007b). The spectre of the literary curriculum. *Curriculum Matters*. pp. 92-107.

_____(2007c). The untold story of assessment. *Curriculum Matters*. pp. 108-122.

_____(2008/forthcoming). Ontological centring and education. *Curriculum Matters*.

_____(2009/forthcoming). Mathematical facts and ideas: Which are which? In R. Averill, R. Harvey and D. Smith (Eds.). *Secondary mathematics and statistics education: evidence based practice. Vol. 1*. Wellington: New Zealand Council for Education Research.

Ricoeur, P. (1992). *Oneself as another*. Chicago: University of Chicago Press [Translated by K. Blamey].

Smyth, J. (1995). What's happening to teachers' work in Australia? *Education Review*. 47. pp. 189-198.

Sumara, D. & Davis, B. (2007). Subjunctive spaces of curriculum: on the importance of eccentric knowledge. *Curriculum Matters*. pp. 79-91.

Varela, F. (1999). *Ethical know-how*. Stanford: Stanford University Press.

AFTERWORD

Contributions to Scholarship in Education from the School of Education

Joanna Kidman and Ken Stevens

The School of Education at Victoria University of Wellington contributed to scholarship through academic publications and research-based teaching for over eight decades; some of these activities are indicated in the preceding chapters. The School also contributed to scholarship in another way – by providing an unusual amount of scholarly leadership in other universities in New Zealand, as well as in other countries. The former Department of Education of Victoria University of Wellington is likely to be remembered for the number of professors of education that it produced. Today it is possible to find professors of education from the School in the United States, Canada, the United Kingdom, Norway, Ireland, and, until recently, in Hong Kong and Malawi. As well as contributing to universities overseas, graduates of this School hold, or have held, Chairs of Education at Otago, Massey and Waikato Universities. Remarkably, six professors of education at the University of Waikato have been either former members of staff or graduates of the Victoria University Department of Education.

The range of professorial appointments from this Department is an indication of its influence in the discipline nationally and internationally. Some former members of the Department appointed to Chairs in Education in other New Zealand universities and wānanga include:

1. Keith Ballard — University of Otago[+]
2. Richard Harker — Massey University[+]
3. Kathie Irwin — Te Whare Wānanga o Awanuiārangi
4. Ian McLaren — University of Waikato[+]
5. Kay Morris Matthews — Eastern Institute of Technology

Graduates of the Department who were later appointed to Chairs in the University include:

1. Rollo Arnold   Internal appointment, by promotion*
2. Cedric Hall   Appointed from the UTDC, VUW
3. Arthur Fieldhouse   Internal appointment, by promotion*
4. Helen May   Appointed from the University of Waikato
5. Deborah Willis   Dean of Humanities and Social Sciences

Graduates of the Department who were appointed to professorial positions in other New Zealand universities include:

1. Peter Freyberg   University of Waikato*
2. Susan Middleton   University of Waikato
3. Peter Ramsay   University of Waikato+
4. Martin Thrupp   University of Waikato
5. Stephen May   University of Waikato

Members of the Department who were appointed to professorial positions in universities overseas include:

1. Graham Feletti   University of Hawaii, USA+
2. David Galloway   University of Durham, UK+
3. Kathy Green   Post-Doctoral Fellow, University of Denver, USA
4. Jane Kroger   University of Tromso, Norway
5. John Nichols   Purdue University and, subsequently, the University of Illinois at Chicago, USA*
6. Bruce Ryan   University of Guelph, Canada+
7. Ken Stevens   Memorial University of Newfoundland, Canada
8. Keith Sullivan   National University of Ireland, Galway

Several professors of education at Victoria University of Wellington were later appointed to Chairs in Education in universities overseas. They include:

1. Gerald Grace University of Durham and, subsequently, The Institute of Education of the University of London, UK
2. Hugh Lauder University of Bath, UK
3. Reg Marsh Baptist University of Hong Kong and, subsequently, The University of Malawi

+ *retired*
* *deceased*

It is possible that there have been other members of the Department and graduates who have become professors of education. The above list is compiled from people we, as editors of this volume, have known during the time we have been associated with Victoria University of Wellington. Over the last two decades of its existence an increasing number of postgraduate students undertook studies for masters and doctoral degrees in education at Victoria University, some of whom are mentioned in the above chapters. From the growing number of post-graduate students there are likely to be other leaders in education who were educated in the former department throughout New Zealand and overseas. For over eight decades, the Department of Education of Victoria University of Wellington nurtured and launched many professional lives. It is through its graduates and former faculty members that the Department will continue to influence education in this country and beyond.

THE CONTRIBUTORS

Lise Bird Claiborne is Director of the Centre for Postgraduate Studies and Associate Professor in the Department of Human Development and Counselling at the University of Waikato School of Education in Hamilton, New Zealand. Her research and teaching interests are in human development and educational psychology, influenced by feminist and poststructural questions about diversity, culture, disability and social justice. She is committed to collaborative research with professionals about our hopes of transformation in an era of global change.

Jim Collinge trained as a teacher at Auckland Teachers College and, for some years, taught in primary schools in Auckland and Nottingham. From 1972 to 2003 he taught in the Department/School of Education at Victoria University of Wellington, specialising mainly in Philosophy of Education and Comparative Education and, from 1986 in Peace Education. He was, from 1988 to 1991, Director of the Stout Research Centre for the Study of New Zealand History, Society and Culture at Victoria University, and, from 1998 to 2004, Associate Dean (Students) in the Faculty of Humanities and Social Sciences. In 1992 he held a Swedish Institute Fellowship at the School of Education, University of Lund, where he worked with Professor Åke Bjerstedt in the programme 'Preparedness for Peace', in addition to studying developments in Swedish education. He has published on Peace Education in journals and books in Sweden, Hungary and Italy. Jim Collinge retired in 2004, but returned to Victoria University in 2005 to be Programme Director of Media Studies, and, for the year 2006, Head of the School of Asian and European Languages and Cultures. He currently chairs the Board of Gender and Women's Studies, and is Acting Programme Director of the Film Programme at Victoria University until June 2010.

Carmen Dalli is Associate Professor in the School of Educational Psychology and Pedagogy at Victoria University of Wellington's Faculty of Education, specialising in Early Childhood Education. She began her academic career at the University of Malta after completing her MEd as a Commonwealth Scholar at Bristol University. She joined Victoria

University in 1986, and there she gained her PhD in 1999. She was involved in establishing the Institute for Early Childhood Studies in 1994, she initiated the Institute's 'Occasional Publication' Series in 1996, and she has served as Director of the Institute for several years. In 2006, she became an associate director of the Jessie Hetherington Centre for Educational Research. She played a leading role in the national working group that developed the early childhood Code of Ethics between 1993 and 1995. Her research focus is on early childhood educational practices, particularly with children aged under three years, and on issues of professionalism in early childhood education.

Jane Gilbert is currently Chief Researcher at the New Zealand Council for Educational Research. She was a senior lecturer in the School of Education at Victoria University of Wellington for nine years (1995–2003), working mainly in sociology/philosophy of education and science/ technology education. Before that she taught Science Education in the School of Mathematics and Computing Sciences at Victoria University of Wellington, and Sociology of Education in the School of Education at the University of Waikato. She was previously a secondary school teacher (of science and biology) for ten years. Her current work mainly involves thinking about and working on how schooling needs to be different in the 21st century. She has published two books: *Catching the Knowledge Wave? The Knowledge Society and the future of education* (2005) and *Disciplining and drafting, or 21st century learning? Rethinking the New Zealand senior school curriculum for the future* (2008, with Rachel Bolstad).

Gerald Grace was Professor of Education and Chairperson of the Department of Education (1987–1989) at Victoria University of Wellington. His inaugural address (5 September 1988) entitled 'Education: Commodity or Public Good?' was a criticism of the New Zealand Treasury document, *Government Management* (see Vol. 2, *Education Issues*, 1987). His address argued that education was not a 'commodity in the market' but a public service and a public good for all New Zealand citizens. Gerald returned to the UK in 1989, having been invited to be Chair of the School of Education at Durham University. He retired from Durham in 1996 and is currently Director of the Centre of Research and Development in Catholic Education at the University of London, Institute of Education. Recent publications include the *International Handbook of Catholic Education* (2 volumes), in 2007, and the journal *International Studies in Catholic Education*, in 2009.

Cedric Hall is Emeritus Professor of Education, having been employed at Victoria University of Wellington (VUW) since 1977. He has held a number of positions at VUW, including Director of the University Teaching Development Centre, Head of School (School of Education), and Deputy Dean of the Faculty of Education when the previous Wellington College of Education merged with Victoria University in 2005. His teaching and research interests have covered: educational assessment and measurement; research methodology; educational psychology; teaching and learning in higher education; educational policy relating to higher education and also senior secondary school assessment systems; quality assurance in higher education; and the design and implementation of professional development for teachers and trainers.

James Irving has had a long career in education in New Zealand and overseas. He has been a teacher in New Zealand and Fiji (1959–65), vocational guidance officer (1965–67), research officer at NZCER (1968–71), lecturer at Victoria University of Wellington (1972–78), and held senior positions in the Department of Education in International Education and Research (1979–89), and in the Ministry of Education (1989–95). As Manager of the Educational Assessment Secretariat (1990–95) he developed policies leading to the National Education Monitoring Project (NEMP) and the Assessment Resource Banks (ARBs). From 1996 to 2002 he was a senior lecturer at Victoria University, teaching postgraduate courses on contemporary education policy in New Zealand and curriculum, learning and assessment. He has worked internationally for UNESCO and the World Bank, on New Zealand surveys for the International Association for the Evaluation of Educational Achievement (IEA), and with the Bernard van Leer Foundation. He has represented New Zealand on the OECD Education Committee and CERI Governing Board in Paris, and from 1990 to 1995 was the National Coordinator for the OECD Educational Indicators Project (INES) and New Zealand representative on the Student Achievement Outcomes Network which set up the OECD Programme for International Student Assessment (PISA). He has written widely on education including comparative education, curriculum, learning and assessment, education policy, educational indicators and development. His most recent publications are *School-wide Assessment: The Big Picture* (NZCER 1997) and (with Warwick Elley) an updating of the Elley–Irving Socio-Economic Index (*New Zealand Journal of Educational Statistics*, Vol. 38, no. 1, 2003).

Joanna Kidman studied in the School of Education in the 1980s and is now a Senior Lecturer in the Faculty of Education at Victoria University of Wellington. She is based in He Pārekereke: Institute for Research and Development in Māori and Pacific Education. Her current research interests are in the sociology of Māori education.

Jane Kroger is Professor of Developmental Psychology at the University of Tromsø, Norway. She holds a PhD in Child Development. Her current research interests are the study of identity in adolescent and adult development. She has published numerous theoretical and research articles on issues of identity and is author of *Identity in Adolescence: The Balance Between Self and Other* (3rd ed., Psychology Press), *Identity Development: Adolescence through Adulthood* (2nd ed., Sage), and editor of *Discussions on Ego Identity* (Lawrence Erlbaum Associates). She has been a visiting scholar at the Erik H. and Joan M. Erikson Center at Harvard University and also at the Henry A. Murray Center for the Study of Lives, Radcliffe College. She is past president of the Society for Research on Identity Formation.

Hugh Lauder has been Professor of Education and Political Economy at the University of Bath since 1996. He was formerly Dean of Education at Victoria University of Wellington. Hugh specialises in the relationship of education to the economy, and has for over ten years worked on national skill strategies and more recently on the global skill strategies of multinational companies. He has co-authored and co-edited several books, including *The Global Auction: The Broken Promises of Opportunities, Jobs and Rewards* (Oxford University Press, forthcoming), *Education, Globalization and Social Change* (Oxford University Press, 2006), *High Skills: Globalisation, Competitiveness and Skill Formation* (Oxford University Press, 2001), and *Capitalism and Social Progress: The Future of Society in a Global Economy* (Palgrave Press, 2001; reprinted in Chinese, 2007). He has also published many academic papers, including some on international education and globalisation, and is editor of the *Journal of Education and Work*.

Helen May is Professor of Education and Dean of the University of Otago College of Education (Dunedin, New Zealand). Her research interests are in early childhood policy, history and curriculum. She has been involved in advocacy work and advisory roles regarding a range of policy initiatives in both New Zealand and international settings. She is the author of a number of books on the history of early childhood education.

Lex McDonald commenced working as a lecturer at Victoria University of Wellington in 2002 and is currently the Head of the School of Educational Psychology and Pedagogy in the Faculty of Education. He has been a teacher, educational advisor and psychologist and has a research interest in training and professional development. Lex has worked in New Zealand, Wales, the Cook Islands and Samoa.

Anne Meade, CNZM, QSO, PhD, MRSNZ, is an education consultant specialising in research and writing focused on early childhood education. Her projects take her overseas as well as around New Zealand. Anne has held three positions at Victoria University over recent decades, and has been the convenor of two major government working groups developing long-term policy for early childhood education in New Zealand, in 1988 and in 2001. She was appointed the Director of the New Zealand Council for Educational Research from 1992 to 1998, and was a Fulbright Senior Scholar in 1999. She has written and edited many books and reports, as well as numerous articles.

Jim Neyland had a long and varied career in education. He was closely involved with Mathematics education and curriculum development. He had an extensive range of research interests within the philosophy of education, which he taught at Victoria University for a period of fifteen years. His book *Rediscovering the Spirit of Education After Scientific Management* was published posthumously in 2010.

Ken Stevens has had three appointments at Victoria University: as a Junior Lecturer (1974–1975), as a Lecturer and Senior Lecturer (1980–1996) and as an Adjunct Professor (since 2005). Currently he is a Professor of

Education at Memorial University of Newfoundland in Canada, where he was appointed to a research chair in e-learning, funded by Industry Canada. From 1976 to 1980 he lectured at James Cook University in Queensland, where he subsequently obtained a doctorate, before returning to Victoria University. In Australia, New Zealand and Canada he has specialised in the provision of education in rural communities and the application of information technologies for teaching and learning in and between schools in sparsely populated areas. He has published widely and his work has been translated into Finnish, Danish, Icelandic, Inuktitut and Portuguese.

Te whānau o He Pārekereke are listed alphabetically: Cherie Chu (New Zealand Tahiti), Joanna Kidman (Te Arawa, Te Aupouri), Wally Penetito (Ngāti Hauā, Ngāti Tamaterā, Ngāti Raukawa), Hazel Phillips (Ngāti Mutunga), Fuapepe Rimoni (New Zealand, Samoa), Kabini Sanga (Solomon Islands), and Pine Southon (Tuhoe).

G. Brian Thompson worked as a psychologist with the New Zealand Department of Education for seven years before taking up a position as senior teaching fellow in the Faculty of Education at Monash University, Melbourne, Australia, where he received his PhD. From 1978 to 2001 he was a senior lecturer in the Department (School) of Education at Victoria University of Wellington, and subsequently a senior research associate of the University; he is currently an associate of the School of Educational Psychology and Pedagogy. Brian was a member of the Literary Experts Group formed by the New Zealand Ministry of Education, 1998–2003, and International Coordinator on the Board of Directors of the Society for the Scientific Study of Reading (USA), 2000–2002. He is the co-author of *Reading Acquisition Processes* (Multilingual Matters, UK, 1993) and *Learning to Read: Beyond Phonics and Whole Language* (Teachers College Press, USA, 1999). Research collaborations across universities, both internationally and within New Zealand, have been a feature of his continuing publications on the learning and teaching of reading.

Martin Thrupp is Professor of Education at the University of Waikato. Previously he was Reader in Education Policy at King's College London and Senior Lecturer in Education Management and Leadership at the Institute of Education, University of London. Martin's research interests include the development of more socially and politically contextualised approaches to education management, the influence of social class on school processes, and the nature and impact of recent school reforms in New Zealand and England. He is a spokesperson for the Quality Public Education Coalition and the Child Poverty Action Group. His publications include *Schools Making a Difference: Let's Be Realistic!* (Open University Press, 1999), *Education Management in Managerialist Times: Beyond the Textual Apologists* (Open University Press, 2003) and *School Improvement: An Unofficial Approach* (Continuum, 2005).

INDEX

fn refers to references in the footnotes only

20 free hours of childcare 75
21st century education 24

Academic Audit Unit 220
academic options, secondary
  education 92
academic politics 44, 46, 130, 148
accountabilities, financial 77
accuracy in reading 242–247
achievement, student 24, 31, 69, 70,
  104
Acland, Sarah 195
acts of parliament *see* legislation
administrative resources 168
adolescents: development and identity
  formation 202–211; counselling of
  208–209
adult education 139, 163
Advanced Placement (AP) 175–181
advisory roles 59, 88, 94, 96, 99, 129;
  in the Pacific 93
agricultural education and training
  163
aid: educational 58, 89; provision of
  97, 100
Alafua Agricultural College, 96
Alcock, Sophie 135
Alton-Lee, Adrienne 132, 148, 198
Arnold, Rollo 43, 214
arts, the: performance, literature,
  visual 235–236
Ashton-Warner, Sylvia 153
assessment: achievement and progress
  33, 113; advice and support for
  89, 93–94; expertise in 116, 215;

of learning 78, 91, 110, 219–220;
  policy changes around 103, 106;
  standards-based 115; tools 113,
  114
Atlantic Canada 173–184
Aubert, Sister Suzanne 151
Australia 85, 93, 94
Australian Catholic University 241
Axford, Ian 240*fn*

Bailey, Colin 121, 124, 214
Baker, Robyn 193
Ballard, Russell 105
ballot systems 75–76
Barrington, John 43, 63, 125
Beeby, C.E. (Clarence Edward) 89:
  Beeby vision 20, 26, 34
Before Five 74, 126, 148
behaviours: adolescent 203; violent
  232
Bell, Marie 122, 123, 145, 148, 151
biculturalism 22, 222
bilingual education 168
Bill of Rights Act (1990) 76
Bird, Lise *see* Claiborne, Lise Bird
birth rates 74
Blennerhassett, Emily 151
Boards of Trustees 48, 74, 231
Book Flood programme 93, 100
Bougainville 98, 101
Brennan, Margaret, 135
Britain *see* United Kingdom
British protectorates 87
Brown, Don 216, 221–223, 228, 235
Bruce, Lynne 132, 134, 145, 148, 150
building of schools 96
bulk-funding for schools 63, 77, 79
bullying 232

Burgon, Jacky 130
Burns, Val 124, 145
Business Round Table 65
Canadian Embassy 210
capitalism 48
Caroline Islands 85
Carr, Margaret 148, 150
Cassidy, Stephen 240
Centre for Distance Learning and
    Innovation (CDLI) 181, 183
Centre for Early Childhood Studies
    122–155, 217
change management 103, 106–107
Cherrington, Sue 136
childcare 139–140
Children's Issues Centre 135
choices, educational 68, 92, 206
Christchurch Health and Development
    Study 203
Chu, Cherie 56, 58
churches 98
Claiborne, Lise Bird 146, 228
classes, social 22, 23–24, 28, 47–48,
    68, 70, 76, 194
Clay, Marie 239
closed learning environments 169,
    176, 179–183
Coalition of Concerned Citizens 231
co-construction of policy 103–104,
    112–115
colleges of education 122, 128, 139;
    see also teacher training colleges
Collinge, Jim 43, 44, 51, 144–146
colonisation 28, 48, 58, 87–88
Committee on Women (International
    Women's Year) 123
committees, governmental: Committee
    on Women (International Women's
    Year) 123; on early childhood
    education 121; Working Group
    on Early Childhood Care and
    Education 123

commodification see marketisation
communities, internet-based 161
community-based early childhood
    education 75
comparative education 42, 43, 45
competency-based paradigms 49
Competent Children study 121, 129,
    132
compulsory education 19, 73, 79
conflict, learning about 229–233
Connelly, Vincent 241
Cook Islands 85–88, 89, 91, 94, 99
Cool Schools programme 231
cooperative learning 234–235
Cornforth, Sue 199
corporal punishment 217
Correspondence School 163–166,
    170–171
Costa, Francesca 195
Cottrell, David 241
Council, Victoria University 124, 148
counselling adolescents 208–209
Crawford, Gwen 124
creativity and imagination, cultivation
    of 90
Croft, Cedric 240
Crooks, Terry 105, 114
Cubey, Pam 145
cultural capital 23–24
cultural diversity 24, 100
curriculum 90, 110, 234: bicultural
    or multicultural 22, 31; changes
    49–50; development 89–90; early
    childhood education 149; expertise
    in 116, 167, 215, 220; hidden
    23; identity-enhancing 206–208;
    national 24fn, 114; opportunities
    182; outcomes-led 113, 254–259;
    policy 46; range of options 162,
    170; reforms 91, 93, 106; resources
    168; secondary 92, 78, 229–230,
    232; The New Zealand 80, 91, 95

cuts to funding 56–60

Daglish, Neil 43
Dalli, Carmen 125–129, 131–135, 148, 151, 153, 217
Davies, Janet 193
Davies, Sonja 145
Davis, Sir Tom 88
decentralisation 104
decile rankings 25, 76, 78, 82
Declaration of the Rights of the Child 228
deficit model 22, 31, 222
deliberative democracy 32*fn*
demographic changes 99
Department of Anthropology 146
Department of Continuing Education 124, 139, 210
Department of Education (NZ) 123, 124, 128, 162, 216–217; publications of 94, 231; working in the Pacific 91, 93
Department of Education (VUW) 41, 45, 63, 121, 123, 129, 213, 229; appointments of staff 124, 127, 190; changes in 155, 199; enrolment with 50, 144–145
Department of Social Welfare (NZ) 123, 128
Department of University Extension *see* Department of Continuing Education
developing instruction materials 181
development, economic 98
development of theories 21–34, 66–67, 70
developmental psychology and development 189–199
devolved (bulk) funding for schools 63, 77, 79,
differences 31–32, 189
digital technology 174, 181

Directors of Education: Ballard, Russell 105; Beeby, C.E. 20, 89–90; Strong, T.B. 21
disability studies 197
discipline in school 90
disciplines of educational study 43, 214: *see also* philosophy, history of education, comparative education, sociology, psychology
distance education 89, 95–96, 161
diversity 189–197
division of labour 23
Douglas, Roger 45
Doyle, Stephanie 223
Drewery, Wendy 197
Dunedin Multidisciplinary Health and Development Study 203
Dunedin Teachers College 91
Dupuis, Ann 71

Early Childhood Council 75, 79
early childhood education 73–75, 95, 96, 109, 121–156, 164, 214, 217, 232: changes in 79, 81–82; quality of 128–130, 140; teacher qualifications 74, 128, 134, 139, 148–150; *see also* education and care centres, kindergartens, home-based care, kōhanga reo
Easter Island 85
economic development 98
economics 26, 44–45, 67, 68
education 27: adult 139, 163–164; advisors 88; agricultural 163; bilingual 168; compulsory 19–20, 73, 79; disciplinary fields of 43, 214; early childhood *see* early childhood education; entrepreneurial 46, 78; evidence-based 222; inclusive 222; non-compulsory 79; policies 33; primary 229; private 78, 79;

programmes 22, 50; provision of 88; quality of 100, 166; secondary 98, 106, 115, 162–171, 177, 229; second-chance 164; special needs 216–217, 221–222; state-funded 19–20; systems 30, 34, 99; tertiary 79, 106, 111, 164–165, 215
Education Act (1877) 19
Education Act (1989) 45, 48, 75, 163
Education Amendment Act (1991) 76
Education Amendment Act (1998) 79
Education Amendment Act (2000) 76
education and care centres 74, 75
Education and Training Support Agency 218
Education Forum 79
Education Review Office (ERO) 78, 105, 113, 218
Education to be More 74, 121, 126–128, 148
educational aid 58, 89
educational choices 206
educational inequalities 20, 24–34, 26
educational opportunities 20, 82, 114, 176
educational planning 97
educational policy 111, 191
educational psychologists 216–217, 221
educational psychology *see* psychology, educational
educational quality 162
educational reforms 20, 45, 107, 109–111
educational research 49–50, 220: assessment and learning 24, 215; early childhood 121, 123, 131, 140, 150; leaning to read 239, 245; Māori 56; role of research institutes 135–136; rural schools 162; in sociology 45; use of 64, 103, 111, 113

educational resources 89, 93, 94–95, 96, 100, 110, 229
educational spaces 256–260
educational structures 24, 189
educational/ecological model 222
efficiency movement 252–260
egalitarianism 31
e-learning 161, 166–170, 173–184
electronic media 177, 180
emotional literacy 232
empiricism 66
employment conditions 75, 81, 100
employment opportunities 19, 30, 33, 100, 193
English as a second language 95, 164
enrolment schemes 76
enterprise, education for 46, 78–80
environments, learning 169
equal opportunities, equal rights 22, 29, 34, 47, 63, 82
equity 27, 46, 75
equivalent full time students (EFTS) 73*fn*
essentialism 29
e-teachers 179–183
evaluation of teaching and learning 89, 93
evidence-based education 105, 222
examinations 89, 90, 91, 93, 114, 115–116, 219
experiential learning (taxonomy of) 111
exploration and commitment dimensions 204–207
Extension Studies (VUW) *see* Department of Continuing Education

fa'a Samoa 195–196
fa'afafine 195–196
face-to-face teaching 183
facts *versus* ideas 258

Faculty of Education 131, 136, 220
family composition 74
feminism 28–30, 32, 145, 190–195
Fieldhouse, Arthur 214, 238–239
Fiji 58, 85–88, 89, 91, 92, 94, 96, 101
Fiji Technical Institute 96
Finland 174
Fletcher-Finn, Claire 241, 245
Flockton, Lester 105, 114
Fraser, Peter 20, 80, 83, 90
free childcare, 20 hours of 75
free-market policies *see* marketisation
French Polynesia 101
FRST funding 56–57
Fulbright scholars 59
Fuli, Everdina (Dina) 56, 194
functionalism 21, 24, 26
funding, schools 77; tertiary education
    45–46, 56; cuts 56

Galloway, David 197
GDP, per capita 86
gender considerations 191, 194
Gilbert, Jane 51
globalisation 46, 104, 255
Gould, Caroline 222
Governance: educational 48; of
    schools 63; of society 48; of
    universities 45
Grace, Dick 222
Grace, Gerald 43, 73, 125–127, 129,
    191, 227
Grace, Shirley Roberson 198
Gray, William 214

Hall, Cedric 153, 197, 219, 223
Hamilton, Carol 195
Harvey, Valerie 197
He Pārekereke: Institute for Research
    and Development in Māori and
    Pacific Education 218, 52–60
health 27, 45, 99–100, 233

high-speed internet connection 177
Hill, Clem 121*fn*
Hill, Kim 65
history of education 43, 46, 141, 149,
    153, 214
Holborow Les, 132
Holmes, Tony 131–132, 148
home-based care 74
housing choices 77
HRC funding 56
Hughes, David 71, 71
human capital 97
human rights 27, 233
Human Rights Commission Act
    (1977) 76

Iceland 174
ideas *versus* facts 258
identities: of students 50; of teachers
    49
identity formation, adolescent
    203–211
identity politics 29
identity reformation processes 205
identity statuses 204–209
imagination and creativity, cultivation
    of 235–236
immigration 99
improving student learning 110
inaugural classes (VUW) 213
inclusive education 21, 106, 109, 222
Inclusive Education Programme 91
independence of Pacific nations 88–90
independent learning 177
indigenous peoples 28, 30, 54
indigenous scholarship 59
individualised learning 105
individualism 27–30, 31–32
industry training 106
inequalities: educational 20, 24–34, 26,
    47–48; social 19, 21, 23–24, 233
influenza epidemic 88

information technology 167–168
Institute for Early Childhood
    Education Studies *see* Centre for
    Early Childhood Studies
instruction materials, developing 181
integrated learning 234
International Association for the
    Evaluation of Educational
    Achievement 104
International Women's Year 123
internet, the 161, 165, 174–175, 175
intranets 170–171, 176–183
Irwin, Kathie 52–53, 54, 56, 130, 195

Jessie Hetherington Centre for
    Educational Research 136, 217
John Ilott Charitable Trust 210
Johnston, Rhona 241
Jones, Liz 222–223
Jones, Vonnie 222

Kalivati, Lianne 222
Kana, Fred 155
kaupapa Māori 53, 56
Kerr, Roger 65
Kerslake-Hendricks, Anne 130
key stage testing 114
Kidman, Joanna 56, 195
Kindergarten Teachers' Association 145
kindergartens 74, 124, 139, 139–140
Kiribati 85–86, 91, 92, 94, 101
Kiribati Teachers College 91
knowledge: digital 174; economy,
    178; in professional learning 111,
    223; views on 27, 29–30, 31
Knowledge Sources theory 243–247
Kōhanga Reo 130, 153
Koloto, 'Ana 53, 56
Kroger, Jane 146, 190

labour, division or organisation of 23,
    48

Labour governments 20, 63, 73,
    74–77, 79, 121, 229, 231
Labrador 173–184
Lange, David 70
languages, Pacific 98–99
Lauder, Hugh 43, 129–130, 198
Laurie, Alison 228
League of Nations 87
League of Nations Union 228
league tables 114
learning environments 169
Learning Media Limited 94–95
learning to read, processes 238–248
learning, students': assessment
    of 105, 113; cooperative 234;
    improvements in 110; independent
    177; integrated 234
legislation: Bill of Rights Act (1990)
    76; Education Act (1877) 19;
    Education Act (1989) 45, 48, 75,
    163; Education Amendment Act
    (1991) 76; Education Amendment
    Act (1998) 79; Education
    Amendment Act (2000) 76; Human
    Rights Commission Act (1977) 76;
    Race Relations Act (1971) 76
lesson preparation 182
letter-sound correspondence 243–247
literacy 100: emotional 232; standards
    94
longitudinal studies 66, 70, 121, 129,
    203, 205, 207, 241
Loveridge, Judith 135

Ma'ai'i, Fanaafi 190
management: of schools 69–71; of
    universities 45
managerialism 45, 49, 78
Manins, Liz 222
Māori academics 53–54, 57
Māori Centre of Research Excellence
    56

Māori education 21–22, 22, 31, 130, 214, 218
Māori knowledge 22
Māori scholarship 52–56, 130
Māori students 24, 30, 53–55, 57, 76, 153, 194
Mara, Ratu Sir Kamasese 88
marketisation 45, 47, 49, 68, 70; effect on education 25, 50, 73, 74, 76–77, 79, 81
Marsden Fund 56
Marsh, Reginald (Reg) 191fn, 221, 240
Marshall Islands 58, 85
Marshall, Russell 229–231
Marxist views 23, 26
Massey University 95, 165
mātauranga Māori 31
Matauranga School 123
mathematics education 252–260
Mau nationalist movement 88
Maui Community College 96
Maxim Institute 79
May, Helen 122, 133–135, 139–156, 153, 198, 214
McCarthy, Marie 56
McCully, Murray 97
McDonald, Geraldine 122, 192, 214
McDonald, Lex 221–222
McKay, Michael 241
Meade, Anne 121, 122, 124, 127, 129–130, 132, 145, 217
Meade Report see Education to be More
media: electronic 177; news 48, 108, 115–116, 161
Memorial University of Newfoundland 173, 177
mental health 203
mentoring programmes 56
mergers: College of Education and Victoria University 59, 135, 140, 199, 214, 219, 223; of schools 163; between teachers colleges

and universities 128, 131, 139, 148, 153
Methodist Mission 98
Middleton, Sue 145–146, 153
minimum rates of pay 74
Minister of Justice 230
Ministers of Education: Fraser, Peter 20, 80, 83, 90; Lange, David 70; Marshall, Russell 229–231
Ministers of Finance, Douglas, Roger 45
Ministry of Education 194, 218, 231: actions of officials from 64, 80, 114, 116; contracts with 129, 193, 221–222; evaluations of policy 110; policy 24, 78, 94–95, 149, 162
Ministry of Foreign Affairs and Trade (MFAT) 97–98
missionaries 98
Mitchell, Jill 122–123
Mitchell, Linda 83, 131
mixed-ability classes 76
Montessori methods 152
Morning Report (radio) 65
Morris, Beverley 124, 139–140, 145
Morris-Matthews, Kay 146, 155, 214
m-teachers and m-teams 183
multiculturalism 22
multimedia resources 168

National Certificate of Educational Achievement (NCEA) 94, 106, 110, 113–114, 115–117, 220
National Education Monitoring Project (NEMP) 105, 114–117
National governments 63, 74–78, 79, 83, 129
National Information and Communications Technology Strategy 168
National Qualifications Framework 113

National Tertiary Teaching Excellence Committee 215
national testing 105, 114
Nauru 85, 94, 99
neo-liberal policies 24, 25, 47, 63, 75, 80–81, 82
neo-Marxism 196
networks of schools, for teaching and learning 166, 169–170, 174
New Caledonia 85
New Right policies *see* neo-liberal policies
New Zealand Agency for International Development (NZAID) 97–98
New Zealand Association for Research in Education (NZARE) 21*fn*, 191
New Zealand Correspondence School 95
New Zealand Council for Educational Research (NZCER) 93–94, 122, 123, 129–130, 132, 150, 239, 240
New Zealand Curriculum 24*fn*, 80, 91, 95, 232
New Zealand Educational Institute 218, 228
New Zealand Foundation for Peace Studies 229
New Zealand Qualifications Authority (NZQA) 48, 106, 115, 131, 218
New Zealand Treasury 83
New Zealand University Grants Committee 241
New Zealand Vice-Chancellors' Committee 48
Newfoundland 173–184
news media 48, 108, 115–116, 161
Ngā Pae o te Māramatanga 56, 218
Nicholls, John 190
Niue 85–88, 89, 91, 94, 99
non-compulsory education 79
normed tests *see* standardised tests

norm-referenced examinations 114
Nuclear Issues Fact Sheets 231
numeracy standards 94

observations, in-class 240
Occasional Publications 134, 151, 217
O'Dell, Betty 124
Oldershaw, Graeme 132, 148, 227
one-off studies 66
online teaching *see* e-teachers
open learning environments 169, 177, 179–183
Open Polytechnic *see* The Open Polytechnic of New Zealand
operational grants 162
opportunities: educational 20, 82, 114, 176; employment 30, 33, 100, 193; vocational options 176
Oral Word Reading Test 238
Otago University 114, 135
outcomes-led curriculum 254–259
Overseas Cambridge exams 92
Overseas Development Assistance programme (ODA) 91, 97
Oxford Brookes University (Oxford, UK) 241

Pacific academics 55
Pacific education 53–54, 55–56
Pacific Forum Basic Education Plan (PFBEP) 97
Pacific languages 86, 95, 98–99
Pacific Literacy and Science booklets 95
Pacific nations 58, 85, 88
Pacific peoples 85
Pacific Regional Initiative for the Implementation and Delivery of Basic Education (PRIDE) 97
Pacific researchers 94
Pacific Senior Secondary Certificate 94
Pacific students 24, 76, 88

Pallotta-Endemann Karl, 196
Pan Pacific Educational and
    Communication Experiment by
    Satellite (PEACESAT) 95–96
Papua New Guinea 85, 98
Parents Centre movement 123
Parkin, Margaret 221
Pasifika Languages Research and
    Guidelines Project 25fn
Pasifika see Pacific
Pathways to the Future – Ngā
    Huarahi Arataki 121
pay parity 74
Peace Foundation 231
Peace Studies: Draft Guidelines 230
Penetito, Wally 51, 56, 60, 218
performance criteria 257
performance pay 77
performance targets 77
Perris, L. 107–108
personalised learning 33–34
Peters, Sally 135
Phillips, Hazel 56
philosophy of education 43, 50, 149,
    214
phonics, explicit 242–247
Picking up the Pace and Shifting
    Focus 25fn
Picot Report 63, 75
Pitcairn Island 85
planning, educational 97
playcentres 123, 124, 139, 139–140
pluralism 31, 32
Podmore, Val 134–135, 150, 151
policy: advice for/informing 65,
    67–68, 71, 129; on assessment
    103–117; co-construction
    103–104, 112–115; educational
    111, 191; implementation
    108–109; reforms 113
politics, academic 44, 46, 130, 148
polytechnics see tertiary education

post-colonialism 30
post-empiricism 68
post-modernism 29, 31, 32, 64, 198
post-positivism 66
Post-Primary Teachers Association
    (PPTA) 105
post-structuralism 196–197
Pouwer, Jan 144, 146–147
practices, teacher 111, 240
pressure groups 108, 116
primary education 25, 95, 114, 229
principals of schools 77, 78, 113
private early childhood education
    centres 75
private schools 78, 79
private sector involvement in
    education 79
privatisation 73, 81
problem solving 90
professional development 222–223; to
    implement new policy 103–104,
    107, 109–112, 116, 168; to
    improve student outcomes 24,
    198; in the Pacific 88, 99, 100
programmes: Book Flood 93, 100;
    Shared Book programme 93; Cool
    Schools 231
projects, research: Christchurch
    Health and Development Study
    203; Competent Children
    121, 129, 132; Dunedin
    Multidisciplinary Health and
    Development Study 203;
    Kōtahitanga research 25fn;
    Pasifika Languages Research and
    Guideines Project 25fn; Picking
    up the Pace and Shifting Focus
    25fn; Progress At School 69;
    Smithfield 24, 65, 68, 69, 71–72,
    129; Strengthening Education in
    Mangere and Otara (SEMO) 25fn
psychoanalytic theory 26, 30, 32

Psychological Assessment Unit (USP) 94
psychological testing 196
psychologists, educational 216–217, 221
psychology: developmental 189–199; educational 43, 192–199, 216, 219, 220–222, 240
Public Choice Theory 68
public education *see* state-funded education
public good service *see* social justice
Pukeatua Kokiri Centre 153
Puketapu, Kara 153
Puketapu, Nanny Jean 153
Purdy, Mary 145

qualifications: 217; early childhood education 74, 128, 134, 139, 148–150
qualifications framework 106
quality: early childhood education 75, 81, 128–130, 140; of education 100, 126, 162, 166; of teachers 89–91, 99, 100; of teaching and learning 215
Quality Public Education Coalition 80
quality rating scale (early childhood education) 130

Race Relations Act (1971) 76
rate (speed) of reading 245–247
Read Pacific Limited 95
reading, beginning learners 238–248
reforms: assessment 106; curriculum 106; educational 20, 45, 107, 109–111; policy 113; social 45
regional education boards, 48
relationship building 32–33, 255–256
relativism 24–34, 31, 64
reliability (of tests) 115–116
religious perspectives 195

Report of the Economic and Educational Viability of Small Schools Review 161
Report of the Ministerial Committee of Enquiry into Violence (Roper Report) 230–231
reporting to parents 105, 113
research: educational *see* educational research; social science *see* social science research; projects *see* projects, research
Resource Teachers: Learning and Behaviour (RTLB) 216, 221–223
resources: administrative 168; curriculum 168; educational 89, 93, 94–95, 96, 100, 110, 168, 229; multimedia 168
restructuring, economic 44–45
rights: human 27; social 19, 27
Rimoni, Fuapepe 59
Robb, Jim 125
Rogernomics 44, 45
roles, social 21
rolls, school 69, 76
Roots of Empathy (ROE) 232
Roper, Sir Clinton 230–231; Roper Committee 231; Roper Report 230
rote memorisation 89–90
Roy McKenzie Foundation 210
Royal, Turoa 54
rural education 161–184
Russia 174

Salmon, Bea 191
Samoa 85–88, 90, 91, 94, 96, 195
Sanga, Kabini 56, 58
Scheme of Cooperation 88–89
Scholarship examinations 115–116
scholarships 89, 96
School Bulletins 94
School Certificate (NZSC) 92–93
school choice 24

school governance 63
School Journal 94
school management 69
School of Education (VUW) 52–56,
    133, 210, 213, 224
School Publications 94; see also
    Learning Media Limited
school rolls 69, 76
school subject areas 234
school zoning 63, 69, 72, 75–77, 79
schools, primary 114
science, women in 192
scientific management 254–259
secondary education: academic
    options 92; assessment and
    qualifications 92, 94, 106, 106,
    115; curriculum 229, 232; in rural
    areas 162–171, 177; in the Pacific
    98; vocational options 92, 168
second-chance education 164
secondments in the Pacific 88, 96
Seddon, Richard 87–88
segregation 76, 82
self-determination 59
self-managing schools 24
separatism 29, 32
Sexton, Stuart 63
sexuality considerations 194
Shallcrass, Jack 43, 51, 144–146, 153,
    154, 214, 228
Shared Book programme 93
Significant Innovations in Teaching
    Award 220
single parents 74
single sex schools 68
Smith, Anne 140, 145, 155
Smith, Linda Tuhiwai 56
Smithfield project 24, 65, 68, 69,
    71–72, 129
Snowling, Margaret 241
social classes 22, 23–24, 28, 47–48,
    68, 70, 76, 194

social inequalities 233
social justice 28, 34, 233; in
    curriculum policy 46–47; in the
    education system 73, 79–82, 106,
    189–197
social reform 45
social rights 27
social roles 21
social science research 64–66, 71, 72,
    202, 211, 227
social services 27
social structures 21, 25, 26, 27, 28, 233
social systems 25
Socialist Unity Party 231
socio-economic change 26
socio-economic factors 21–26
socio-economic indicators 87
socio-economic status 76, 78
sociology of education 19–34, 41–51,
    58, 125, 140, 214
software packages 178
Solomon Islands 58, 59, 85–86, 94,
    101
Solomon Islands Teachers College 91
Somerset, Crawford 42, 124, 140, 214
Somerset, Gwen 139–140
South Pacific Board for Educational
    Assessment (SPBEA) 93–94, 96
South Pacific Form Seven Certificate 94
South Pacific Option (for
    examinations) 92
Southon, Pine 57
Special Education 2000 196, 222
special education 216, 221–222
stages of educational development
    (Beeby's thesis) 89
standardised tests 25, 214, 238
standards: educational 93; unit and
    achievement 78, 254
standards-based examinations 114, 115
State Services Commission 79, 115, 123
state-funded education 19–20, 28, 46

Stevens, Ken 43, 50, 146
strategic plans 77
Strathdee, Rob 71
Strengthening Education in Mangere
  and Otara (SEMO) project 25*fn*
Strong, T.B. 21
structuralism 26
structures: educational 24, 189; family
  74; occupational 48; social 21, 25,
  26, 27, 28, 233
student achievement 24, 25, 33, 69,
  70, 104
student crèche 126, 143–145
student-centred learning 97
students' learning, progress in 105,
  110, 113; *see also* learning
student-teacher interactions 255–256,
  182
Sutherland, Alison 198
Sutton-Smith, Brian 238
Sweeny, Mark 222
systems: educational 24, 30, 34, 99;
  social 25

taha Māori 22
Tasker, Gillian 198
Tate Oral English Scheme 93
Te Kupenga o MAI 57
Te One, Sarah 135
Te Tauihu o Ngā Wānanga 218
Te Wānanga-o-Raukawa 218
Te Whare Wānanga o Aotearoa 57
Te Whare Wānanga o Awanuiārangi
  52, 57, 218
Te Whāriki 133, 136*fn*, 149–151, 232
Teacher Education Quality
  Improvement Project 91
teacher education *see* teacher training
teacher qualifications *see*
  qualifications
teacher training 49, 88, 89–91,
  100, 131, 245: early childhood

education 122, 124, 126, 133,
  140
teacher unions 77, 79, 105, 145
teacher-only days 112
teacher training colleges 91, 96, 140,
  150, 227, 229 *see also* colleges of
  education
teachers 89, 99, 116: identities of 49;
  practices of 90, 111–112, 240;
  quality of 69–71, 89–91, 99, 100
teacher–student interactions 182,
  255–256
Teaching Matters Forum 215
technological advancements 48, 96
technology, digital 181
Tennant, J.S. (John Smaillie) 41, 214
tertiary education: distance education
  95, 164–165; funding 44, 46,
  56, 79; Māori 57; in the Pacific
  96; qualifications 106; student
  learning 111
Tertiary Education Commission 48
tests, standardised 25, 214
textbooks 90, 93–94
The Open Polytechnic of New
  Zealand (TOPNZ) 95, 165–166
The South Pacific Bible College 95
theories, development of 66–67, 70
theory of control 254–259
third spaces 32
Thompson, G. Brian 239
Thomson, Charlotte (Lottie) 221–223,
  235
Thrupp, Martin 71, 80
Tokelau 85–87, 94, 98
Tomorrow's Schools 48, 63, 75, 104,
  121, 127, 191
Tomorrow's Standards 114
Tonga 85–88, 92, 94, 98, 101
Town, Shane 195, 198
Treaty of Waitangi 194, 218
truancy 197

Tu, Sheur-er 195
Tupou College 98
Tupu series 94–95, 100
Tupuola, AnneMarie 197
Tuvalu 85–86, 92, 94, 96, 101
twenty free hours of childcare 75
twenty-first century education 24

unions, teacher 77, 79, 105, 145
United Kingdom 33, 93, 114
United Nation, 87, 97
United States of America (USA) 174, 178
Universal Declaration of Human Rights 233
universal truths 27
universities see tertiary education
University Entrance (UE) 92–93
university funding see tertiary funding
University of Auckland 56, 222, 239, 241
University of Hawaii 96
University of New Zealand 213
University of Otago 241
University of South Pacific (USP) 96, 93–96
University of St Andrews 241
University of Waikato 150, 222
University Teaching and Development Centre 219

validity (of tests) 115–116
values, personal 204
Vanuatu 58, 85–86, 94, 98, 99
Vice-Chancellors 48
VicLink 222
Victoria University College 213
Victoria University Council 124, 148
violence 229–233
virtual classrooms 169, 173–184
Vista School District Digital Intranet 176–179

vocational options, secondary education 92, 168, 176, 204
Volunteer Service Abroad (VSA) 97–98

Waitangi, Treaty of 194, 218
Walker, Michael 56
Waslander, Sietske 71
Watson, Susan 71, 198
Webster, Peter 144, 145
welfare state 19, 45
Wellington College of Education 126, 148, 214, 228; collaboration with VUW 122, 133–134, 150, 153, 217; see also mergers
Wellington Polytechnic 96
Whāriki Papatipu 153
Wilkie, Margaret 57
Williams, Les 57
Willis, Deborah 193, 215
women in science 192–193
Women into Science Education 193
Women's International League for Peace and Freedom 228
word accuracy in reading 242–247
working classes 28, 70
Working Group on Early Childhood Care and Education 123
working women 74
workshops 112
World Indigenous Higher Education Consortium 218
World War I 87–88
World War II 88, 221
Wylie, Cathy 129–130, 146

zoning, school 63, 69, 72, 75–77, 79